Demand and Exchange in Economic Analysis

A History from Cournot to Marshall

John Creedy

The Truby Williams Professor of Economics
University of Melbourne

Edward Elgar

Published by
Edward Elgar Publishing Limited
Gower House
Croft Road
Aldershot
Hants GU11 3HR
England

Edward Elgar Publishing Limited
Distributed in the United States by
Ashgate Publishing Company
Old Post Road
Brookfield
Vermont 05036
USA

CIP catalogue records for this book are available
from the British Library and the US Library of Congress

ISBN 1 85278 530 6

Printed in Great Britain by
Billing and Sons Ltd, Worcester

Contents

Figures

Tables

Acknowledgements

This book would not have been written without the constant encouragement and support of Denis O'Brien, whose help is greatly appreciated. His knowledge, judgement and friendship are of enormous value to me. However, he has not read all of the chapters, and cannot be held responsible for the shortcomings of this book. I am grateful to John Whitaker for asking me to contribute a chapter on Marshall and international trade to *Centenary Essays on Alfred Marshall*. This request led me to look closely at the analyses of trade by Cournot, Mill and Whewell and to build a mathematical and diagrammatic 'bridge' between their works and that of Marshall. When the chapter was completed I found, by accident while looking for something else, that the route I had taken was identical to that of Walras. This at least confirmed, despite the denial by some other writers, that the models of Marshall and Walras were essentially the same. Indeed, the fairly sophisticated structure of the theory of exchange, which reached a peak in the work of Edgeworth, is based on the seemingly platitudinous conception of reciprocal demand combined with the specification of demand as a schedule depending on relative prices. John Stuart Mill must surely take the credit for combining and exploiting these ideas more clearly than any of his predecessors.

I should also like to thank the following for their cheerful and highly efficient word processing: Margaret Lochran, Sally Nolan, Marnie Jenkin and Lynne Ki. The preparation of the manuscript would have been much more difficult without their skilful contribution. I have also benefited from a faculty teaching relief award for the second semester of 1990. Mention should also be made of the excellent research environment provided by the Economics Department at Melbourne, enhanced by the unstinting contribution of Robert Dixon as Head of Department. Some of the material has previously appeared (in a very different form) in papers published in the *Scottish Journal of Political Economy*, the *Journal of the History of Economic Thought*, the *Scandinavian Journal of Economics*, *Oxford Economic Papers* and the *Manchester School*. I am grateful for permission to use these papers. The material from Appendix A is taken from joint work with Vance Martin, who kindly allowed me to use it here. Mark Casson, who encouraged me to write as well as buy books, again gave useful advice.

1 Introduction

In view of the central role of 'demand and exchange' in modern economic analysis, and the difficulty in producing a title that is both succinct and accurate, it seems useful to begin by trying to clarify the precise nature of this book. One way to describe it is to say that Part 1 of the book examines some major problems in the analysis of demand, taking as its central focus the mathematical treatment of demand conceived as a schedule or functional relationship. Part 2 then examines some major contributions to the analysis of exchange, involving the combination of the idea of demand as a schedule with the fundamental interpretation of the 'rate of exchange', or price ratio, in terms of the amount of one good offered in return for a unit of another good.

These basic beginnings, the use of a schedule combined with the interpretation of price in terms of the *quid* and the *pro quo*, allied with the use of some fairly straightforward mathematics, appear to the modern economist to be so elementary as hardly to require comment. Yet these simple materials, modelled with a powerful tool, can be seen to have generated some extremely important, and not entirely obvious, insights into economics. There are no doubt many people, including at times Marshall, who would argue instead that the tool of analysis has been used to produce too many results that can only be assigned to the 'toy shop' as 'academic playthings', but it is not intended to enter this heated debate here.

In considering the nature and importance of some of the very early insights, it is worth keeping in mind the point made by Schumpeter that, 'it is much more difficult for the human mind to forge the most elementary conceptual schemes than it is to elaborate the most complicated super-structures when these elements are well in hand' (1954, p. 602). A fundamental insight is always in danger of being dismissed by later generations as a platitude. A conceptual scheme that Schumpeter had in mind was in fact the idea of demand as a schedule. This 'proved unbelievably hard to discover and to distinguish from the concepts – quantity demanded and quantity supplied' (1954, p. 602). There has been some debate on the precise meaning attached to the concept of demand used by the classical economists, but this debate is not rehearsed below in view of the emphasis on studies which can be said to have used a mathematical approach. For example, even though Say had a fairly clear view of demand as a schedule, whose form was significantly influenced by the distribution of income, he made no attempt to develop it mathematically.

1

Some comments on the sub-title of this book are also necessary. Many people would perhaps readily accept that this type of book would begin with Cournot. After all, Cournot is usually regarded as the originator of the partial equilibrium demand curve expressed in terms of quantity as a function of price. As Edgeworth later exclaimed, 'how much logomachy is saved by this appropriate conception!'. Yet the story really begins, as in Chapter 2, with the King–Davenant law, which dates from the end of the 17th century. Not only does this clearly conceive of demand as a schedule, emphasizing the inelastic nature of the demand, but it appears that a mathematical approach (more sophisticated than anything used for many years afterwards) may well have been used by the originator. Despite the many later references to this law, the gap in time between its first statement and the next step taken is quite remarkable. Furthermore, it was Whewell who took this 'law', a decade before Cournot's famous contribution, and formulated the first measure of price elasticity as part of his statement of a demand function. John Stuart Mill's first formulation of reciprocal demand, in his analysis of international trade, also took place a decade before Cournot's book, but he did not actually publish it until later. The use of Cournot's name in the sub-title therefore arose largely from the need to have a readily recognized 'signal' which, while not entirely accurate, is not too misleading. The role of Cournot, particularly with regard to Marshall and Walras, will indeed be seen to be central to this volume. It should also be stressed that no attempt has been made to provide a comprehensive treatment of the subject. Rather, attention is focused on a number of issues, or problems, which are regarded as warranting close analysis. The words 'problems in. . .' or 'landmarks in . . .' the history of demand and exchange might justifiably have appeared in a longer title.

The concentration on mathematical treatments of demand and exchange should not be taken to imply that this book is in any sense intended to be a history of mathematical economics. But while the emphasis is on the economic issues, it has not been possible to 'imitate the parsimony of symbols' which characterizes the majority of books on the history of economic analysis. An attempt has been made to find an appropriate middle ground between an 'exuberance of algebraic foliage' and an 'excessive circumlocution to which the purely literary method is liable' (these words are Edgeworth's), but it is never easy to find the right balance.

Most books in the history of economics may be said to be 'painted' with a 'broad brush'. These require an enormous breadth of knowledge, a fine judgement and an unusual facility for compression in order to be successful, but fortunately there are some splendid examples of this approach.

However, the present approach concentrates on the detail that would otherwise be overlooked. One cost is that the degree of selectivity is much greater; the knowledgeable reader will find it easy to think of contributions which might have been included. There is of course a useful role for both types of approach. The present book is based on the belief that a great deal can be learned about economics, its methods and limitations, by the close study of previous writers, and the attempt to understand as clearly as possible precisely what they were doing. This is not always easy. Indeed, to the modern student the early writers often seem to be using a different language, their methods are often concealed and their models and assumptions are often implicit. There is of course no substitute for study of the original works, but it is hoped that this book is useful to those wishing to learn something about both the economic theory of exchange *and* its history. Yet another alternative title might have included something along the lines of 'the theory of exchange from an historical point of view'.

It is also necessary to stress that several closely related aspects of demand and exchange are not examined here. In particular, this book is *not* about the history of the utility analysis of demand, nor of empirical studies of demand, nor of the concept of consumers' surplus, despite the fact that each of these issues is mentioned at various points. Fortunately, extensive treatments of these subjects are already available.

In order to avoid cluttering the text with too many references to the literature, or with additional detail that would otherwise reduce the continuity of the argument, each chapter has been given a final section on notes and further reading. It is hoped that this method provides the interested reader with the information in a somewhat more readable form than the usual sequence of footnotes. In the majority of cases, no biographical information about earlier writers has been given. There are fortunately several good reference works which are readily available in most libraries.

Notes and further reading
For an extensive discussion of the use of 'demand' in classical economics, see Smith (1951). For a flavour of a more recent debate on the role of demand, particularly in Ricardo's work, see Rankin (1980) and Garegnani (1983). The origins of the terminology 'supply and demand' have been examined in detail by Thweatt (1983) who does not, however, examine the role of clearly perceived schedules. The history of mathematical economics has yet to be written and presents a huge challenge, but essential references are Robertson (1949), Theocharis (1961) and Baumol and Goldfeld (1968).

PART 1

PARTIAL EQUILIBRIUM ANALYSES

2 The first demand schedule

It is generally recognized that the first demand schedule was stated by Charles Davenant (1656–1714) in his *Essay upon the Probable Methods of Making a People Gainers in the Balance of Trade* (1699). Davenant's brief statement of the schedule, or 'law of demand', is as follows:

We take it, that a defect in the harvest may raise the price of corn in the following proportions:

Defect		Above the common rate
1 tenth		3 tenths
2 tenths		8 tenths
3 tenths	Raises the price	1 + 6 tenths
4 tenths		2 + 8 tenths
5 tenths		4 + 5 tenths

so that when corn rises to treble the common rate, it may be presumed that we want above one-third of the common produce; and if we should want five-tenths or half the common produce, the price would rise to near five times the common rate. (Davenant, 1699, p. 83.)

It is of interest that this first schedule was stated in which may be called 'elasticity' form. It stresses the point that a reduction in supply, as a result of a poor harvest, is associated with an increase in total revenue. Despite the extent to which this schedule was quoted in the literature, the idea of demand and price viewed as a functional relationship and the concept of price elasticity were very slow to emerge as tools of analysis. Indeed, it was very many years before anything comparable was produced. Indeed, Jevons wrote that he knew 'nothing more strange and discreditable to statists and economists than that in so important a point as the relations of price and supply of the main article of food, we owe our most accurate estimates to writers who lived from one to two centuries ago' (1957, p. 154). Similarly, Schumpeter regarded it as remarkable that 'it did not occur to economists either to improve upon it... or to apply the same method to other commodities' (1954, p. 213).

It is perhaps no less remarkable that over a period of about 280 years there have been very few really serious analyses of what was so often referred to as the 'celebrated' law of demand. The most serious discussions of the law include those of Whewell (1850), Jevons (1871, 5th ed. 1957), Wicksteed (1889, reprinted in 1933), and Yule (1915a). The purpose of this chapter is therefore to draw the various threads of the literature together, and especially to examine the methods of analysis used by each of these four authors. Sections 2.1 to 2.4 take each of the authors in chronological order, and then section 2.5 considers the possible implications of the analysis for the possible origins of the law. The questions relating to these origins are thus raised in the following subsection.

It is first necessary to acknowledge that the association of the above schedule with a 'law of demand' requires what is now referred to as an identifying restriction. The relationship between price and quantity changes gives the demand curve on the assumption that the variability is produced by shifts in the supply curve along with the idea that equilibrium values are observed. But the context is clearly one in which price changes are indeed generated by exogenous changes in supply caused by harvest failures. Although the identification problem was not formally clarified until more than two centuries later, there is no doubt that all those who discussed the schedule saw it in terms of demand. The later pioneering statistical studies of demand also concentrated on agricultural goods, for which the assumption that supply exhibits relatively more variability is warranted.

The origins of the law
There is much uncertainty about the origins of this famous law. In his *Essay*, Davenant reproduced, with permission and acknowledgements, material from the earlier unpublished report by Gregory King (1648– 1712) on *Natural and Political Observations and Conclusions upon the State and Condition of England* (1696). It was generally thought that Davenant also borrowed the law from King, and it was often simply referred to as 'Gregory King's Law'. Jevons (1957, p. 156) reported that although the law was commonly attributed to King, he was unable to find it in the full reproduction of King's *Observations* contained in George Chalmer's *Estimate of the Comparative Strength of Great Britain* (1802). The fact that Davenant elsewhere fully acknowledged King led Jevons to suggest that in fact the law was due to Davenant.

In attempting to trace the origin of the law, Evans (1967) explored the previously unpublished writings of King, and found only one sentence, in King's working journal, which relates the price of corn to its scarcity. This reference, reproduced by Evans (1967, pp. 486–7), does not however provide anything like the information given in Davenant's schedule, and Evans suggested that it is 'more appropriate to refer either to King–

Davenant or to the Davenant–King Law of Demand – or even to the Davenant Law of Demand' (1967, p. 483). Evans made no reference to Jevons's discussion and did not discuss the nature of the law itself. However, it is argued below that the precise nature of the law provides an important clue to its possible originator.

The second and perhaps more important point on which the literature is uncertain concerns the basis of the law itself. Schultz (1938, p. 397) made it clear that he did not regard it as being derived from 'actual statistics of crops and prices'. Stigler (1965, p. 213) used quotation marks when referring to the law as the first 'empirical' demand schedule, and went on to discuss what he called 'real empirical' investigations. On the other hand, there were those such as Jevons and Marshall who clearly thought that the law was based on observations. The classic work on the history of prices by Tooke (1838) provided a convenient source for many later references to the law and it is of interest to read Tooke's confident statement, after quoting Davenant, that 'It is perhaps superfluous to add, that no such strict rule can be deduced; at the same time there is some ground for supposing that the estimate is not very wide of the truth' (1838, reprinted in 1938, Vol. I, p. 12). The kind of ambivalence shown in Tooke's comment will be discussed further in section 2.5.

2.1 Whewell's analysis

William Whewell (1794–1866) was one of the great polymaths of the 19th century, of whom a contemporary said, 'science is his forte, and omniscience his foible'. He was master of Trinity College, Cambridge from 1841, and held professorships in mineralogy (1828–32) and moral philosophy (1838–55). A surprising aspect of the literature is that Whewell's discussion of the King–Davenant Law has been entirely neglected even by those who referred in other connections to his works. As shown in the next section, Jevons seems to have been the only person to refer to Whewell's comment on the law, but even Jevons missed the most important part of his contribution. It is however very easy to miss the relevant section, since Whewell (1850, p. 5) made no mention of either King or Davenant, but only referred to the 'data given by Mr Tooke' (*High and Low Prices*, p. 288). Whewell's own presentation must also take some of the blame for this neglect; his substantial point occurs in the only footnote in his 1850 paper, and the law is discussed very briefly only as an example of a situation in which his general 'formula of demand' would not be appropriate.

Whewell's general discussion of supply and demand was to a considerable extent restricted by his special formulation in which price, p, was assumed to change by a proportion, x, so that the new price, p' is given by

$p' = p(1 + x)$. The initial and new quantities were denoted q and q' respectively, and the new total expenditure was written as $p'q' = pq(1 + mx)$, where m had to be determined in any given situation. This specification will be examined in greater detail in Chapter 3. He took several cases of supply reduction directly from the statement of the King–Davenant law and showed that the value of m varied, but for small x was about 0.5. After concluding that $pq(1 + mx)$ is not really the true formula in this context, Whewell (1850, p. 6) stated in a footnote:

> It would be easy to devise a formula which should more nearly represent Mr Tooke's progression; but even if his numbers were derived from facts, they would, of themselves, be insecure grounds for generalisation. And the nature of the progression makes it probable that ⸝he progression is hypothetical merely: the third difference being constant: as appears thus:

$$
\begin{array}{ccccccc}
0 & & 3 & & 8 & & 16 & & 28 & & 45 \\
& 3 & & 5 & & 8 & & 12 & & 17 \\
& & 2 & & 3 & & 4 & & 5 \\
& & & 1 & & 1 & & 1
\end{array}
$$

> The general term of the series 3, 8, 16, 28, 45 is
> $$\frac{n(n + 1)(n + 2)}{6} + 2n.$$

He then concluded that the law must be 'hypothetical merely'. The numbers on the top row of Whewell's table are the increases in price, in tenths, resulting from equal decreases of supply of one tenth, as displayed in Davenant's presentation. The second row (of first differences) is obtained by calculating the differences between the successive items in the first row; thus $3 = 3 - 0$, $5 = 8 - 3$, and so on. The last part of Whewell's terse comment reveals two useful points about the function. First, the demonstration that the third differences are constant immediately indicates that the demand function relating price to quantity must be cubic. Second, having obtained the form of the progression, the equation could have been obtained by direct substitution; this is shown in the following subsection.

The solution from Whewell's series
Whewell's hint at the end of his footnote enables the equation of the King–Davenant law to be obtained by direct substitution. If the initial values (or 'common rates') of q and p are normalized to unity, then the law states that as q takes the values, 1, 0.9, 0.8,. . .,0.5 then p takes the values 1, $1 + 3/10$, $1 + 8/10$,. . ., $1 + 45/10$, respectively. Hence q takes the values

$(1 - n/10)$ for n $1, \ldots, 5$. Similarly, using Whewell's result, p takes the values $1 + [\{n(n + 1)(n + 2)/6\} + 2n]/10$ for $n = 1, \ldots, 5$. Thus

$$p = 1 + n(n + 1)(n + 2)/60 + 0.2n \qquad (2.1)$$

and making the substitution $q = 1 - n/10$, so that $n = 10(1 - q)$, equation (2.1) becomes, after a little manipulation, the following cubic:

$$p = 25 - 62\tfrac{1}{3}q + 55q^2 - 16\tfrac{2}{3}q^3 \qquad (2.2)$$

This formula fits the normalized Davenant figures exactly.

2.2 Jevons's formula

Jevons's specification
Although Jevons did not draw a demand curve in his *Theory of Political Economy* he specified a functional form and attempted to estimate its parameters using the information contained in Davenant's table. Jevons wrote the dependent variable as the price, with the quantity as the independent variable, which is natural when following Davenant's statement. Jevons clearly regarded the law as being based on direct observation, and quoted the high authority of Tooke as stating that it 'is not very wide of the truth' (Jevons, 1957, p. 156). He attempted 'to ascertain the law to which Davenant's figures conform', and proceeded by imposing a priori restrictions on the nature of the schedule. He argued that it would be asymptotic to the quantity axis, and that the price would approach infinity before q approached zero. Thus:

> It is probably that the price of corn would never sink to zero, as, if abundant, it could be used for horses, poultry or cattle, as for other purposes for which it is too costly at present. . . . On the other hand, when the quantity is much diminished, the price should rise rapidly, and should become infinite before the quantity is zero, because famine would then be impending. . . a total deficiency of corn could not be made up by other food. (1957, p. 157)

On the basis of these arguments, and 'inspection of the numerical data' . (adopting the same normalization as used above in section 2.1), Jevons suggested the function:

$$p = a/(q - b)^n \qquad (2.3)$$

Equation (2.3) does not transform to one which is linear in the coefficients, so estimation of the parameters a, b, and n would have presented

Jevons with an awkward numerical problem. However, Jevons only said that 'inspection of the numerical data shows that *n* is about equal to 2, and, assuming it to be exactly 2, I find that the most probable values of *a* and *b* are $a = 0.824$ and $b = 0.12'$ (1957, p. 157). He then used these values to calculate estimated values of *p* corresponding to each *q*, compared them with Davenant's values, and concluded, 'we may safely substitute the empirical formula for his numbers' (1957, p. 158). Rather surprisingly, after taking the trouble to introduce the parameter *b*, Jevons goes on to state:

> Roughly speaking, the price of corn may be said to vary inversely as the square of the supply, provided that this supply be not unusually small. I find that this is nearly the same conclusion as Whewell drew from the same numbers. He says: 'If the above numbers were to be made the basis of a mathematical rule, it would be found that the price varies inversely as the square of the supply, or rather in a higher ratio'. (1957, p. 158)

This statement is surprising for a further two reasons. First, he was quoting from Whewell's *Six Lectures on Political Economy* (1862), rather than the more detailed discussion of 1850 examined above. However, Jevons knew of the 1850 paper and earlier papers: they are mentioned in his list of mathematico-economic literature (1957, pp. 322–40) and in his preface to the second edition of *The Theory of Political Economy* (1957, p. xxv). Jevons therefore missed Whewell's most perceptive remarks on the law; perhaps he too rapidly judged Whewell as one who used mathematics, but 'built upon the sand' (1957, p. xxv). The second surprising aspect of the statement is in fact the quotation from Whewell. Section 2.1 above has shown that Whewell's comment of 1850 leads to the recognition that the equation must be a cubic. It seems that in 1862 Whewell forgot what he had written in 1850.

Further properties of the formula
The formula used by Jevons is one of the forms considered by Pareto over 25 years later for graduating income distributions. The non-linearity in the coefficients means that estimation of the parameters would have been very difficult. If the value of $n = 2$ is imposed, along with Jevons, it is possible to estimate values of the parameters *a* and *b* using only two pairs of points, say (p_1, q_1) and (p_2, q_2). The two simultaneous equations can be solved to give $b = (\sigma q_1 - q_2)/(\sigma - 1)$, where $\sigma = \sqrt{(p_1/p_2)}$, and *a* is easily obtained by substitution into equation (2.3). If Jevons used this approach he did not use two points taken directly from the King–Davenant table, but two taken perhaps after drawing a free-hand curve through the six points.

The parameters of equation (2.3) can be estimated using an iterative procedure based on the method of maximum likelihood; see Creedy (1985). The use of this procedure with the King–Davenant data gives values for a, b and n respectively of 2.299 (± 0.505), -0.631 (± 0.110) and 4.736 (± 0.384), with standard errors in parentheses. The important point to note is that the value of b is negative, rather than being positive as Jevons supposed; the demand curve is given by $p = 2.299/(q + 0.631)^{4.736}$. Also, the exponent is much larger than Jevons imagined, and of course the value of b implies that the curve intersects the ordinate. In fact, had Jevons plotted his fitted curve alongside the curve obtained much more easily by setting b to zero, he would have seen that the latter gives a closer fit. Thus Jevons, having missed Whewell's hint, provided an a priori specification of the demand curve but did not reject his assumptions, because his own approach gave what seemed a reasonable fit to the data. His use of economic arguments to provide a nonlinear specification may nevertheless be regarded as a pioneering piece of applied econometrics. It was however the particular set of a priori assumptions used which formed the starting point of Wicksteed's later criticisms.

Before turn to Wicksteed's contribution it is worth mentioning Pareto's brief discussion of the law. It does not seem to be widely recognized that Pareto first introduced his famous law of income distribution in 1895 (one year earlier than the essay usually cited), in connection with the King–Davenant law and the analysis of demand. He gave no bibliographical details, but mentioned Jevons's name. However, none of the other relevant authors was noted, and Pareto did not examine Jevons's treatment. Pareto's paper is of interest mainly for his explicit discussion of aggregation in demand analysis. By specifying a simple relationship between demand, income and price, Pareto obtained the aggregate relationship between demand and price by aggregating over the relevant range of incomes (using his simple functional form to describe the income distribution).

2.3 Wicksteed's solution
Wicksteed's criticism of Jevons
Wicksteed's (1889) analysis of the King–Davenant law arose directly from his close analysis of Jevons's work. In his opening comments, Wicksteed stated that, 'empirical or hypothetical data may be seriously misinterpreted, even by experts, for a want of a sufficiently close preliminary analysis of the mathematical instrument of investigation' (1889, reprinted in 1933, p. 734). He then criticized Jevons for his assumptions that the demand curve would be asymptotic to the quantity axis (the abscissa) but that the price would approach infinity before the quantity is reduced to

zero, leading to Jevons's shifting of the vertical axis to the left by taking the power of $q - b$ rather than q.

Wicksteed objected to Jevons's consideration of the use of wheat for purposes other than human food. Thus, 'the law connecting the six points which constitute our data must be independent of such possible uses of wheat as are wholly inoperative throughout the region over which our observations (or conjectures) extend' (1933, p. 736). He also argued 'it is pitiable to think how slight the rise would probably have to be in order to induce incipient "famine", and how false the inference that if people are dying for want of a thing the price of that thing must be "infinite" ' (1933, p. 737). Wicksteed's sharp treatment of Jevons in this context contrasts with his more usual laudatory comments. Wicksteed's argument that the curve 'will cut both axes' was not however used to suggest a specification of the mathematical form of the curve, but was kept in reserve, 'to act as a check upon our results' (1933, p. 737). Wicksteed did not follow Jevons's reference to Whewell and therefore missed the latter's useful contribution.

Bridge's formula
After rejecting Jevons's approach Wicksteed states that a third degree polynomial fits the points exactly, and gives the formula as:

$$60p = 1500 - 374q + 33q^2 - q^3 \qquad (2.4)$$

Wicksteed had transformed the data such that $q = 10$ when $p = 1$, and substitution confirms that equations (2.4) and (2.2) are equivalent (remembering that Whewell and Jevons set $q = 1$ when $p = 1$). Wicksteed wrote in a footnote that the formula, 'may be conveniently found by the method of differences' and added 'I am indebted to Mr John Bridge, of Hampstead, for suggesting the application of this method' (1933, p. 737, n. 1). Bridge was a mathematics tutor at University College London, and Wicksteed had been supplementing his mathematical training by taking lessons in calculus from Bridge (see Herford, 1931, p. 200, n. 1). Wicksteed's presentation does not really suggest a confident handling of the technique, and for this reason it seems appropriate to refer to the solution as 'Bridge's formula', rather than Wicksteed's formula.

Just like Whewell before him, Wicksteed was led by his investigation to question the origin of the law. For example, he commented that, 'These results have a *resemblance* which is truly remarkable. . .Such an outcome of our investigations can hardly fail to stimulate curiosity as to the origin of this most interesting estimate, and the grounds on which it was formed' (1933, p. 738). But Wicksteed could not have been particularly curious, as he immediately moved on to criticize Jevons's treatment of the dimensions of economic quantities. Wicksteed gave no indication of whether he would have agreed with Whewell that the law is 'hypothetical'.

The 'method of differences'

Wicksteed refers only to the use of the 'method of differences', giving no further references and no explanation, except to add rather cryptically (1933, p. 737, n. 1)

Take four points:

```
10 . . . 1
              3
 9 . . . 1.3    2
              5    1
 8 . . . 1.8    3
              8
 7 . . . 2.6
```

Wicksteed had in fact provided part of what is called a table of 'differences'. This should be compared with the table produced by Whewell and quoted in section 2.1 above. The first column represents the first four values of q, while the second column gives corresponding values of p, and the following columns give appropriate first, second and third differences, except that Wicksteed omitted the decimal points (the third column should read 0.3, 0.5, 0.8, and so on). There is enough information in this hint to indicate that Wicksteed was actually referring to a method of interpolation which is based on the representation of a polynomial by factorials. In the case where, as in the present context, the values of the argument of the function increase by equal intervals, interpolation may proceed using what is generally known as the Gregory–Newton formula. It is now rare for economists to be trained in methods of numerical analysis, so the approach may perhaps be worth briefly presenting here.

Suppose that a number of values of p corresponding to values of q are available, and the unknown relationship is written as $p = \mathrm{f}(q)$. Denote the first value of q by q_0, and suppose that the available values of q have equal intervals of w. It is required to estimate the value of p corresponding to an unobserved value of q, of $q_0 + xw$; where x is some specified proportion. An infinite number of curves can of course be drawn to pass through the observed points, but the method is based on the use of a polynomial of appropriate degree, which is basically the simplest type of curve to satisfy the requirement. The Gregory–Newton formula states:

Table 2.1   Part of a table of differences

q	$f(q)$	$\Delta f(q)$	$\Delta^2 f(q)$
q_0	$f(q_0)$		
$q_0 + w$	$f(q_0 + w)$	$f(q_0 + w) - f(q_0)$	
$q_0 + 2w$	$f(q_0 + 2w)$	$f(q_0 + 2w) - f(q_0 + w)$	$f(q_0 + 2w) - 2f(q_0 + w) + f(q_0)$
$q_0 + 3w$	$f(q_0 + 3w)$	$f(q_0 + 3w) - f(q_0 + 2w)$	$f(q_0 + 3w) - 2f(q_0 + 2w) + f(f_0 + w)$

Table 2.2   The table of differences for the King–Davenant law

q	$f(q)$	$\Delta f(q)$	$\Delta^2 f(q)$	$\Delta^3 f(q)$
10	1			
		0.3		
9	1.3		0.2	
		0.5		0.1
8	1.8		0.3	
		0.8		0.1
7	2.6		0.4	
		1.2		0.1
6	3.8		0.5	
		1.7		
5	5.5			

$$p = f(q_0) + x\Delta f(q_0) + \frac{x(x - 1)}{2!}\Delta^2 f(q_0) +$$
$$... + \frac{x(x - 1)...(x - n + 1)}{n!}\Delta^n f(q_0) \qquad (2.5)$$

where $\Delta f(q_0)$ is by definition the first difference $f(q_0 + w) - f(q_0)$ and $\Delta^2 f(q_0)$ is the second difference $\{f(q_0 + 2w) - f(q_0 + w)\} - \{f(q_0 + w) - f(q_0)\}$. The top left-hand corner of the appropriate table of differences can therefore be written as shown in Table 2.1.

The approach is tractable because for a polynomial of degree n, all the values of $\Delta^n f$ are constant, and values of $\Delta^{n+s} f$ are zero for $s \geq 1$. In practice, a table of differences would be constructed using all observed values of q and $p = f(q)$, and the degree of the polynomial would be chosen as the value of n for which the differences $\Delta^n f$ are roughly constant. In the present context, the table of differences is shown in Table 2.2, using

Wicksteed's adjustment that $q = 10$ when $p = 1$. It is immediately apparent that a third-degree polynomial is appropriate.

$$p = 1 + x(0.3) + \frac{x(x - 1)(0.2)}{2} + \frac{x(x - 1)(x - 2)(0.1)}{6} \quad (2.6)$$

Interpolation may therefore easily be carried out for any specified value of the proportion x. But more importantly for the present context, equation (2.6) may be used to find the coefficients of the polynomial relating p to powers of q by using the fact that by definition $q = q_0 + xw$. Here $q_0 = 10$ and $w = -1$; hence $x = 10 - q$. Substitution into (2.6) gives:

$$p = 1 + (10 - q)(0.3) + (10 - q)(9 - q)(0.1) + \\ (10 - q)(9 - q)(8 - q)(0.1/6). \quad (2.7)$$

Inspection of equation (2.7) shows that the easiest way to simplify is first to multiply both sides by 60 in order to eliminate the decimals, whence it can be seen that:

$$60p = 1500 - 374q + 33q^2 - q^3 \quad (2.8)$$

which is precisely the formula given by Wicksteed. The calculation of equation (2.8) has used only the first four values in Table 2.2 but the same result would be obtained using any four consecutive points.

It was stated above that Jevons did not see Whewell's footnote on the law. There is, however, no doubt that he would have recognized the importance of the table. Indeed, Jevons was familiar with the 'method of differences' and would have had no difficulty in using it to produce the correct formula, but his a priori argument led him away from the use of a simple polynomial. Jevons gave a clear summary of the method in his *Principles of Science* (1909, pp. 495–9), where he warned of the dangers of extrapolating beyond the range of observations.

2.4 Yule's equation

There had been 21 years between the analyses of Whewell and Jevons, with a further 28 years between the latter and Wicksteed. The next, entirely independent, contribution was published by Yule a further 26 years later, in 1915. Yule's (1915a) brief note was stimulated by his reading of Moore's book on *Economic Cycles* (1914). Moore had estimated a number of third-degree polynomials for various commodities and Yule wished to compare his results with those generated by the King–Davenant law. However, Yule mentioned no other literature relating to

Table 2.3   Table of differences for Yule's problem

x	$f(x)$	$\Delta f(x)$	$\Delta^2 f(x)$	$\Delta^3 f(x)$
0	0			
		30		
−10	30		20	
		50		10
−20	80		30	
		80		10
−30	160		40	
		120		10
−40	280		50	
		170		
−50	450			

the law, and simply wrote: 'I do not know whether anyone has noticed the form of this law. The figures given form a three-difference series with the third difference unity' (1915, p. 296). He went on to state (p. 297)

If we express the defect in production in its more usual modern form of a percentage x, and the rise in price similarly as a percentage y, the relation is

$$y = -\frac{7}{3}x + \frac{1}{20}x^2 - \frac{1}{600}x^3$$
$$= -2.33x + 0.05x^2 - 0.00167x^3$$

Moore had used percentage deviations from trend values, which explains Yule's transformation. Yule gave no details of his method of solution, but his reference to third differences, with an accompanying table, clearly suggests that he used the same method as Bridge. However, Yule's approach is not obvious since the table shown by Yule (the same as that given by Whewell) could not have been the one he actually used to derive the formula quoted above. Yule expressed the relationship in terms of percentage deviations from the initial values, so that the appropriate values are shown in Table 2.3.

The variable x is used to maintain consistency with Yule's notation (and the variables y and x do not correspond to p and q used earlier). Thus in using the representation of a polynomial by factorials, as in equation (2.5) above, the variable r is substituted for x. Using Table 2.3, substitution gives

$$y = 0 + 30r + 10r(r - 1) + 10r(r - 1)(r - 2)/6 \qquad (2.9)$$

In this case $x = x_0 + rw$, and $x_0 = 0$, with $w = -10$. Hence $r = -x/10$, and substitution into equation (2.9) gives, after some simplification, the result stated by Yule. Schumpeter reproduced Yule's equation and described it simply as a demand equation without commenting on the transformation of the data.

Yule showed the similarity with Moore's results for maize and potatoes, but noted that the price rise for a given percentage deficiency was lower for Moore's data. Yule then commented that, 'The comparison makes one more curious than ever to know what estimates of production King used as a basis for his Law, and what suggested the particular form he gave to it' (1915a, p. 298). He could not resist what must have been a rather hastily considered suggestion, acknowledged to be 'pure speculation', which actually amounted to the view that the law was almost entirely hypothetical and that it was pure coincidence that it followed exactly a third-degree polynomial.

The publication by Yule of his result of the King–Davenant law virtually coincided with the birth of modern studies in demand analysis in 1914. This literature now forms a significant branch of the literature of economics, but it appears that the pioneers of this modern field treated the King–Davenant law with contempt and stressed the huge gap in time and technique between this early work and the work of their own generation. Even Schultz, the most widely read of any of the demand analysts, did not take the law seriously and in his great book of 1938 he cited none of the relevant literature. The same applies to the later scholarly treatment of Wold (1953).

2.5 Possible origins

Having considered the major analyses of the King–Davenant law, the question remains: Does this literature shed any fresh light on the issues, raised in the introduction, of the origins and nature of the law? Consider the following alternative hypotheses concerning its origins.

First, the majority of early writers who quoted the law took the view that while it did not reproduce exact observations it was based on well-informed guesswork. Although there was not a vast amount of data by modern standards, Schultz (1938, p. 657) clearly exaggerated their scarcity, and King and Gregory were well placed to have access to the best data available. For a valuable account of commercial statistics at the time of King and Davenant, see Clark (1938). The belief that King was associated with the law adds weight to the idea that it was not purely hypothetical. For example, Studenski's view is quite representative: he stated that King, 'was modest and unassuming, meticulously careful with his figures, and extremely cautious in his conclusions' (1958, p. 30). However, the knowledge that the law follows precisely a third-degree polynomial means that this simple explanation must be rejected. It is highly unlikely that informed estimates would by coincidence follow such a formula.

The second possibility, that the law is purely hypothetical, was suggested by Whewell and Yule (Wicksteed was less explicit in his reaction). It is of course possible that hypothetical values of coefficients were used with a cubic equation in order to generate the basic 'data', and then the results converted into the familiar elasticity form. It may however be objected that a more simple equation, with less awkward parameter values, would have served the same purpose equally well. But it may perhaps also be suggested that Davenant actually wished to conceal the use of a hypothetical formula by making its nature less than obvious. Against this point it could be argued that small adjustments to the numerical values in the table would have served the same purpose more effectively.

The suggestion that the law is hypothetical because it is discovered to be exactly a third-degree polynomial ignores the important point, made by neither Wicksteed nor Yule, that their discovery was made using an approach devised by the mathematicians James Gregory and Isaac Newton. This method of interpolation was introduced by Gregory in 1670. It became more widely known through Newton's publications, as early as 1672, but especially through the *Principia* of 1687. It is therefore quite possible that, using the 'method of differences', a third-degree polynomial was fitted to actual observations. The presentation of the cubic by Davenant would have been quite out of place and for his wider readership the table is much more suitable. The suggestion that the Gregory–Newton method was used to estimate a cubic demand curve using genuine data can of course only remain speculation, but it is not unreasonable.

If the possibility that the Gregory–Newton approach was used with available data is taken seriously, are there any implications for the question of who first produced the law? Although, as seen above, there is no direct evidence that the law was derived by King, the hypothesis presented here does lend some support to the suggestion that the basic work was carried out by him. King at one time supported himself by teaching mathematics, while it was unlikely that Davenant had sufficient knowledge of mathematics. The possibility that the first demand curve was estimated using a sophisticated numerical procedure does indeed place it in a different light from that in which it is usually viewed. The view that the law was generated using an interpolation method also qualifies somewhat the judgement of Robertson (1949, p. 523) that, 'There is nothing in the literature of political arithmetic ... which may properly be regarded as mathematical . . ., contrary to what we might expect in view of their preoccupation with quantities'.

Notes and further reading

In quoting the schedule at the beginning of this chapter, the last three rows have used the notation of, for example, 1 + 6 tenths (that is, 16 tenths). This differs from the original statement, in which the potentially confusing notation of 1.6 tenths was used.

A good example of the importance attached to the law is the following remark by Rogers (1891, p. 250):

> Now there is one law of prices which you must know and understand before you can make the least progress in interpreting the simplest problem. It is known to some economists, I do not say all, for it is most unaccountably neglected or obscured in most treatises on the subject, as Gregory King's Law.

Published versions of King's writings, other than those in Chalmers (1802), are contained in the editions by Barnett (1936) and Laslett (1973). King's role in early population estimates is examined in detail in Glass and Eversley (1965). References to manuscripts of King are also given by Deane (1974). Evans (1967, p. 485) mentions the reference to the law by Schumpeter (1954, p. 212, n. 4), who claimed incorrectly that Chalmers (1802) contains, in sections VI and VII, the 'famous demand schedule'. Stigler (1965, p. 214) reported that the law was attributed to King by Lord Lauderdale in the latter's *Inquiry into the Nature and Origin of Public Wealth* (1804), although Stigler added that this was made 'without any known basis'. While Wicksteed (1933, p. 735) and Wold (1953, p. 331) acknowledge Jevons's tentative support for Davenant, it is strange that Schultz actually said (1938, p. 397) that the law was attributed to King by Davenant. But he gave no primary reference and in a footnote simply referred to the relevant section in Jevons's *Theory of Political Economy*. It is of interest to note that using the information given by Lowe (1823, pp. 151–3), who made no reference to King or Davenant, similar results can be obtained for the elasticity at the normal harvest. Furthermore, Stigler (1965, p. 215, n. 32) pointed out that Engel's estimate of the elasticity of demand at the normal harvest was close to that of King.

Jevons's attitude to Whewell did not help later perceptions of his work, but see Schumpeter (1954, p. 488, n. 7), and the brief discussion by Robertson (1949). In the more recent examinations of Whewell's work by Henderson (1973) and Rashid (1977), there is still no mention of his comments on the King–Davenant law.

Jevons's discussion of the law has been much neglected. It is not mentioned by S. Stigler (1982), and although Stigler (1965, p. 214, n. 30) seems to be the only person to refer to Wicksteed's contribution, he did not go back to Jevons, and via Jevons to Whewell. Jevons is the only author who both took the schedule seriously and took a scholarly interest in the origin of the law.

Pareto mentioned the name of Thorold Rogers, but gave no bibliographical reference. In addition to the discussion mentioned above, Thorold Rogers suggested that (1884, p. 484):

> The seven barren years at the conclusion of the seventeenth century were long noted for the distress of the people and for the exalted profits of the farmer, as they probably gave occasion to the celebrated law of Gregory King, that when there ensues a scarcity in an absolute necessity of life, and the quantity falls off in an arithmetic ratio, the price is exalted in a geometric one.

However, it can easily be seen that the assumption of a simple 'Malthusian' type of relationship is not supported by the data. Pareto may also have had in mind Thorold Rogers (1891), where he attributed the law to King and said that, 'though undoubtedly sound in principle, [it] is hypothetical in form' (1891, p. 252; see also p. 55). A rare but brief reference to Pareto (1895) in connection with the law of demand is contained in Marget (1938, p. 209). Schultz (1938, p. 127) referred to Pareto's aggregation procedure, and pointed out that Moore (1908) was the first demand analyst to draw attention to the approach, but neither Schultz nor Moore mentioned that the King–Davenant law was the starting point of Pareto's paper. It is of interest that later work of Moore led indirectly to Yule's publication discussed above.

Wicksteed first stated the equation of the King–Davenant law in a footnote to his *Alphabet* (1888, p. 44), but he gave no explanation or reference. As noted above, Wicksteed's analysis has suffered considerable neglect. It seems odd that Schumpeter (1954, p. 832) actually praises Wicksteed's 1889 paper for its analysis of Jevons's theory of dimensions in economics, but in connection with the King–Davenant law (1954, p. 213, n. 5) he only mentions Yule's (1915a) note. Reference may also be made here to a brief comment on Jevons's assumptions by a perceptive correspondent, R.O. Williams; see Black (1977, p. 138). Jevons's brother Thomas Edwin Jevons (1841–1917) replied to Wicksteed's criticism. T.E. Jevons (1889) devoted part of his reply to a further justification of Jevons's a priori assumptions, and in doing this he ignored completely the implication of Wicksteed's (Bridge's) formula that it cuts both the ordinate and the abscissa. Jevons's younger brother Thomas had much earlier moved to the United States where he pursued a successful career, but there was an extensive correspondence between the two brothers; see Black (1982). On Jevons's treatment see also Bostaph and Shieh (1987).

For a good account of the method of differences see Whittaker and Robinson (1944, pp. 8–10). At one time, economists with an interest in statistics would have received training in numerical methods of interpolation; for example Bowley (1926) devotes a chapter to interpolation. A curious feature of Yule's contribution is that it has been cited more often than the others discussed here. In addition to Schumpeter (1954, p. 213, n. 5), it has been cited by Deane (1974, p. 386), Spiegel (1971, p. 142), and Evans (1967, p. 488). The omission of Yule by Stigler is surprising in view of the fact that he elsewhere quoted from Yule's (1915b) review of Moore's book; see Stigler (1965, p. 356). This review is only a few pages away from Yule (1915a). More surprising perhaps is the act that Evans did not mention Wicksteed, even though he quoted from the same page in Stigler (1965) which contains the footnote reference to Wicksteed.

In the first edition of his *Principles*, Marshall stated the law and then added that, 'This is the famous estimate quoted by Gregory King' (1961, II, p. 250). But this was later revised and extended to the remark that the law is, 'commonly attributed to Gregory King. Its bearing on the law of demand is admirably discussed by Lord Lauderdale' (1961, I, p. 106, n. 2). Although Marshall made no reference to Jevons, it is likely that his position was probably influenced by Jevons's discussion. In his footnote discussion of the law, Marshall (1961, I, p. 106, n. 2) made no mention of Jevons or Wicksteed. But he produced a diagram to reinforce his statement that, 'where the price of wheat is very low, it may be used, as it was for instance in 1834, for feeding cattle and sheep and pigs and for brewing and distilling' and 'when the price is very high, cheaper substitutes can be got for it'.

Mention should also be made of a study, published in the same year as Schultz's classic, by Guitton (1938). A rare reference to this book is in Spiegel (1971, p. 142), who nevertheless gave no details of its content. This interesting study concentrated on the non-proportionality of the price response to the supply shortfall, and examined later data for France. No mention was made of Whewell, Wicksteed, Pareto, or Yule, but Guitton (1938, p. 27, n. 1) reproduced Jevons's result. He referred to it as a Newtonian formula since it involves the reciprocal of a square: but as shown above, there are other and perhaps better reasons for regarding the basic law as 'Newtonian'. In the same footnote, Guitton reproduced a statement by Bouniatian (1927, p. 64) that $y = 0.757/(x - 0.13)^2$ is an improvement on Jevons's estimate. Guitton (1938, p. 76, n. 2) also repeated the incorrect suggestion that prices vary in a geometric progression, but made the more interesting point (1938, p. 58) that the price response may not be symmetric with respect to an increase in supply, giving rise to a hysteresis effect. There is also a brief discussion of the law by Einaudi (1943), but of the authors discussed here he mentioned only Jevons. See also Endres (1985, 1987).

It is appropriate to mention another colourful figure who emerges from this investigation of the famous law. Gregory first made his results known to John Collins (1625–83), who was the former's sole contact with the outside world while at the University of St Andrews. Collins had a varied career, including work in the Excise Office, the Royal Mint and the Royal Fishery Company, but he is best remembered through his corresponding with Newton and Gregory. As Letwin (1963, p. 107) states: 'At any time between 1668 and 1680, Collins, it is quite safe to say, knew more about the frontiers of mathematical inquiry than any other man'. Collins played an important role not only in spreading knowledge but in persistently placing practical problems before these two great mathematicians. See especially the Newton correspondence (which includes letters of Gregory and Collins) edited by Turnbull (1959, pp. 46, 49, 61–2, 342–5). Turnbull (1959, p. 327, n. 2) shows that the interpolation formula (based on third differences) must have been known to Michael Dary (1613–79) before Gregory or Newton, which is of interest in view of the fact that Dary was an assistant of Collins at the Royal Mint.

As Letwin (1963, pp. 97–113) shows, Collins was also a political arithmetician *manqué*. He had a large collection of books on trade, and Letwin (1963, p. 112) reproduces an interesting letter from Collins to Shaftsbury of about 1670 in which he gave an outline of projects in political arithmetic which he wished to carry out. Collins never really had the opportunity to fulfil his plans. Although no direct link between Collins, King and Davenant has been traced, it is rather a nice thought that this economist *manqué* might have had an indirect role, through providing an important stimulus to Gregory and Newton, in the production of the celebrated law of demand.

3   The elasticity of demand

It has been seen in Chapter 2 that the King–Davenant law of demand was presented in what may be described as 'elasticity' form. This was fully recognized by the many subsequent writers who made use of the schedule to point out that farmers gain when the supply falls as a result of crop failure. The relationship between the proportional changes in price and quantity and the change in total expenditure involved was reasonably well understood. However, it seems something of an exaggeration to say with Stigler that the idea of elasticity was so prevalent that 'the whole literature of the pre-Marshallian period teems with discussion of it' (1965, p.2). In the non-mathematical literature no-one used the relationship between price, quantity and revenue changes better than J.S. Mill in his analysis of international trade, but he cannot be said to have defined the concept of elasticity. This important work will be examined in Part 2 of the present book.

It seems that the earliest explicit treatment of an elasticity concept, related to the idea of demand as a schedule, was by Whewell. Section 3.1 is devoted to Whewell's treatment, which was an important ingredient in his international trade model (examined in Chapter 7 below). It is sometimes suggested that Cournot was very close to the concept of elasticity. Although Section 3.2 will argue that Cournot was not in fact very close, it will be seen that his analysis of changes in total expenditure is very important for the insights it can provide into exchange. However, Cournot's partial equilibrium approach prevented those insights being exploited by Cournot himself. Section 3.3 turns to Marhsall's famous treatment of elasticity, where it is shown that his diagrammatic approach may owe something to one of Cournot's diagrams.

3.1   Whewell and elasticity
Whewell's first treatment
Whewell's recognition in 1850, that the King–Davenant law of demand describes a progression whose third differences are constant, has been discussed in Chapter 2. However, his first analysis of the law appeared in 1829 in the course of his criticisms of Ricardo. At this early stage, Whewell gave a clear definition of the price elasticity of demand and suggested that in general it will vary along the demand curve.

Whewell (1829, p.10) first considered the possibility that the expenditure on a good is constant, but argued that, 'probably the approximation is a very loose and inaccurate one. According to this estimate, the failure of 1/4 the crop of corn, for instance, would increase the price by 1/3.' Whewell did not explain his calculation, but suppose that the initial price and quantity are p and q respectively while the new values are p' and q'. If expenditure remains constant then $pq = p'q' = $ k, say. If q changes such that $q' = (3/4) q$, then $p'q' = (3/4) p'q' = $ k and substitution for $q = $ k$/p$ gives the result that the proportional increase in the price is equal to (p'/p) $- 1 = (4/3) - 1 = 1/3$. Most modern students would probably have answered that constant expenditure implies an elasticity of $- 1$, with equal and opposite proportional changes in quantity and price, so that the price must increase by 25 per cent rather than 33 per cent. But this standard result applies only to small changes. It will be seen below that Whewell's later approach was restricted to small changes too, but that he, along with some later commentators, did not fully appreciate the nature of the restriction.

Whewell immediately contrasted his figures with the values given in the King–Davenant schedule, which he quoted in full, and suggested that, 'the increase of the price is much more rapid than the diminution of the supply. And according to this table the increase of the price varies according to no simple power of the defect of the supply' (1829, p. 11). He argued that in the cases he wished to consider (such as the effects of tax changes) the changes are small and 'we cannot be far wrong' in assuming that 'the increase of price is proportional to the deficiency of the supply'. Based on the first row of the King–Davenant table, Whewell stated that the constant of proportionality is three (a defect of 1/10th raises the price by 3/10 ths), and then added that 'I shall however use the general number e instead of 3 in most cases'. This term, $e,$ is of course $-$ the *reciprocal* of the price elasticity of demand.

Whewell added, 'It is manifest, that whatever more accurate data we may hereafter obtain for establishing the law of this dependence, the increase of price *ceteris paribus* must be a *function* of the defect of supply, and may in this manner be introduced into the calculation' (1829, p. 11). Two years later, Whewell very briefly discussed demand and referred to his earlier paper. The assumption of small changes was implicit when he wrote that, 'If the supply diminish in the ratio 1:1 $- y$, the price increases in the ratio 1:1 $+ ey$: (e being greater than 1)' (1831, p. 10). In this statement, y is the proportional reduction in the supply. Hence the proportional increase in the price is ey, with $(dq/q)/(dp/p) = - (1/e) = -y/(dp/p)$. The statement that e is greater than unity implies an inelastic demand, of course.

It was 20 years before Whewell again considered the 'law of demand', in the context of his examination of Mill's analysis of international trade. This will form the subject of Chapter 7, but the remainder of this section concentrates on Whewell's development of his treatment of demand. His later focus on changes in total expenditure is retained from his treatment of 20 years earlier, which was so strongly influenced by his examination of the King–Davenant table. The discussion of Mill, with its emphasis on changes in total expenditure as a result of trade, would clearly have suggested the applicability of Whewell's earlier formulation.

The basic framework

The new focus of analysis (Mill's treatment of trade) required a change from the emphasis of the King–Davenant law on the effect of supply reductions in the price. In 1850, Whewell's starting point was a change in the price. As before, he made no use of calculus, but his approach implicitly required an assumption of small changes. Denoting price and quantity demanded as p and q respectively, Whewell considered the new price and quantity, p' and q', that would result from a proportionate increase, of x, in the price of the good. The new price becomes:

$$p' = p(1 + x) \tag{3.1}$$

Whewell wrote the new total expenditure as

$$p'q' = pq(1 + mx) \tag{3.2}$$

This shows that planned expenditure changes by a proportion, mx, that is expressed as a multiple of the proportionate change in the price. Whewell called m the 'specific rate of change' of the commodity and distinguished goods according to its value. When $m = 0$, total expenditure is unchanged and the good is called an 'article of fixed expenditure'; goods for which $0 < m < 1$ are 'general necessaries' for which expenditure rises; when $m = 1$ the quantity is unchanged and such goods were called 'conventional necessaries'; for 'popular luxuries' $m < 0$ and expenditure decreases. In his discussion of the practical application of his approach, Whewell suggested that m would vary along the demand curve, and showed that this point is true of the King–Davenant schedule. Combining (3.1) and (3.2), Whewell sometimes found it convenient to write:

$$q' = \frac{q(1 + mx)}{(1 + x)} \tag{3.3}$$

Demand elasticities

In examining Whewell's approach it is first useful to write total expenditure as R. The proportionate change in R from R to R' is, as already noted, given by mx. Hence for small changes (3.1) and (3.2) give:

$$\frac{dp}{p} = \frac{p'}{p} - 1 = x \text{ and } \frac{dR}{R} = \frac{R'}{R} - 1 = mx \tag{3.4}$$

Thus the price elasticity of total expenditure is:

$$\frac{dR/R}{dp/p} = m \tag{3.5}$$

and is the 'specific rate of change' of the good. The relationship between this term and price elasticity of demand can be seen as follows. The total derivative dR is equal to qdp is $+pdq$, so that:

$$\frac{dR}{R} = \frac{dp}{p} + \frac{dp}{q} \tag{3.6}$$

If η denotes the 'Marshallian' price elasticity of demand $(dq/q)/(dp/p)$, dividing equation (3.6) by dp/p gives:

$$m = 1 + \eta \tag{3.7}$$

It seems that this property was first noted, without any explanation, by MacGregor (1942, p. 316). In terms of Whewell's term, e, introduced in his 1829 and 1831 papers, the same approach confirms that, for small changes, $m = 1 - 1/e$.

Further insight may be gained by considering directly the proportional change in the quantity demanded. Writing:

$$q' = q(1 + y) \tag{3.8}$$

Then total expenditure after the price change is given by:

$$\begin{aligned} p'q' &= pq(1 + x)(1 + y) \\ &= pq(1 + x + y + xy) \end{aligned} \tag{3.9}$$

For small changes:

$$y = \frac{dq}{q} = \frac{dq}{dp}\frac{p}{q}\frac{dp}{p} = \eta x \tag{3.10}$$

Substituting (3.10) into (3.9) and neglecting the resulting term in x^2 gives:

$$p'q' = pq\{1 + x(1 + \eta)\} \qquad (3.11)$$

Hence comparision of (3.11) with (3.2) immediately gives the result already established in (3.7) that $m = 1 + \eta$. The limitation of Whewell's representation to the analysis of small changes in price is clearly brought out by the above arguments.

Now consider the expression in (3.3), used by Whewell. It would perhaps be tempting to rewrite this as

$$\frac{q'}{q} = \frac{1 + mx}{1 + x}$$

and hence

$$\frac{\mathrm{d}q}{q} = \frac{q'}{q} - 1 = \frac{x(m-1)}{1 + x} \qquad (3.12)$$

However, the latter approach would give the incorrect result for the price elasticity, of $(m - 1)/(1 + x)$; this converges to the result in (3.7) only as x approaches zero. This argument suggests that instead of using Whewell's equation (3.3.) it would be more appropriate to return to (3.4) and (3.6), which together give:

$$\frac{\mathrm{d}R}{R} = mx = \frac{\mathrm{d}p}{p} + \frac{\mathrm{d}q}{q} = x + \frac{q'}{q} - 1$$

Rearrangement then gives:

$$q' = q\{1 + x(m - 1)\} \qquad (3.13)$$

When $m = 1$ both (3.3) and (3.13) give the result that the quantity demanded is unchanged. When $m = 0$ (the elasticity is $-$ unity) equation (3.13) gives the appropriate result that $q' = q(1 - x)$; that is, the quantity decreases by the same proportion as the price increases. But equation (3.3. gives $q' = q/(1 + x)$, so that the two results are consistent only if it can be assumed that $x^2 \approx 0$, in which case $(1 - x)(1 + x) \approx 1$. It is worth bearing this point in mind in Chapter 7, when considering Whewell's analysis of Mill, where he used equation (3.3). Whewell's failure to write down an explicit demand function, but to concentrate on changes in total revenue that result from small price changes, was very useful for his special purpose but certainly created unforeseen difficulties.

3.2 Cournot and total expenditure

Nine years after Whewell's clear statement of the reciprocal of elasticity, Cournot published his now much more famous *Researches* (1838, translated 1927), though he too suffered considerable neglect for many years. It has sometimes been suggested that he came very close to stating the concept of elasticity, though it will be argued that this claim is somewhat misleading.

Cournot began his discussion of demand by arguing that the words sales and demand 'are synonymous, and we do not see for what reason theory need take account of any demand which does not result in a sale' (1927, p. 46). It seems best to interpret this strong statement as implying that only 'effective demand' is relevant, rather than ruling out the possibility of excess demand or supply. Cournot then took a pathbreaking step and wrote market demand as a general function of price: 'Let us admit therefore that the sales or the annual demand D is, for each article, a particular function $F(p)$ of the price p of such article' (1927, p. 47). This has the characteristic of many original and important contributions, that with hindsight it appears rather obvious.

He went on to say that if $F(p)$ is continuous, *'The variations of the demand will be sensibly proportional to the variations in price so long as these last are small fractions of the original price.* Moreover, the variations will be of opposite signs' (1927, p. 50). It should be recognized that Cournot was here talking about absolute, not proportional variations. He was really suggesting that, for small changes, the relevant range of the demand curve can be regarded as linear. His examples were of quantity changing by one unit for each ten cents change in price. This linearization of the range of the demand curve is fundamental to Cournot's approach to comparative statics throughout the *Researches*. The technique most frequently used by Cournot was that of a Taylor series expansion. Thus if the price changes by an amount δ, the new demand is $F(p + \delta)$, which can be expanded as:

$$F(p + \delta) = F(p) + \delta F'(p) + (\delta^2/2) F''(p) + \ldots \qquad (3.14)$$

Cournot neglected the squares and higher order powers of δ in this expansion, giving the convenient linearization:

$$F(p + \delta) = F(p) + \delta F'(p) \qquad (3.15)$$

Since the variations are of 'opposite signs', the demand curve is downward sloping, enabling Cournot to assume that $F'(p) < 0$. He went on to consider total expenditure, making the important point that:

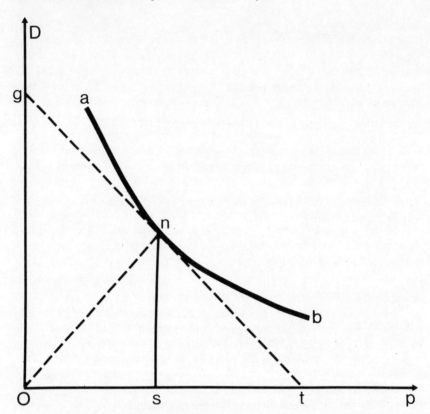

Figure 3.1   Cournot and total expenditure

Since the function F(p) is continuous, the function pF(p), which expresses the total value of the quantity annually sold, must be continuous also. This function would equal zero if p equals zero. . .[and] disappears also when p becomes infinite . . . Since the function pF(p) at first increases, and then decreases as p increases, there is therefore a value of p which makes the function a maximum, and which is given by the equation.

$$F(p) + pF'(p) = 0$$

(1927, pp. 52–53)

Cournot then refers to a diagram, reproduced in Figure 3.1 with a slight change in notation. He points out that the root of the above equation 'will be the abscissa of the point n from which the triangle Ont, formed by the tangent nt and the radius vector On, is isosceles, so that we have Os = st' (1927, p. 53). No proof is given, but it is clear that since the slope of the tangent gt is F'(s), its equation is:

$$D = g + F'(s)p \qquad (3.16)$$

and

$$F(s) = g + F'(s)s \qquad (3.17)$$

subtracting $F(s) + sF'(s) = O$ from (3.17) and rearranging gives $F(s) = g/2$, whence:

$$Os = Ot/2 \qquad (3.18)$$

It is of course a simple step from Cournot's condition for maximum expenditure to write:

$$\frac{pF'(p)}{F(p)} = -1 \qquad (3.19)$$

so that the left-hand side is the elasticity; this is (minus) unity when expenditure is a maximum. But Cournot did not take this step and to state the condition for maximum expenditure is not to define elasticity. His classification of goods was based on which side of the point n the market is currently placed. Thus there is a need:

> to separate articles of high economic importance into two categories, according as their current prices are above or below the value which makes a maximum of $pF(p)$. We shall see that many economic problems have different solutions, according as the article in question belongs to are or the other of these two categories (1927, p. 54).

Cournot uses this classification to produce *sufficient* conditions for several results to apply; an example will be examined in detail in Chapter 6 below. But Cournot's failure to produce an elasticity concept meant that he was unable to produce the *necessary* conditions.

A further difficulty with this classification is that the equation, $F(p) + pF'(p) = 0$, may have multiple roots. Cournot recognized this and showed that, with $F'(p) < 0$, there will be only one maximum if the demand function 'turns its concave side to the axis of the abscissas' (1927, p. 55). Although he did not rule out the general possibility of multiple maxima, he argued that it is highly improbable that there would be 'several intermediate maxima and minima inside of the limits between which the value of p can vary' so that 'all problems are the same as if the function $pF(p)$ only admitted a single maximum' (1927, p. 55). Again, Cournot is seen to be restricting his analysis to small changes, over which the demand curve is linear. With a linear demand curve over the whole range, the total revenue curve is parabolic.

Cournot's treatment of total expenditure has further implications which were not fully exploited until much later. First, the total revenue curve can usefully be added to Cournot's figure. It seems that this addition was first made by Lardner (1850, p. 249), whose diagram showed the case where there is a single maximum, with price on the vertical axis instead of the horizontal, as in Cournot's diagram. Lardner made no reference to Cournot, but there seems little doubt that he was directly influenced by the *Researches*. Lardner followed Cournot in stating that profit maximization requires marginal revenue to be equal to marginal cost, though of course these modern terms were not used. The second stage, not taken by Lardner, is the recognition that the total expenditure curve actually represents a *supply curve*. In the present context this is the supply or offer of money in return for the good. If the price is expressed instead as a relative price, then the total expenditure curve becomes a supply curve of the other good offered in exchange for the good in question. Such a supply curve is immediately seen to be 'backward bending'. All that is required for the supply curve to be backward bending is that the corresponding demand curve has an elastic range, since the turning point occurs where the elasticity is (minus) unity. All this leads to a general equilibrium analysis, so that further discussion must be deferred until Part 2.

3.3   Marshall and elasticity

In view of Marshall's acknowledgements to Cournot, some writers have expressed surprise at the long time taken to develop the concept of elasticity. However, it has been seen that Cournot was much further from such a concept than has sometimes been claimed. What is much more surprising is that Marshall does not seem to have been aware of Whewell's treatment. But some writers have suggested that Marshall made use of Whewell's work; these include Hutchison (1953, p. 64), Henderson (1985, p. 422) and Cochrane (1975, p. 398). One argument to support this claim is that Marshall's signature has been found on other volumes of the *Transactions* in which Whewell's papers first appeared; see Collard (1968, p. xviii). But Marshall's only reference to Whewell seems to be to the latter's role as editor of Richard Jones's works; see Pigou, (1925, p. 296) and Marshall, (1975, II, p. 264).

It does not seem possible to attribute any particular analytical contributions of Marshall to the work of Whewell. Indeed, the fact that there are valuable aspects of Whewell's work which were not used by Marshall suggests the absence of any familiarity. It has also been seen in Chapter 2 that Whewell hinted that the famous King–Davenant 'law of demand' follows a third-order polynomial precisely, yet when Marshall discussed the law in the *Principles*, he simply reproduced some of Jevons's arguments about the shape of the demand curve. Furthermore, Whitaker (in Marshall, 1975, I, p. 45, n. 26) has pointed out that Marshall made no reference to Whewell's criticisms of Ricardo.

While it may seem surprising for Marshall not to be familiar with Whewell's work, it is worth recalling a query raised by Hutchison (1955) in connection with Cournot's *Researches*. The possible significance of Cournot's book was suggested to Jevons in 1875 by the mathematician Todhunter who added that, 'I never found any person who had read the book' (Hutchison, 1955, p. 8). Yet Todhunter was. like Marshall, a fellow of St John's College and Marshall stated that he read Cournot in 1868. The lack of communication between Todhunter and Marshall, at least on the subject of Cournot, must also have extended to Whewell, about whom Todhunter had considerable knowledge.

Marshall certainly did not arrive at the terminology quickly. In his early notes, he is seen using such clumsy expressions as 'guided by the rate' (1975, I, pp. 260-80). Mary Paley Marshall describes the circumstances of Marshall's adoption of the term.

> We were five months at Palermo, on a roof, and whenever I want something pleasant to think about I try to imagine myself on it. It was the roof of a small Italian hotel, the 'Oliva', flat of course and paved with coloured tiles, and upon it during the day Alfred occupied an American chair over which the cover of the travelling bath was rigged up as an awning, and there he wrote the early chapters of his *Principles*. One day he came down from the roof to tell me how he had just discovered the notion of 'elasticity of demand'. (1947, p. 28)

By the time of its first appearance in chapter IV of the *Principles* (1961, p. 102), Marshall had certainly advanced the concept well beyond any previous writers, including Whewell. He presented, as always in a footnote, a very simple and elegant diagrammatic method of measuring elasticity. This is shown in Figure 3.2 where 'the elasticity at the point P is measured by the ratio of PT to Pt, that is of MT to MO – and therefore the elasticity is equal to one when the angle TPM is equal to the angle OPM' (1961, p. 103, n. 1). It is quite possible that Marshall was led to this form of analysis by Cournot's figure examined in the previous section. Marshall showed in his mathematical appendix that elasticity is:

$$\frac{P'R}{OM} \Big/ \frac{PR}{PM} = \frac{(P'R)\,(PM)}{(PR)\,(OM)} = \frac{(TM)\,(PM)}{(PM)\,(OM)} = \frac{TM}{OM} = \frac{PT}{Pt} \quad (3.20)$$

The statement regarding unit elasticity is, like Cournot's, a description

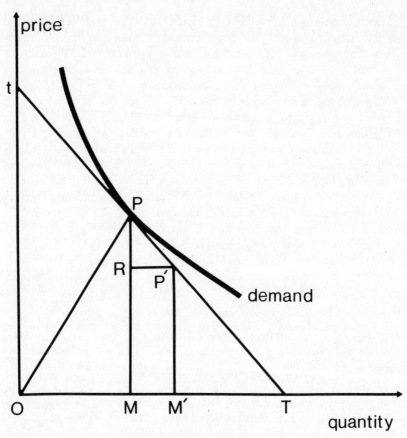

Figure 3.2   Marshall and elasticity of demand

of the result; to find it geometrically would be rather tedious, involving drawing alternative tangents and then using the standard method of bisecting a line using a set of compasses. But Marshall suggested that a point of unit elasticity can easily be found using a set of rectangular hyperbolas, which he called 'constant outlay' curves. This follows from the fact that a constant unit elasticity implies that the demand curve is a rectangular hyperbola. Hence the tangency position (or positions) of a demand curve with a rectangular hyperbola gives the point (or points) on the demand curve of unit elasticity. He recommended 'tracing constant outlay curves on thin paper, and then laying the paper over the demand curve. . .it will be found that practice of this kind makes it easy to detect the nature of the assumptions. . .which are implicitly made in drawing a demand curve of any particular shape' (1961, pp. 839–40). The use of a set of rectangular hyperbolas was also recommended for the analysis of monopoly, in particular to find the point or points of maximum profit; see Creedy and O'Brien (1990). Their use in the analysis of exchange is discussed in Chapter 8 below.

Marshall and Giffen goods

It is perhaps appropriate to discuss briefly Marshall's suggestion that the elasticity of demand may be positive, and his disagreement with Edgeworth over this issue. In the course of a review of a book by Rea, Edgeworth argued that an upward sloping demand curve was highly *improbable*. He added that, 'Even the milder statement that the elasticity of demand for wheat *may* be positive, though I know it is countenanced by high authority, appears to me so contrary to *a priori* probability as to require very strong evidence' (1904, p. 104). The high authority alluded to was of course Marshall, who made the suggestion in the *Principles* (1961, p. 132). Marshall wasted no time in responding by letter, and wrote:

> I have just noticed your review of Rae...I don't want to argue. But the hint that a rather rash and random guess has been made by those who suggest that a (moderate) rise in the price of wheat might increase its consumption in England (not generally) provokes me to say that the matter has not been taken quite at random. (in Pigou, ed., 1925, p. 438)

The following day he sent another, much longer, letter to Edgeworth concerning both the supply and demand of wheat. The Giffen good has provoked an enormous literature, but an argument used by Marshall in his second letter seems to have received little attention. Marshall gave an example involving the choice of transport in order to minimize travel time, subject to a fixed budget, and suggested:

> I believe that people in Holland travel by canal boat instead of railway sometimes on account of its cheapness. Suppose a man was in a hurry to make a journey of 150 kilos. He had two florins for it, and no more. The fair by boat was one cent a kilo, by third class train two cents. So he decided to go 100 kilos by boat, and fifty by train: total cost two florins. On arriving at the boat he found the charge had been raised to 1¼ cents per kilo. 'Oh: then I will travel 133⅓ kilos (or as near as may be) by boat, I can't afford more than 16⅔ kilos by train'. Why not? Where is the paradox? (in Pigou, ed., 1925, p. 441).

If the person were to travel 100 kilometres by boat at the higher price, he would not be able to pay for 50 kilometres by rail, and so would be unable to complete the required distance. He therefore has to travel further by the slower method. If the price of boat travel were to increase to 1⅓ cents, the traveller would have no choice but to go the whole distance by boat. Since the objective is to minimize the total journey time, this is achieved by maximizing the time spent on the fastest mode of transport. But this can only be maximized subject to constraint that sufficient money is left to complete the journey in the slower mode. Suppose that the cost of train and boat travel per unit of distance is denoted c_t and c_b respectively, and that the distance travelled by each method is L_t and L_b. It is required to travel a total distance L with a fixed budget of B. Hence the individual may be regarded as maximizing L_t subject to the constraint that:

$$B - c_t L_t = c_b(1 - L_t) \tag{3.21}$$

Substitute for $L_t = L - L_b$ and collect terms in L_b to get:

$$L_b = \frac{c_t L - B}{c_t - c_b} \tag{3.22}$$

By definition, $c_t > c_b$, and the problem is only interesting if $c_t L > B$; that is, if the cost of travelling the total distance by the fastest method exceeds the budget. Marshall chose his numbers so that the numerator of (3.22) is unity. It is thus easily confirmed that $\partial L_b / \partial c_b > 0$, so that an increase in the cost of boat travel increases the distance travelled by boat. Notice that the relative speed of alternative methods is irrelevant. Marshall could obviously have made his basic point using only intuition, yet he nevertheless devoted some energy to solving the model explicitly in order to give numerical illustrations to Edgeworth. Marshall simultaneously concealed his mathematics and criticized Edgeworth for an excessive use of mathematics. This type of ambivalence characterizes much of Marshall's work.

Notes and further reading

In considering Mill and elasticity, it has been claimed by Bladen (1965, p. 43) that the concept of elasticity 'was clarified in Mill and only waited to be christened by Marshall'. But this type of comparison does not seem very useful when discussing such major figures. Stigler (1965, p. 2) suggested that Cournot 'almost wrote' the 'equation defining elasticity' and referred to Whewell 'for a crude definition of elasticity'. The above analysis obviously questions this judgement.

The major account of Whewell's work is by Todhunter (1876). Whewell's role in the scientific community can be seen in the history of the British Association by Morrell and Thackray (1981). Whewell's work has received more sympathetic treatment in recent years; see for example Cochrane (1975), Henderson (1973, 1985, 1989) and Campanelli (1982).

It is surprising that Henderson (1973, p. 337) recognized the result in equation (3.5) but then said that 'MacGregor erred when he stated that "this measure is $1 + [\eta]$, where $[\eta]$ is Marshall's elasticity"'. Ironically, Cochrane (1975, p. 398) criticized Henderson's comment on the relationship between Whewell's and Marshall's measures for the wrong reason, but reconsideration led Henderson (1975, p. 402) to recognize that MacGregor was correct. Chipman (1965, p. 492) stated that m is 'one minus the elasticity of demand' which is true of absolute values. Cochrane (1975), used equation (3.12) to produce a half-page table giving 'the proper taxonomy of outcomes' (1975, p. 399). Henderson then described Cochrane's *incorrect* interpretation as, 'fascinating, though not necessarily the only possible one' (1975, p. 403). Unfortunately Rashid (1977) got as far as equation (3.9), but incorrectly wrote y as $(dq/dp)xp$ instead of the result in equation (3.10).

Whewell knew of Cournot's work (see Rashid, 1977, p. 388) but did not seem to make any use of it in his 1850 paper. Whewell's approach may be compared with the result of using a Taylor series expansion, Cournot's favourite simplification. If the new demand is written as $q' = q(p') = q(p + x)$, then a Taylor series expansion, neglecting second and higher order terms, gives $q' = q + x \, dq/dp$. Then $p' \, q' = q\{p + x(1 + \eta)\}$, where η is the elasticity of demand. This is not the same as Whewell's statement.

Lardner's discussion of total expenditure and profit maximization makes no reference to Cournot, but the influence is highly likely. Hicks (1934, fn. 5) points out that Lardner and Cournot were both living in Paris in 1850 and that in 1835 Cournot had translated a book by Lardner on mechanics into French. For an amusing discussion of Lardner, and his controversy with Brunel over steam ships and railway gauges, see Morrell and Thackray (1981, p. 473). The controversy ended when in 1840 Lardner eloped with a married woman and lost a court action for seduction. It is well known that Jevons was influenced by Lardner (1850); for discussion and further references, see Bostaph and Shieh (1987). The relationship between the demand curve and total expenditure, and its connection with exchange, was discussed at length in Pantaleoni (1889, trans 1898, pp. 156–7).

When discussing Jevons's awareness of Cournot, Hutchison adds that Jevons could not have been aware of Newcomb's review of *The Theory of Political Economy,* which compares Jevons's work with that of Cournot, or of Marshall's brief reference to Cournot in his 1876 paper on Mill. Anyone with a reasonable library knows too that ownership does not imply familiarity: Jevons had owned a copy of *Researches* since 1872.

It is worth noting the following comment of Marshall on the use of constant elasticities:

'It is to be understood that the supposition of an elasticity that is even approximately constant, cannot reasonably be made in relation to amounts of trade either much smaller or much larger than that of the time and under the circumstances in view. Similar limitations apply to nearly all mathematical and diagrammatical illustrations of any part of economic theory'. (1923, p. 388, n. 1)

See also his comments on constant unit elasticities (1923, p. 355, n. 3).

Marshall's example of a Giffen good is examined in more detail in Creedy (1990). In a discussion of the origins of the concept, Dooley (1985, p. 203) stated that Marshall's example, in his letter to Edgeworth, is similar to one given by Pareto. Marshall was quite prepared to use a highly-artificial example, in which individuals can instantaneously transfer between boat and train at any point in the journey. But he was not alone in his use of an artificial example to illustrate the Giffen good phenomenon. Bowley (1924, p. 52) referred to an example of a utility function given by Johnson (1913, p. 500). He then gave his own illustration of an individual wishing to spend a fixed sum in order to maximize the area of land purchased, but with a constraint on the length of the frontage required. Wicksell (1934, pp. 60–2) gave an example of an individual exchanging wheat for rye in order to achieve 'maximum nourishment', up to a specified limit or target. As the price of rye in terms of wheat increases, the individual must sell more wheat to meet the target, up to the point where the price is so high that even by selling all his wheat, the dietary aim is not achieved. Neither Wicksell nor Bowley made any reference to Marshall or Giffen, and their discussions have been neglected in the extensive literature on Giffen goods.

The use of the concept of elasticity is now ubiquitous in economics. It is perhaps unfortunate, though not surprising, that such familiarity has led to it being treated with contempt in some quarters. Thus Samuelson stated that, 'Through the influence of Alfred Marshall economists have developed a fondness of certain dimensionless expressions called elasticity coefficients. On the whole, it appears that their importance is not very great except possibly as mental exercises for beginning students' (1947, p. 125).

4   Inter-related goods

Inter-related goods present particularly awkward analytical difficulties, and it is not surprising that early treatments of demand concentrated on partial equilibrium analyses of a single good. This chapter concentrates on a pioneering analysis of inter-related goods by Hans Karl Emil Von Mangoldt (1824–68). Although he is often briefly cited in histories of economic analysis as making an important contribution to economic theory, the details of his compressed analysis have rarely been given close attention. A major exception is Edgeworth, with his wide knowledge of the literature in numerous languages. Edgeworth concentrated on Mangoldt's analysis of international values, but referred briefly to his use of demand and supply curves and suggested that, 'By virtue of these constructions, Mangoldt, writing without reference to his predecessors Cournot, Dupuit and Gossen, may claim to be one of the independent discoverers of the mathematical theory of Demand and Supply' (1925, II, pp. 52–3).

Schneider (1960) judged Mangoldt's most important contribution to supply and demand theory to be the analysis of price formation with joint supply or demand, and made an interesting attempt to 'rescue Mangoldt's work from oblivion' (1960, p. 392). However, it is suggested that Schneider's analysis was incomplete. This chapter will argue that Mangoldt did not derive a demand curve at all, as he claimed. Instead, he showed the path taken to reach an equilibrium position by a numerical process of iteration. This may alternatively be viewed as the path taken by a highly stylized adjustment process, from an arbitrary position of disequilibrium. Mangoldt's problem gives rise to a set of non-linear equations which can only be solved using an iterative search procedure. His procedure is in fact a neat way of solving the model, but the resulting curve which he generated bears no relation to a demand curve. Mangoldt's basic analysis is described in Section 4.1. In view of the symmetrical treatment of joint supply and demand, for present purposes it is only necessary to concentrate on the case of joint demand. The alternative interpretation is contained in Section 4.2.

4.1   Mangoldt's analysis

Mangoldt considered the situation in which two goods are consumed in fixed proportions, but the supply curves are not inter-related. He was explicit about the assumptions required for a partial equilibrium analysis.

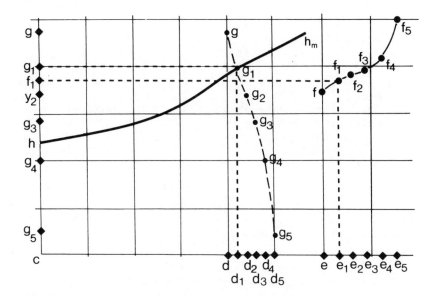

Figure 4.1   Mangoldt's diagram

The determination of a set of equilibrium prices and quantities of the two goods is not straightforward with this constraint operating. An equilibrium does not necessarily exist for an arbitrary set of demand curves. Mangoldt further assumed that the total amount spent on the two goods is fixed. The resulting loss of a further degree of freedom means that there is only a finite number of equilibrium prices and quantities. Mangoldt's assumptions also imply, as shown below, that the demand curves must be (with a suitable shift of axes) rectangular hyperbolas. But he seemed to believe that his analysis generated the demand schedule for one of the goods. It is best to quote Mangoldt at length in order to give the full flavour of his approach.

> Let us again illustrate the argument by a diagram (Figure 16 [Figure 4.1]). The data are the ratio (n) of A-demand to B-demand, a certain amount (F) of funds available for the purchase of A and B together, and the supply curves for A($f \ldots f_5$) and for $B(h \ldots h_m)$. We are looking for the demand curve for B. We proceed as follows. For every possible volume of demand for B (measured along the abscissa from origin up to the variables $d, d_1, \ldots$), we determine the possible price by deducting the expenditure for the corresponding quantities of A (that is $n \times cd$, or $ce, ce_1, \ldots$ times the necessary price of $ef, e_1f_1, \ldots$) from the total available purchase funds F, and then dividing the rest by the volume of B-demand. This gives us the price ($cg, cg_1, \ldots$) which can be paid for B at different levels of demand. The general formula is

$$ce = n \times cd$$

$$cg = \frac{F - ce \times ef}{cd}$$

By joining together the points obtained by marking off the resulting distances on the perpendiculars over $d, d_1, \ldots$, we get the demand curve for B which we are looking for, and its intersection point with the supply curve is the new centre of gravity for the B-price.

The above formula can be simplified. If we divided F by cd, we obviously get the price which could be paid for B if a corresponding amount of A were to be had free. If we then enter this price on the price scale as $cG, cG_1 \ldots$, we get

$$cg = cG - \frac{ce \times ef}{cd}$$

Since ce/ed is the same as n, we can also write

$$cg = cG - n \times ef$$

Figure 16 is drawn on the assumption that the ratio of demand for A and B is 3:2 and that a total of 4000 is available for the purchase of both goods. The results of our calculation would then be as shown in the table.

cd	cG	ce	ef	cg
40	100	60	35	$47\frac{1}{2}$
42	$95\frac{5}{21}$	63	37	$39\frac{39}{42}$
44	$90\frac{10}{11}$	66	38	$33\frac{10}{11}$
46	$86\frac{22}{23}$	69	39	$28\frac{21}{40}$
48	$83\frac{1}{2}$	72	42	$20\frac{1}{3}$
50	80	75	50	5

At the given supply curve $h \ldots h_m$ for B, equilibrium between demand and supply would come about at a price indicated by the point g_1, so that the consumption pattern would be

42 B at a price of $39\frac{39}{42}$ and
63 A at a price of 37.

(Mangoldt, 1962, pp. 43–4)

The two columns labelled ce and ef give the supply schedule of good A, while the column headed cd gives consumption levels of good B such that the values in this column are 2/3 those in the ce column. Consider the first row of Mangoldt's table. If 60 units of good A are purchased at a price per unit of 35, then the fixed budget of 4000 means that 4000 minus (35)(60) = 1900 is available for spending on good B. But with fixed proportions it is required to purchase 40 units of good A. The maximum price consumers are willing to pay for these units is thus 1900/40 = 47.5 per unit. This is the figure in the final column headed *cg*. Mangoldt does not give the supply schedule of good B in the table, but says that the output and price of 42 and $39\frac{31}{42}$ respectively give one point on that curve; this is the equilibrium.

Mangoldt regards the relationship between the columns *cg* and *cd* as showing the demand schedule for good B. But it is seen that Mangoldt appears to have derived a demand curve for one good, from the supply curve of another good and two constraints, one on total expenditure and the other on the ratio of amounts demanded. Schneider (1960, p. 386) recognized that this is unusual, saying; 'It has to be noted, however, that this demand function is not a demand function in the ordinary sense. It is rather a demand function ... *under the assumption that the market for commodity* [A] *is always in equilibrium*'. It is argued in the following section that the schedule under consideration should not be referred to as *any* kind of demand function.

It should be stressed that Mangoldt's procedure is entirely numerical; the schedules in his table are transferred directly to his Figure 16, shown here as Figure 4.1. Schneider provided an elegant geometrical construction using a four-quadrant diagram. His construction requires a set of parallel straight lines *cg* = (F/*cd*) − (*ef*)*n*, for alternative values of *cd*, to be drawn. Other quadrants give the supply curve of good A, and a straight line for the proportionality constant, showing *ce* = *n*(*cd*). The so-called demand curve for good B is projected in the fourth quadrant, which can also show the supply curve of good B and hence the point of intersection between the two curves.

4.2 An alternative interpretation
It is convenient to introduce different notation from that used by Mangoldt. Let x_i^d and x_i^s denote the quantities demanded and supplied of goods i (i = 1, 2), at price p_i. The two constraints imposed by Mangoldt are sufficient to generate the two demand curves. These constraints require:

$$x_2^d = nx_1^d \tag{4.1}$$

and

$$K = p_1 x_1^d + p_2 x_2^d \tag{4.2}$$

The substitution of (4.1) into (4.2) gives:

$$p_1 = \frac{K}{x_1^d} - \frac{p_2}{n} \tag{4.3}$$

and

$$p_2 = \frac{K}{x_2^d} - \frac{p_1}{n} \tag{4.4}$$

Hence (4.3) and (4.4) are the demand curves, expressed with price as the dependent variable. Each demand curve is simply a rectangular hyperbola, with suitable shift of axis. Each demand curve shifts downwards as the price of the other good rises. The inter-relationship through (4.1) should be kept in mind, so that it is not possible to move independently along each demand curve.

Consider Figure 4.2, which shows the markets for the two goods in separate diagrams. Each diagram has upward sloping supply curves which are independent. Begin by taking a demand curve for good 1, labelled $D_1^1|p_2 = p_2^0$. This is the demand curve, drawn for a price p_2^0 of good 2. With this demand curve, equilibrium in the market for good 1 occurs at point e_1, which is associated with a price of p_1^1 for good 1. Now move to the market for good 2 and draw the demand curve. $D_2^1|p_1 = p_1^1$; that is, the demand curve with vertical position determined by the price p_1^1 obtained from the market for the good 1. The 'equilibrium' in this market is at E_1, which has an associated price of p_2^1. This situation can of course only be a true equilibrium if $p_2^1 = p_2^0$, and $x_2 = nx_1$. The figure shows a situation in which $p_2^1 > p_2^0$. Another way of viewing this is to say that with x_1^1 being consumed of good 1, the consumption of $x_2^1 = nx_1^1$ of good 2 along that good's demand curve would be at the point I_1. This is obviously not a point of equilibrium in that market.

Hence the search for an equilibrium set of prices requires an adjustment to the vertical position of the demand curve for good 1. Since $p_2^1 > p_2^0$. A small increase, of say δ, will shift the demand curve for good 1 down to $D_1^2|p_2 = p_2^0 + \delta$, which gives a new equilibrium at e_2 with a price of p_1^2, which is less than p_1^1. Thus the demand curve for good 2 shifts upwards to $D_2^2|p_1 = p_1^2$, with a new equilibrium of p_2^2. But $p_2^2 \neq p_2^0 + \delta$ and general equilibrium in the two markets has not been reached. Indeed, the consumption of $x_2^2 = nx_1^2$ along the demand curve D_2^2 is at point I_2. It can be seen that a gradual process of adjustment would eventually lead to an equilibrium in which the prices underlying the position of each demand curve are consistent with the equilibrium prices in the other market.

If the points I_1, I_2 ... are joined together, they produce a locus labelled GG in Figure 4.2. It may be said that, beginning with price p_2^0, which is gradually increased, the line GG describes the path of adjustment from the disequilibrium situation to the general equilibrium solution. It is precisely such an adjustment path that Mangoldt has traced in his figure; the points g_5, g_4 ..., g in his Figure 16 correspond to GG in Figure 4.2. The position and shape of this path depend on the constraints K and n and the shape of the supply curve of good 1.

This adjustment procedure is just one of several that may be followed; for example, arbitrary starting points for both prices may be taken (rather than just p_2^0) and adjusted at each iteration following a simple rule. An approach to finding the solution could be to take high and low values of p_1^0 in order to obtain points on GG on each side of the equilibrium position. An iterative process of taking the middle value would then converge to the equilibrium. But the procedure described above is clearly more efficient in searching for the equilibrium. However, it is merely a numerical procedure for solving the problem. It cannot be interpreted in any sense as a demand curve.

The approach of Figure 4.2 can also be used to examine the comparative static properties of the model more clearly. Suppose that there is a change in the production of good 1 which shifts the supply curve down. Equilibrium can only be restored by an upward shift in the demand curve for good 2, resulting from the fall in the price of good 1. This involves a rise in the price of good 2, which is associated with a downward shift in the demand curve for good 1.

Mangoldt did not use functional forms to describe his supply curves and indeed he stressed the variety of shapes that they can take. Hence a numerical search procedure is necessary to solve the model. But it is necessary to ask if fairly simple functional forms would allow the equilibrium to be solved explicitly, although it should be borne in mind that Mangoldt's schedules are far from linear and in many cases are closer to cubics. Consider linear supply functions and write the model, with the two constraints, as follows:

$$x_2^d = nx_1^d \tag{4.5}$$

$$x_1^d = \frac{K}{np_2 + p_1} \tag{4.6}$$

$$x_1^s = \alpha + \beta p_1 \tag{4.7}$$

$$x_2^s = \gamma + \delta p_2 \tag{4.8}$$

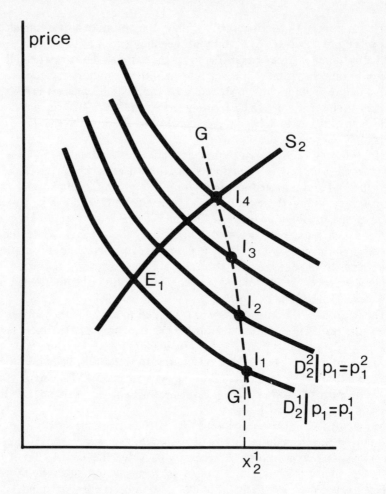

Figure 4.2   Solving the model

These four equations must be used to solve for the four unknowns x_i and $p_i (i = 1,2)$, given the equilibrium conditions for the two markets, that $x_i^s = x_i^d$. Substituting into these conditions gives:

$$\alpha + \beta p_1 = \frac{K}{np_2 + p_1} \qquad (4.9)$$

$$\gamma + \delta p_2 = \frac{nK}{np_2 + p_1} \qquad (4.10)$$

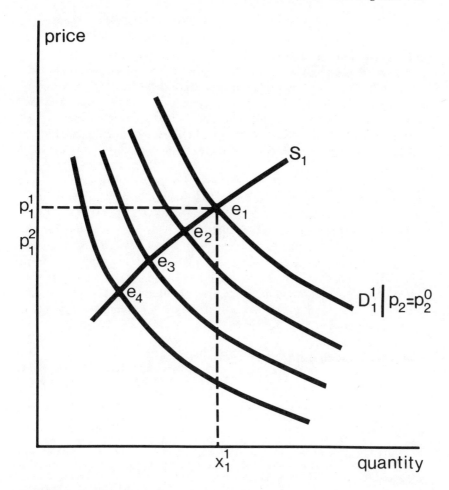

Figure 4.2 continued

Dividing (4.10) by n and equating the result with (4.9) gives, after rearrangement:

$$p_1 = \frac{\gamma + \delta p_2}{n\beta} - \frac{\alpha}{\beta} \tag{4.11}$$

Substituting for p_1, from (4.11), into (4.10) and collecting terms in p_2 gives:

$$p_2^2\left(n\delta + \frac{\delta^2}{\beta n}\right) + p_2\left(\gamma n + \frac{2\gamma\delta}{n\beta} - \frac{\alpha\delta}{\beta}\right) + \left(\frac{\gamma^2}{n\beta} - \frac{\alpha\gamma}{\beta} - nK\right) = 0 \tag{4.12}$$

The equilibrium value of p_2 is thus the positive root of equation (4.12). It can be seen from the structure of the model that the polynomial determining the equilibrium price is one degree higher than that of the supply function. Hence anything other than linear supply functions create awkward difficulties, and the iterative procedure described earlier would be very useful. It can be shown that with a linear supply curve the GG schedule is downward sloping and convex to the origin. The explicit solution could of course have been found by first deriving the equation of GG and then finding the point of intersection with the supply curve of good 2.

It has been seen that Mangoldt devised a very convenient numerical procedure for finding the equilibrium set of prices, faced with a non-linear set of equations, and provided useful comparative static analyses. Mangoldt identified his solution procedure with the derivation of the demand curve for one of the goods. But this can at best be regarded as a very unusual demand curve, depending as it does only on the supply curve for one of the goods and a proportional relationship between amounts consumed of the two goods. This chapter has reinterpreted Mangoldt's procedure in terms of iterative search procedure, involving the systematic movement between demand curves.

Notes and further reading
The publishing history of Mangoldt's major work (1863) is somewhat ironic. The second edition was prepared by Kleinwächter in 1871 and excluded the geometrical analysis, on the grounds that 'it is utterly inconceivable to me that graphs or mathematical formulae could facilitate the understanding of economic laws'. However, the section containing the diagrammatic analysis was for long the only part of the book to have been translated into English, in the shortlived but invaluable *International Economic Papers* (1962). The technical appendix on international values was later translated in Mangoldt (1975). Hutchison (1953, pp. 133–7), among historians of economic thought, devotes relatively more attention to Mangoldt and states that, 'The work of Mangoldt represents a culminating point in German theoretical economics but it received little or no recognition either from Marshall or from the Austrian school' (1953, p. 137). Viner (1955, pp. 458–63) follows Edgeworth's analysis quite closely. Other brief references to Mangoldt are mentioned by Schneider (1960). Hennings (1980, p. 659, n. 3) states that there are no references to Mangoldt in the work of Wicksell. However, Wicksell (1954, p. 89) complained about the elimination of the diagrams from the second edition of the *Grundriss*, although his description of the diagrams was misleading.

Mangoldt's references to other authors such as Rau were excluded from the translation in 1962. On Mangoldt's likely awareness of Cournot, see Schneider (1960, p. 382). The tabular form of presentation was adopted in the translation, but does not appear in the original in such a clear presentation. Notice that equations (4.3) and (4.4) could be combined to produce, for example, $p_1 = \{Kn^2/(1+n^2)\}\{1/x_1 - 1/nx_2\}$. But the above approach yields more insight into the problem.

5 Commodity taxation

In view of the importance of indirect taxes and customs duties for raising government revenue, it is not surprising that their properties were debated at length by the classical economists. A fundamental issue concerns the incidence of such taxes, the extent to which they may be shifted. However, the present chapter concentrates on several highly original contributions which have had a significant impact on modern economic theory. First, Cournot's analysis of the taxation of a monopolist producing a single good is examined in Section 5.1. Cournot's analysis was enhanced by his specification of demand as a schedule, which stimulated Edgeworth to exclaim, 'how much logomachy is saved by this appropriate conception', and by his clear statement of the first-order conditions required for profit maximization. Cournot extended his approach to deal with taxes and subsidies in the context of international trade; discussion of this is deferred until Chapter 6 below.

It has been seen in the previous chapter that inter-related goods presented awkward analytical problems. Edgeworth considered that taxation of a monopolist producing two inter-related goods and showed that it is possible to obtain the paradoxical result that the price of one of the goods can fall. The surprising nature of this result stimulated later important work on demand theory, but Section 5.2 concentrates on a simplified discussion provided by Wicksell (1934). He gave a remarkably succinct summary of a mathematical problem which is not entirely straightforward, yet he adapted the model in such a way that only basic algebra is required.

5.1 Taxation of a monopolist

Profit maximization

Cournot's results on taxation followed directly from his treatment of profit maximization and the effect of cost changes. With demand expressed as a function of price, so that $D = F(p)$, Cournot wrote the cost of making D units of the good as $\phi(D)$. Thus $\phi(D)$ is a function of a function, $\phi\{D(p)\}$. Net receipts, or profits, are thus $pF(p) - \phi(D)$, so that the price which maximizes profit is obtained by differentiating this expression with respect to p and setting the result equal to zero. Hence:

$$F(p) + F'(p)\{p - \phi'(D)\} = 0 \tag{5.1}$$

Cournot treated $\phi'(D)$ as 'a new function of D, the form of which exerts [a] a very great influence on the principal problems of economic science' (1927, p. 59). This is of course now referred to as marginal cost, and Cournot argued that for manufacturing industries it will initially decrease and then increase. Since this can be treated as a function of p, Cournot wrote $\phi'\{D(p)\} = \psi(p)$, whence the profit maximizing price is the root of:

$$F(p) + F'(p) \{p - \psi(p)\} = 0 \qquad (5.2)$$

For the modern economist it is a small step to rearrange (5.2) into the form:

$$\psi(p) = p(1 + 1/\eta) \qquad (5.3)$$

where η is the price elasticity of demand, $F(p)/pF'(p)$, and the right-hand side is equal to marginal revenue. A great deal of fuss was made over the rediscovery of this simple first-order condition, concerning the equality of marginal cost and marginal revenue, in the 1930s. However, not only had Marshall, with acknowledgement to Cournot, stated the condition clearly in his *Principles* (1961, p. 856), but he had stressed, unlike Cournot, that equation (5.2) may have more than one root. Indeed, except for very simple functional forms, equation (5.2) is very likely to produce multiple roots that are feasible (that is, are non-negative). This led Marshall to devise his ingenious geometrical method of finding the global maximum, involving the use of a set of rectangular hyperbolas; but his approach has been largely ignored, or even ridiculed, by later economists who did not recognize the nature of his contribution.

Cournot pointed out that any fixed costs will not affect $\psi(p)$ and hence will not affect the profit maximizing price and output. Hence it is clear that a lump sum tax cannot affect output, so long as the firm remains in operation. The effect of a tax on each unit of the good is equivalent to a fixed rise in marginal costs. Suppose that $\psi(p)$ increases by u and as a result the price changes to $p + \delta$. The first-order condition of equation (5.2) now becomes:

$$F(p + \delta) + F'(p + \delta) \{p + \delta - \psi(p + \delta) - u\} = 0 \qquad (5.4)$$

Cournot's method of examining this type of comparative static problem, also used in Chapter 6 below, is to write $F(p + \delta)$ as $F(p) + \delta F'(p)$; that is, he used a Taylor series expansion but neglected the squares and higher powers of δ. By expanding equation (5.4) in this way and subtracting equation (5.2), it can be shown, after also neglecting cross-product terms δu, that:

$$\delta/u = F'(p) [F'(p)\{2 - \psi'(p)\} + F''(p)\{p - \psi(p)\}]^{-1} \qquad (5.5)$$

Then using equation (5.2) to substitute $-F(p)/F'(p)$ for $p - \psi(p)$ in equation (5.5), and dividing numerator and denominator of the latter by $F'(p)$, it can be shown that $\delta/u > 1$ if:

$$\{F'(p)\}^2 \{1 - \psi'(p)\} - F(p) F''(p) < 0 \qquad (5.6)$$

which is Cournot's (1927, p. 63) result. Cournot certainly entertained the possibility that the price could increase by more than the increase in marginal cost (or by more than the increase in the tax). When discussing the result, Edgeworth suggested that the increase will 'probably be less, at least for the case of decreasing returns' (1925, p. 90; see also n. 3). In view of Cournot's concentration at this point on a monopolist, he did not wish to rule out the case where $\delta > u$.

The imposition of a tax

The analysis of a shift in marginal costs was directly applicable to the imposition of a tax. Cournot could therefore immediately state that a fixed absolute amount of tax will leave the price unchanged and that a tax on gross receipts is equivalent to a unit tax which raises the same revenue. If u now denotes the unit tax, the tax revenue is equal to $uF(p + \delta)$. Furthermore, the extra amount paid by consumers who continue to purchase the good is equal to $\delta F(p + \delta)$; this can only exceed the tax revenue in the (unlikely) situation that $\delta > u$. However, the total expenditure on the good must fall. He was also able to show that the loss of net income to the monopolist will exceed the amount of tax revenue. In Marshall's later analysis, mentioned above, the possibility of multiple roots to the first-order condition for profit maximization means that the price change resulting from a small unit tax may involve a discontinuous jump. Even where the price change is quite small, the associated change in quantity can be very large. This type of behaviour that can result from non-linear models which admit of multiple solutions is of much interest to modern economists interested in 'chaos', but was ignored for many years. It will be seen in Part 2 of this book that the same is true of multiple equilibria in exchange models.

The popular treatment of commodity taxation which appears in so many elementary textbooks is somewhat simpler than Cournot's monopoly case, and uses the concepts of consumers' and producers' surplus which Cournot himself used when examining import taxes (see Chapter 6 below). The usual presentation closely follows that pioneered by Dupuit (1844) and independently by Jenkin (1871) which produces the well-known result that the 'deadweight loss' is approximately equal to one half of the tax rate multiplied by the change in the quantity produced. This approach uses standard supply and demand diagrams and shows that the price of the taxed good will either remain constant, in the extreme case of inelastic supply, or will increase. Edgeworth's paradoxical result that the price of the taxed good can *fall* in certain circumstances is the subject of the following section.

5.2   Inter-related goods

Edgeworth showed that when inter-relationships between commodities are explicitly allowed, there are circumstances in which the price of the taxed good will fall. His statement of the paradox is as follows:

> When the supply of two or more correlated commodities – such as the carriage of passengers by rail first class – is in the hands of a single monopolist a tax on one of the articles – e.g. a percentage of first class fares – may prove advantageous to the consumers as a whole . . . The fares for *all* the classes might be reduced. (1925, I, p. 139)

Edgeworth regarded this as an example of a situation where, 'the abstract reasoning serves as a corrective to what has been called the "metaphysical incubus" of dogmatic *laisser faire*' (1925, I, p. 139; see also 1925, II, pp. 93–4). He first stated the argument in his Italian paper on monopoly in 1897, not translated until 1925. The two commodities must be substitutes in consumption and production, and the result arises partly because the monopolist has an incentive to increase the supply of the untaxed good. Edgeworth (1925, II, p. 63) also recognized that the result could occur in competitive markets.

The result was initially greeted with a certain amount of incredulity. For example, Seligman (1921, p. 214) referred to it as 'a slip of Mr Edgeworth' and went on to suggest that the result, 'will surely be a grateful boon to the perplexed and weary secretaries of the Treasury and ministers of finance throughout the world'. The paradox was not a subject of continuous development, but a major development occurred when it attracted the attention of Hotelling, who consequently produced another of his seminal papers (1932). Hotelling demonstrated the conditions under which the result can occur in competitive and monopolistic markets. He later stated that the 'paradoxical discovery . . . is one proposition of economic importance which cannot be proved, apparently, without the use of formulae; moreover, it is very suggestive of further developments' (quoted by Garver, 1933, p. 402). It will be seen below that Wicksell's more pedagogic discussion required only basic algebra. Wicksell's modification of the problem avoided the need to deal with the complexities arising from the general treatment of interrelated goods. He also provided a neat diagrammatic treatment illustrating the point that the paradox cannot be ruled out on a priori grounds.

As Hotelling suggested, the further developments are also important. His own analysis led him to show for the first time how restrictions derived from utility theory could be used in the estimation of systems of demand equations. Bailey (1954) later showed the conditions under which the phenomenon could be 'one way'; that is, may occur when one of the monopolized goods is taxed, but not the other. In a volume of papers in honour of Hotelling, further analyses were carried out by Vickrey (1958) and Ferguson (1958). The problem has thus had a significant influence on the development of demand theory. A detailed diagrammatic treatment of the paradox was provided by Coase (1946). But none of these authors mentioned Wicksell's analysis.

Wicksell's discussion

This section reproduces Wicksell's brief discussion so that easy reference may be made in the formal analysis that follows. Although the paradox was initially stated in terms of first and third class fares, Wicksell uses second and third class fares.

The mathematical treatment of monopoly profits and their taxation abounds in interesting and often very surprising features. Suppose, for example, that a railway company which has a monopoly in passenger traffic, with only two classes, second and third, is taxed on the basis of the number of second class tickets sold. Who would suppose, at first sight, that this taxation might make it economically advantageous for the company to *reduce* the price of both second and third class tickets? And yet Edgeworth has fully proved that, on certain assumptions, this can be the case.

This can, if necessary be understood without the use of higher mathematics. For the sakes of simplicity we shall assume – an assumption not very far removed from reality – that *ceteris paribus* the number of second class passengers is determined exclusively by the price difference between the two classes; in other words, the passengers would travel in any case, though the difference in price decides whether they will travel second or third class. In such a case it is in the interest of the railway company to *increase* this difference in order to force some passengers to go over from second class to third class – and thereby save in taxation. That this can always happen without a corresponding reduction in the total revenue is implied in the very concept of maximization – at least in most cases. A slight change in the most advantageous price combination produces a relatively very small reduction in traffic revenue, whereas the corresponding saving in taxation is considerable. Now a given increase in the price difference can be brought about in *three* different ways:

(a) by a moderate increase in second class fares and a reduction in third class fares;

(b)   by a greater increase in the former and a slight increase (or, at any rate, no reduction) in the latter; and

(c)   by a slight reduction (or, at any rate, no increase) in second class fares and a greater reduction in third class fares.

By all three methods the railway company makes an equal saving in taxation. It remains an open question, therefore, which of the three will produce the least decrease in the traffic revenue. As a rule it would be the first method, but in special cases the second and even the third may be preferred.

Thus, if second class traffic is very considerable and third class traffic not particularly elastic, it may happen that the most profitable course would be to increase both fares (although, apart from taxation, this increase must always reduce the traffic revenue, since it alters the combination of prices existing before the imposition of the tax, which must be assumed to be, in those circumstances, the most advantageous). But if third class traffic is very elastic – so that reduced fares would attract a number of new passengers (to the third class) – and the second class traffic is not very great, then, however paradoxical it may at first sight appear, the last of the three methods will be the most advantageous to the railway company. (1934, pp. 93–4)

A formal analysis

The first problem in understanding Wicksell's discussion is to decide precisely what was meant by his assumption that, 'the number of second class passengers is determined exclusively by the price *difference* between the two classes; in other words, the passengers would travel in any case, though the difference in price decides whether they will travel second or third class'. The interpretation pursued here is that there is a demand function for railway travel that depends *ceteris paribus* on the price of the third class fare. If there is no differential between second and third class tickets then obviously all passengers will travel second class, but the *proportion* of total passengers travelling second class tends to zero as the price differential increases. Two basic functions are therefore relevant: these are the demand for railway travel itself, and the function that divides customers into second and third class travellers.

Suppose that the total number of passengers, n, is determined by the third class fare, p, so that $n = n(p)$. Furthermore, the number of second class fares, n_2, is a proportion of n, and that proportion is determined by the price difference between second and third class fares. Hence if the second class fare is p_s, then:

$$n_2 = n(p)\, g(p_s - p) \qquad (5.7)$$

with $0 < g(\cdot) < 1$; $g(0) = 1$. The number of third class fares, n_3, is given by:

$$n_3 = n - n_2 = n(p) \{1 - g(p_s - p)\} \tag{5.8}$$

Wicksell was not explicit about costs, but suppose that total costs are fixed at C. This is reasonable for the context of railway travel. The profit Π is therefore $\Pi = p_s n_2 + p n_3 - C$. Writing $p_s - p = v$, and substituting for n_2 and n_3 gives:

$$\Pi = n(p) \{p + vg(v)\} - C \tag{5.9}$$

The objective of the monopolist is to choose p and v in order to maximize Π. The first-order conditions give:

$$\frac{\delta \Pi}{\partial p} = \{p + vg(v)\}\frac{\partial n}{\partial p} + n = 0 \tag{5.10}$$

$$\frac{\partial \Pi}{\partial v} = nv\frac{\partial g}{\partial v} + ng = 0 \tag{5.11}$$

These conditions can be rearranged to give:

$$\frac{p\partial n}{n\partial p} = - (1 + vg/p)^{-1} \tag{5.12}$$

$$\frac{v\partial g}{g\partial v} = - 1 \tag{5.13}$$

The term $(p/n)(\partial n/\partial p)$ represents the elasticity of the total number of passengers with respect to the third class fare. The term $(v/g)(\partial g/\partial v)$ measures the elasticity of the proportion of total fares travelling second class, with respect to the price differential between second and third class fares.

The precise implications for p and v depend on the forms chosen for $n(p)$ and $g(v)$. Wicksell gave no hint concerning the forms he had in mind. Since Wicksell (1934, p. 288) was the first person to use what is now referred to as a Cobb–Douglas production function, it is perhaps not unreasonable to use a demand function for which the elasticity is constant. Thus:

$$n = ap^{-\beta} \tag{5.14}$$

Substitution of (5.14) into (5.12) and rearranging gives the profit-maximizing third class fare, p, as:

$$p = gv/(\beta^{-1} - 1) \tag{5.15}$$

The function g must satisfy several conditions; in particular that $g(0) = 1$, $g(\alpha) = 0$, with $\partial g/\partial v < 0$. A flexible functional form satisfying these conditions and involving a single parameter, $\delta > 1$, is:

$$g(v) = \{\theta/(\theta + v)\}^\delta \tag{5.16}$$

This function has the elasticity:

$$\frac{v\partial g}{g\partial v} = -\left\{\frac{\delta v}{v + \theta}\right\} \tag{5.17}$$

which, on substitution into (5.13), gives

$$v = \theta/(\delta - 1) \tag{5.18}$$

Finally, the price, p, can be solved by substituting (5.16) and (5.18) into (5.15), giving after some manipulation:

$$p = \theta\{(\delta - 1)(\beta^{-1} - 1)\}^{-1} \{(\delta - 1)/\delta\}^\delta \tag{5.19}$$

The introduction of a tax
The problem is to examine how the introduction of a tax of t on each second class fare affects the prices as given by (5.18) and (5.19). The introduction of the tax changes the profit function in (5.9) to:

$$\Pi = n(p) \{p + (v - t) g(v)\} - C \tag{5.20}$$

Maximization of (5.20) with respect to p and v can be seen to give after differentiation and rearranging:

$$\frac{p\partial n}{n\partial p} = -\{1 + g(v - t)/p\}^{-1} \tag{5.21}$$

and

$$\frac{v\partial g}{g\partial p} = -v/(v - t) \tag{5.22}$$

The substitution of (5.17) into (5.22) gives the result that:

$$v = (\theta + \delta t) / (\delta - 1) \tag{5.23}$$

Hence (5.23) shows clearly that, by comparison with (5.18), the introduction of the tax increases the absolute difference between the prices of second and third class fares. The new third class price is obtained by substituting the constant elasticity $-\beta$ into (5.21), along with the form of $g(v)$ given in (5.16) and the new solution for v given in (5.23). It can be found after some manipulation that the new price is:

$$p = (\theta + t)(1 + t/\theta)\{(\delta - 1)(\beta^{-1} - 1)\}^{-1}\{(\delta - 1)/\delta\}^{\delta} \quad (5.24)$$

For the post-tax price of third class fares to be less than the price of pre-tax fares, it is required that the ratio of the price in (5.24) to that in (5.18) is less than unity. Making the appropriate division, and rearranging, gives the condition:

$$(1 + t/\theta)^{1-\delta} < 1 \quad (5.25)$$

Now $t/\theta > 0$ as θ must be > 0, hence the inequality (5.25) always holds. Therefore a tax on the number of second class fares always leads to a reduction in the price of third class fares.

This result is difficult to reconcile with Wicksell's second possibility, numbered (b) above, which allows for a 'slight increase (or at any rate no reduction) in [the third class fare]'. However, his discussion of this possibility is not entirely clear, as he then says that, 'apart from taxation, this increase must always reduce the traffic revenue, since it alters the combination of prices existing before the imposition of the tax'. Perhaps Wicksell intended to acknowledge that case (b) would not be a profit-maximizing strategy even though it would provide a 'saving in taxation'.

Although there is no doubt that the third class fare is reduced, and the difference between the second and third class fares is increased as a result of the tax on the second class passengers, the effect on the price of second class fares is ambiguous. A comparison of pre- and post-tax second class fares is therefore required. This proceeds as follows. The pre-tax second class fare is obtained by adding (5.18) to (5.19), and the post-tax second class fare is obtained by adding (5.23) to (5.24). For the tax to lower the price of second class travel it is required that the difference between pre- and post-tax fares is positive. This condition is quite tedious to examine, but it can be shown that the second class fare is reduced if the following condition holds.

$$1 - \{(\theta + t)/\theta\}^{t-\delta} > (\beta^{-1} - 1)\,\delta(t/\theta)\{\delta/(\delta - 1)\}^{\delta} \quad (5.26)$$

Suppose, for example, that θ, δ and t take the values 6, 1.2 and 1 respectively; which give sensible values for the function $g(v)$. The substitution into (5.26) gives the condition that the second class fare falls if β > 0.98. A value of β greater than unity will unequivocably cause the fare to fall, confirming Wicksell's statement that the tax paradox occurs when the elasticity of demand is high (in absolute terms).

Wicksell also suggests that the paradox occurs when the number of second class passengers is not very great. At first sight this statement may seem surprising since the condition (5.26) is in terms of the elasticity of demand for total traffic, and the parameters of the function $g(v)$ that affects the division of passengers between classes. However, this can be explained as follows. The above numerical example implies a pre-tax price differential of 25, which means that only 11.6 per cent of passengers travel second class. The low value of δ implies a relatively high preference for second class travel, and profit is maximized by having a very high differential. Even if the value of δ is raised to 2.0, only 25 per cent of passengers travel second class, and the paradox can occur so long as the value of β exceeds 0.905. Wicksell's desire not to introduce any mathematics makes it difficult for him to summarize the conditions precisely.

Wicksell's diagrammatic treatment

Continuing his discussion of the tax paradox, Wicksell (1934) presented an alternative approach involving a simple diagram. This approach is perhaps best regarded as an illustration of the possibility of the paradox taking place, rather than a diagrammatic treatment which generates the conditions required. He suggested:

> Let us draw up a series of combinations of prices which, apart from taxation, would yield the company a *certain given net income* slightly less than the maximum. Geometrically, this series could be represented by a closed curve (roughly elliptical in shape) enclosing the maximum point; we have then to find the point on this curve at which the difference between the co-ordinates (the difference between second and third class fares, and consequently the saving in taxation) is a maximum. This point is clearly the point of contact of the upper of the two tangents to the curve which make an angle of 45° with the axes. (1934, p. 94)

It is useful to refer to Figure 5.1, which shows just the crucial part of Wicksell's diagram. The axes measure deviations of prices from the pre-tax profit maximizing fares, and the locus of points giving constant gross profit is indicated. The lines LL and L'L' are inclined at 45°. Consider moving away from point A along the constant profit locus in a south-westerly direction. As the slope exceeds 45°, the rate at which the second class fare decreases is higher than the rate of decrease in the third class fare; hence the price differential falls. Similarly, the differential again falls

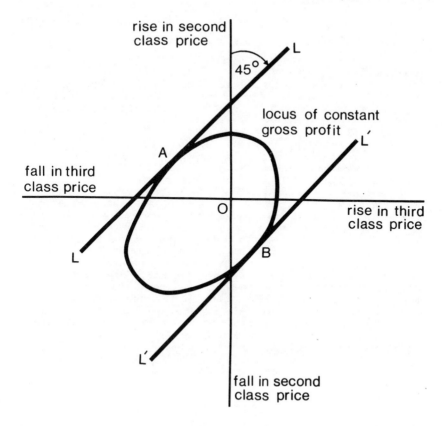

Figure 5.1   Taxation of inter-related goods

when moving in a north-easterly direction from A. Thus position A represents the highest differential consistent with the given gross profit rate and thereby minimizes the amount of tax to be paid on second class passengers. The point B on the tangent L'L' represents the minimum difference between second and third class fares. The gross profit level for the locus of Figure 5.1 is arbitrary, but there is clearly a locus and a resulting tangency position that maximizes net profit. The tangency position could be in the negative orthant, where both fares are lower than the pre-tax position. As Wicksell suggested, 'The same construction may then be repeated with a succession of new curves (new series of price combinations) the process being continued so long as the saving in taxation increases more than the traffic revenue decreases' (1934, p. 94). Thus his diagram neatly illustrates the argument that there are no a priori grounds for ruling out the tax paradox, and that the outcome will depend on the shape of the constant gross profit locus.

Notes and further reading

Marshall's treatment of monopoly is examined in detail in Creedy and O'Brien (1991). When Wicksell (1934, pp. 91–3) examined monopoly taxation, he took Cournot's model and simplified it by assuming constant marginal costs throughout. For a more general discussion of indirect taxation see Creedy (1984) and the references therein.

Wicksell (1958, p. 208) also mentioned the tax paradox. There is no mention of this analysis in Uhr (1960). It is understandable that Hotelling did not know of Wicksell's analysis, since he wrote before the English translation was available. On personal contact between Edgeworth and Wicksell, see Gärdlund (1958, pp. 230, 320, 323, 331). Hotelling too had his critics; see Garver (1933) and the reply by Hotelling (1933).

Like numerous other technical discussion in Wicksell's *Lectures*, the section quoted above appeared in smaller type and was slightly indented. The third edition was published in Sweden after Wicksell's death under the editorship of Somarin; see Robbins's introduction to Wicksell (1934, p. xviii). Furthermore, in the Swedish edition Wicksell only referred to Edgeworth's treatment in the *Economic Journal*, but a reference to the *Papers* is added in the English edition (without any indication that it is an editorial addition). The English edition also added 'in that order' to the end of the penultimate paragraph, and in the second paragraph omitted the word 'not' from the second sentence. Using the model examined above, it can be seen that the constant profit locus has a rather awkward form. Haavelmo dicussed this in his lectures on Wicksell (notes of which, in Norwegian, are in a memorandum from Socialökonomisk Institutt, Oslo, Sept. 1951). Haavelmo suggested that Wicksell may have had a Taylor series expansion of the profit function in mind, disregarding terms of degree larger than two. This is to some extent supported by the fact that a more accurate translation of Wicksell's comment is 'with sufficiently small deviations elliptical'.

6   Trade between regions

The previous chapters have concentrated on various aspects of the demand side of markets. The present chapter takes a step towards the analysis of exchange, involving the interdependence between demand and supply, by examining Cournot's treatment of some implications of the 'communication' of markets which were previously isolated. This is contained in chapter 10 of the *Researches* (1838). Cournot's analysis has received very little attention. It was not considered in Chipman's (1965) survey, and while Viner (1955) provided a detailed criticism of Cournot's treatment of the gains from trade, he did not examine chapter 10. However, when discussing the possibility of gain from tariffs, Schumpeter noted tersely that 'Cournot's contribution to the theory of international values lies in this field' (1954, p. 615, n. 21). More attention was given to this contribution by Edgeworth, who commented, not without sympathy, that:

> ' The lesson of caution in dealing with a subject and method so difficult is taught by no example more impressively than by that of Cournot. This superior intelligence . . . seems not only to have slipped at several steps, but even to have taken a wholly wrong direction. (1925, II, p. 47)

A close examination of Cournot's treatment is therefore warranted. It will also be seen in Chapter 9 below that an understanding of Cournot's model helps to see the later work of Marshall and Walras in a clearer perspective.

Cournot's basic framework is described in Section 6.1, which examines his demonstration that both the quantity demanded and the value of an exported commodity may fall as a result of trade. The analysis of the change in the value of output was incomplete; a full treatment is given here. Cournot established conditions in terms of the slopes of the relevant demand and supply curves, but it is shown that they can be expressed in terms of elasticities. Section 6.2 then examines Cournot's analysis of taxes. The error in Cournot's argument that an export tax lowers the price in the exporting market and may also lower it in the importing market is examined. His incomplete discussion of a tax imposed in the exporting country is extended, and an inconsistency in the use of his favourite method of 'development and reduction', when examining a tax-cum-subsidy, is discussed. A diagrammatic form of the model is examined in Section 6.3. In order to facilitate comparison with the original, Cournot's notation has been used throughout and references will be made to the

1927 reprint of Bacon's translation. A fundamental problem, raised by Walras and Marshall, is that the partial equilibrium model of Cournot is not really appropriate for the analysis of exchange. This is considered in Section 6.4, which shows how the model can easily be converted into general equilibrium form.

6.1   Cournot's basic model
The framework
Cournot considered a single good which is produced and consumed in two separate markets A and B. In isolation the equilibrium price of the good is p_a and p_b in markets A and B respectively, with demand functions $F_a(p)$ and $F_b(p)$, and supply functions $\Omega_a(p)$ and $\Omega_b(p)$. The prices are given by the intersection of the separate supply and demand curves; that is, they are the solutions to:

$$\Omega_a(p_a) = F_a(p_a) \tag{6.1}$$

and

$$\Omega_b(p_b) = F_b(p_b) \tag{6.2}$$

If $p_a < p_b$ and the difference exceeds the cost of transporting the good between the two markets, ϵ then the good is exported from A to B. Trade equalizes the price of the good in the two markets, except for the transport costs. If the new equilibrium price in market A is denoted p'_a, Cournot (1927, p. 119) stated that this is given as the solution to:

$$\Omega_a(p'_a) + \Omega_b(p'_a + \epsilon) = F_a(p'_a) + F_b(p'_a + \epsilon) \tag{6.3}$$

This expression simply states that total supply is equal to total demand in both markets combined. Cournot then writes:

$$p'_a = p_a + \delta \text{ and } p_b = p_a + \omega \tag{6.4}$$

so that δ is the change in the price in market A and ω is the pre-trade absolute difference between prices in the two markets. Trade takes place only if $\omega > \epsilon$. Substitute for $p_a = p_b - \omega$ in the first of the expressions in (6.4) and add ϵ to get:

$$p'_a + \epsilon = p_b + \delta + \epsilon - \omega \tag{6.5}$$

Equation (6.3) can then be rewritten as:

$$\Omega_a(p_a + \delta) + \Omega_b(p_b + \delta + \epsilon - \omega) = F_a(p_a + \delta) + F_b(p_b + \delta + \epsilon - \omega)$$
$$(6.6)$$

Cournot then applied his method of 'development and reduction', his standard approach used throughout the *Researches*. This involves taking the Taylor series expansion of each function of the form $F(p + \delta)$ and neglecting squares and higher powers of δ. Thus:

$$F(p + \delta) = F(p) + \delta F'(p) \qquad (6.7)$$

Expanding each term in (6.6) in this way, and using (6.1) and (6.2), Cournot (1927, p. 120) obtained:

$$\delta\{\Omega_a'(p_a) - F_a'(p_a)\} = (\delta + \epsilon - \omega)\{F_b'(p_b) - \Omega_b'(p_b)\} \qquad (6.8)$$

Since demand curves are assumed to slope downwards and supply curves to slope upwards, the term in curly brackets in the left-hand side of (6.8) is positive, while that on the right-hand side is negative. Since $\delta > 0$, then $\delta + \epsilon - \omega < 0$ and $\delta < \omega - \epsilon$. Hence the increase in price in market A must be less than the difference between the initial price differential and the unit transport cost.

Changes in output
For demand in the two markets combined to increase it is necessary to have:

$$F_a(p_a + \delta) + F_b(p_b) + \delta + \epsilon - \omega + F_b(p_b) > F_a(p_a) + F_b(p_b) \, (6.9)$$

Using the Taylor series expansion, (6.9) reduces to:

$$\delta F_a'(p_a) + (\delta + \epsilon - \omega) F_b'(p_b) > 0 \qquad (6.10)$$

Using equation (6.8) to substitute for $\delta + \epsilon - \omega$ in (6.10), gives after some rearrangement, Cournot's condition (1927, p. 120) that total demand is increased if:

$$F_b'(p_b)\Omega_a'(p_a) - F_a'(p_a)\Omega_b'(p_b) < 0 \qquad (6.11)$$

The inequality is reversed because the term in curly brackets on the right-hand side of (6.8) is negative. Cournot commented that the inequality 'may or may not be satisfied according to the numerical relations of functions F' and Ω'' but he did not explore the conditions further. Edgeworth later described the condition in terms of the concept of elasticity, without giving the mathematics, as follows:

> The increase of the production in A may not compensate the decrease in B; when the demand in A is very inelastic, and the rise in the cost of production with the amount produced very steep, while the contrary properties are true of B. (1925, II, p. 47)

and added that 'it is among the few that are not open to suspicion'. But Edgeworth's summary is not quite accurate. Rearranging (6.11) gives:

$$\frac{F_b'(p_b)}{\Omega_b'(p_b)} < \frac{F_a'(p_a)}{\Omega_a'(p_a)} \tag{6.12}$$

The elasticity of demand in market A is $p_a F_a'(p_a)/F_a(p_a)$ which may be denoted η_a. Using (6.1) and (6.2), and denoting supply elasticities by ξ_a and ξ_b, (6.12) becomes:

$$\eta_b/\xi_b < \eta_a/\xi_a \tag{6.13}$$

The condition therefore depends on the ratio of demand to supply elasticities in each country, remembering that the demand elasticities have been defined to be negative. If absolute values are taken, then the inequality must again be reversed. This condition is intuitively clear since a low elasticity of supply in country B, combined with a high demand elasticity, means that the reduction in price in that country which results from the 'communication of markets' is associated with a relatively small reduction in supply with a large increase in demand. If the demand elasticity in the exporting country, in which the price rises, is low, then the combination of this with a large supply elasticity in that country will produce an increase in total output.

Changes in the value of output
Cournot (1927, pp. 121–2) then considered the question of whether the total *value* of output would increase. He simply wrote the basic expressions for total expenditure before and after trade and stated that the 'inequality will or will not be satisfied, according to the numerical relations of the quantities which enter into the inequality' (1927, p. 122). However, in a very terse statement he suggested that the total value of output would *fall* if:

> the value of p_a is greater than the value of p, which would render the function $pF_a(p)$ a maximum, and, on the other hand, that the value of p_b is less than that which would render the function $pF_b(p)$ a maximum. (1927, p. 121)

This can be translated into modern terms by noting that revenue is maximized where marginal revenue is zero; that is, when the elasticity of demand is equal to -1. Cournot's division of goods, according to whether or not the price is above or below that which maximizes total revenue, has been discussed in Chapter 3 above in connection with his failure to produce the concept of elasticity.

But Cournot's analysis was incomplete, as the following analysis shows. First, it is useful to consider the simpler problem for a single market in which the price changes from p to $p + \delta$. The new total revenue is $(p + \delta)$ $F(p + \delta)$, which becomes, after expansion by a Taylor series, $(p + \delta)\{F(p) + \delta F'(p)\}$. Neglecting terms in δ^2 this is $pF(p) + \delta F(p)(1 + \eta)$ where, as before, η denotes the elasticity of demand. Hence the *change* in total revenue is given by $\delta F(p)(1 + \eta)$. This gives the result familiar to all modern economists that if $\eta < -1$ the total revenue decreases when the price increases. For Cournot's problem the value of output after trade takes place is given by:

$$p'_a \, F_a \, (p'_a) + (p'_a + \epsilon) \, F_b(p'_a + \epsilon) \qquad (6.14)$$

Using (6.4) and (6.5) this becomes:

$$(p_a + \delta)F_a(p_a + \delta) + (p_b + \delta + \epsilon - \omega)F_b(p_b + \delta + \epsilon - \omega) \quad (6.15)$$

Expanding (6.15) it can be seen that the *change* in total revenue, ΔR, is given by:

$$\Delta R = \delta F_a(p_a)(1 + \eta_a) + (\delta + \epsilon - \omega)F_b(p_b)(1 + \eta_b)$$

Equation (6.8) can again be used to substitute for $\delta + \epsilon - \omega$. After some manipulation it can be found that total revenue increases if:

$$(1 + \eta_a)\left\{\frac{F'_b(p_b) - \Omega'_b(p_b)}{F_b(p_b)}\right\} < (1 + \eta_b)\left\{\frac{F'_a(p_a) - \Omega'_a(p_a)}{F_a(p_a)}\right\} \qquad (6.16)$$

Using (6.1) and (6.2) and the definitions of the relevant elasticities given above, (6.16) reduces to:

$$(1 + \eta_a) \, (\eta_b - \xi_b)p_b < (1 + \eta_b)(\eta_a - \xi_a)p_a \qquad (6.17)$$

Since $\eta - \xi$ is always negative it can be seen that a sufficient condition for (6.17) to be satisfied is that $\eta_a > -1$ and $\eta_b < -1$. Hence market A, where the price rises, has an inelastic demand while market B, for whom the price falls, must have an elastic demand. From Cournot's comment, quoted above, it can now be seen that he had recognized the *sufficient* condition for revenue to decrease. But his failure to formulate the elasticity concept prevented him from deriving a clear statement of the *necessary* conditions.

6.2   The effects of taxation

An import or export tax

In examining the effects of taxes, Cournot began (1927, p. 122) by noting that 'a tax on exportation or on importation will produce the same effects as an increase in the cost of transportation, equal to the amount of the tax'. In order to simplify the notation, he wrote $p'_a = p$ for the pre-tax, post-trade, price of the good in the exporting market. Thus (6.3) can be rewritten as:

$$\Omega_a(p) + \Omega_b(p + \epsilon) = F_a(p) + F_b(p + \epsilon) \tag{6.18}$$

The tax of u per unit is assumed to lead to a new price of $p + \delta$. The equilibrium condition becomes:

$$\Omega_a(p + \delta) + \Omega_b(p + \delta + \epsilon + u) = F_a(p + \delta) + F_b(p + \delta + \epsilon + u) \tag{6.19}$$

Following Cournot's usual approach it is then necessary to expand the terms in both (6.18) and (6.19) using a Taylor series (neglecting the second and higher powers), subtract the expanded form of (6.18) from that of (6.19), and finally collect terms in δ and u to give:

$$\delta = u\left(\frac{F'_a(p) - \Omega'_a(p)}{\Omega'_b(p) - F'_b(p)} - 1\right)^{-1} \tag{6.20}$$

However, Cournot gave the incorrect result that:

$$\delta = -(\epsilon + u)\frac{\Omega'_b(p) - F'_b(p)}{\Omega'_a(p) - F'_a(p) + \Omega'_b(p) - F'_b(p)} \tag{6.21}$$

The expressions (6.20) and (6.21) are only equivalent if ϵ is deleted from (6.21). The fact that Cournot had made an algebraic error seems first to have been noted by Edgeworth (1894, reprinted 1925, II, p. 49). Edgeworth added 'I am confirmed in this view by Mr A. Berry and Mr C.P. Sanger, who have independently made a similar correction'. Both Berry and Sanger were very close to Marshall and it is not unlikely that they were led to examine Cournot's analysis by Marshall himself. As Edgeworth pointed out, Cournot should have spotted his error because δ must be zero when u is zero. The error was later pointed out by Fisher in 1989 (reprinted in Cournot, 1927, p. xxiv), who did not mention Edgeworth. Neither Edgeworth nor Fisher gave the form of the solution shown in (6.20) above. Indeed, Edgeworth argued that Cournot was led to make his error because of his method of expanding terms such as $F_b(p + \delta + \epsilon + u)$. Cournot clearly used an expansion of the form $F_b(p) + (\delta + \epsilon + u) F_b'$ (p), but Edgeworth argued that transport costs are not necessarily negligible and that it is more appropriate to use $F_b(p + \epsilon) + (\delta + u)F_b' (p + \epsilon)$. Only for linear demand and supply curves will the two methods give precisely the same result.

Consideration of the signs in (6.20) shows that δ is unambiguously negative and in absolute terms is less than u. The duty always lowers the price in the exporting market and raises it in the importing market, whereas Cournot's error led him to believe that the price may fall in the importing market. It should be added that (6.20) cannot conveniently be converted into an expression involving elasticities since it is no longer true that, for example $F_a(p) = \Omega_a(p)$.

A tax-cum-subsidy
Cournot briefly mentioned the case where, instead of an export or import tax, a tax of u is imposed only in the country of origin. The pre-tax post-trade equilibrium price, p, is given by (6.18), as before but the new price, $p + \delta$, is given by:

$$\Omega_a(p + \delta - u) + \Omega_b(p + \delta + \epsilon) = F_a(p + \delta) + F_b (p + \delta + \epsilon) \quad (6.22)$$

He did not pursue this problem, but it can be found that

$$\delta = u\left[1 + \frac{\Omega_b'(p) - F_a'(p) - F_b'(p)}{\Omega_a'(p)}\right]^{-1} \quad (6.23)$$

Hence $\delta > 0$ and the price must increase.

He went on to consider the effects of tax 'imposed on a commodity in the country of its origin, that in order to favour its exportation, the government reimburses or restores the amount of the impost to the merchant who exports the commodity' (1927, p. 125). Cournot argued that if p'' is the price after the imposition of the tax-cum-subsidy of u, then the new equilibrium condition is:

$$\Omega_a(p'' - u) + \Omega_b(p'' + \epsilon - u) = F_a(p'') + F_b(p'' + \epsilon - u) \quad (6.24)$$

He then showed, following the familiar method used above, that the policy raises the price of the good in the exporting market and lowers it in the importing market. He also demonstrated that the policy unequivocally increases the volume of exports. This is intuitively clear, since production in the importing country must fall as a result of the price fall there.

Cournot's solution for the change in price, δ, is given (1927, p. 125) as:

$$\delta = u \left[\frac{\Omega'_a(p) + \Omega'_b(p + \epsilon) - F'_b(p + \epsilon)}{\Omega'_a(p) + \Omega'_b(p + \epsilon) - F'_a(p) - F'_b(p + \epsilon)} \right] \tag{6.25}$$

It can therefore be seen that thre is some inconsistency in his method of applying the Taylor series expansion, when compared with his earlier treatment of an import tax. In equation (6.25) Cournot is seen to be expanding $\Omega_b(p + \delta + \epsilon - u)$ as $\Omega_b (p + \epsilon) + (\delta - u) \Omega'_b (p + \epsilon)$, which is precisely the way Edgeworth argued that the method should proceed. The consistent application of Cournot's method would give:

$$\delta = u \left[1 - \frac{F'_a(p)}{\Omega'_a(p) + \Omega'_b(p) - F'_b(p)} \right]^{-1} \tag{6.26}$$

6.3   Diagrammatic analysis

The back-to-back diagram

It has been seen that Cournot's basic framework of analysis, used mainly to examine the effects of various tariffs, was a relatively simple one in which a single good is initially produced in two countries that are isolated from each other. When 'communication' between the markets occurs, the good is produced and exported by the country in which it is initially cheaper, allowing for transport costs. The equilibrium requirement is that the supply (in the exporting country) is equal, at the new price, to the aggregate demand of both countries combined. Although Marshall published nothing on this analysis, some early notes are reproduced in Marshall (1975, II, pp. 246–8). These notes show Marshall's early attempt to cast Cournot's model into diagrammatic form, mainly for the purpose of examining the gains from trade using measures of producers' and consumers' surplus.

The diagrammatic analysis of Cournot's model was later refined by Marshall's former student Henry Cunynghame (1892, 1903), who produced the machine used by Marshall for drawing his rectangular hyperbolas. Cunynghame argued that 'the method of treating economics graphically is probably due to Cournot' and added, 'the chief credit of reviving an interest in this method rests with Professor Marshall' (1892, p. 36).

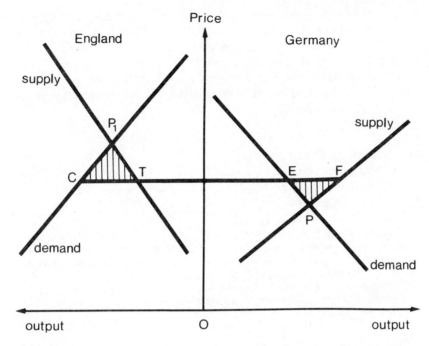

Figure 6.1   Cournot's model

After an unsatisfactory start (1892, p. 44), Cunynghame produced the now familiar 'back-to-back' diagram without any reference to Cournot but virtually paraphrasing the latter's introduction to his model (1903, p. 317). It does not seem to be widely recognized that Cunynghame's treatment stems directly from Cournot. Even Viner (1955, p. 589), who also refers to Barone's use of the same diagram to measure the gains from trade, does not seem to recognize that the diagram represents Cournot's model. The origins are, however, recognized by Samuelson (1952).

Ignoring transport costs, the diagram is shown in Figure 6.1 where the equilibrium price is such that CT = EF. The essential feature of the model is of course that it involves only one good and the demand and supply schedules are specified in terms of the absolute price of the good, in terms of units of a common currency. Marshall's notes on Cournot show clearly the influence on Marshall's analysis of consumers' and producers' surplus. His diagrammatic version of Cournot's model translates his analysis (of Cournot's chapter XII) into the now familiar triangles. Using the back-to-back version of Figure 6.1 the left-hand side shows that the gain to English consumers arising from the price reduction outweighs the loss to producers, so that the net gain is equal to the shaded area P_1CT. The price increase in Germany produces a net gain equal to the shaded area EPF in the right-hand side of the figure. Marshall added that if in each country the cost of production is independent of output, then the exporting country gains nothing from trade (1975, II, pp. 247–8). Although these notes are not dated, there seems little doubt that Cournot was the sole influence and that Jenkin's brilliant analysis was quite independent, as Marshall himself insisted.

6.4   General equilibrium

A fundamental criticism of Cournot's model is that it deals with only one good. This point was acknowledged by Cournot towards the end of the *Researches*, where he wrote:

> It will be said that it is impossible for exportation of a commodity to fail to involve importation on the exporting market of a precisely equal value; and reciprocally, importation on a market involves exportation of an equal value. . . It would be necessary to consider each of these nations as acting simultaneously the part of an importing nation and that an exporting nation, which would greatly complicate the question and lead to a complex result (1927, pp. 161–2).

Cournot did not, however, pursue this question. The fundamental problem is that the partial equilibrium apparatus cannot be used to answer a general equilibrium question. It is more complex than simply adding another good and imposing a balance of payments constraint. Additional partial equilibrium demand and supply curves cannot by their nature cope with the interdependence which is at the heart of the problem. The use of simple partial equilibrium schedules involving money prices is precisely what Marshall rejected when it came to the analysis of foreign trade. It was the recognition that the 'ordinary' demand and supply curves are inadequate for international trade contexts that led Marshall to develop his 'offer curves' capturing the reciprocal nature of supply and demand stressed by Torrens and Mill. He argued that, 'Students frequently fall into errors which they may easily avoid if they will resolve that when discussing the pure theory [of foreign trade] they will not speak of the imports or exports of a country as measured in terms of money' (1975, II, p. 131).

Marshall added that the complexities become 'wholly unmanageable', so it is necessary to produce a barter model rather than a model along the lines of Cournot. There are also some brief but illuminating remarks on the contrast between Mill's and Cournot's analyses of exchange values in domestic and international contexts, made by Marshall in his first major paper in economics on *Mr Mill's theory of value* (1876, reprinted in Pigou, ed., 1925, p. 129).

A simple extension

This subsection shows briefly how Cournot's model can be converted into a general equilibrium model involving two goods. Suppose that there are two goods, X and Y, and comparative advantage is such that A exports good X to country B, while the latter exports good Y to A. Assume complete specialization, and denote the relative price of good X as p. This relative price can be interpreted as the amount of good Y that must be given in order to obtain a unit of good X. For present purposes it is necessary to express B's demand for X and A's demand for Y as $F_b(p)$ and $F_a(p^{-1})$ respectively; p^{-1} is the relative price of Y.

The essential feature of this type of exchange model is that the demand for one good, at a given price, automatically carries with it a supply of the other good. B's supply of Y, corresponding to the demand $F_b(p)$, is given by:

$$\Omega_b(p) = p \, F_b(p) \tag{6.27}$$

while A's supply of X is given by:

$$\Omega_a(p) = p^{-1} \, F_a(p^{-1}) \tag{6.28}$$

The equilibrium price is that value of p for which the demand for and supply of, say Y, are equal. This requires:

$$\Omega_b(p) = pF_b(p) = F_a(p^{-1}) \tag{6.29}$$

which is equivalent to the equilibrium condition for good X, given by:

$$\Omega_a(p) = p^{-1} \, F_a(p^{-1}) = F_b(p) \tag{6.30}$$

The conversion of Cournot's partial equilibrium model to a general equilibrium model is therefore in principle fairly straightforward. It requires the specification of the two demand function in terms of the relative price, p. But in historical terms the short step involved in generalizing Cournot's model had to wait some time, however, and forms the subject of Part 2 of this book.

Notes and further reading

When discussing the possibility of gain from tariffs, Schumpeter (1954, p. 615, n. 21) commented that 'Cournot's contribution to the theory of international values lies in this field'.

Viner (1955, pp. 583–6) has some interesting comments on partial and general equilibrium analyses of international trade. Although Viner uses 'terms of trade' diagrams and notes the relationship between supply and demand elasticities (1955, pp. 539–40), he does not explore the shapes of the curves or refer to Walras's analysis.

The following brief but illuminating comment by Cournot on the need for, and difficulty of, a general equilibrium treatment is worth quoting here.

> in reality the economic system is a whole of which all the parts are connected and react on each other. An increase in the income of the producers of commodity A will affect the demand for commodities B, C, etc., and the incomes of their producers, and, by its reaction, will involve a change in the demand for commodity A. It seems, therefore, as if, for a complete and rigorous solution of the problems relative to some parts of the economic system, it were indispensable to take the entire system into consideration. But this would surpass the powers of mathematical analysis and of our practical methods of calculation, even if the values of all the constants could be assigned to them numerically. (1927, p. 127)

The problem was indeed to surpass the powers of analysis until the middle of the 20th century, and the methods of calculation until more recently. But Walras later concentrated on stating the structure or form of the general equilibrium model, without attempting to specify the precise nature of the equations and solve them. This statement by Cournot is worth keeping in mind when considering the influences on Walras, in Chapter 9 below.

PART 2

GENERAL EQUILIBRIUM ANALYSES

7 Exchange and reciprocal demand

It has been argued that Cournot's analysis of trade between two previously isolated regions was limited by its partial equilibrium concentration on a single good. It was rejected by Walras and Marshall for
precisely this reason. The most important early contribution to the general
equilibrium analysis of exchange was made by J.S. Mill in the context of
international trade. This is justly famous, and is discussed briefly in
section 7.1 below. Less well-known is Whewell's mathematical analysis,
based on Mill's basic framework. A significant result of Mill's analysis was
that it stimulated his old adversary Whewell to produce his third paper
(1850) on mathematical economics. When writing to Richard Jones about
this paper, Whewell stated that it 'really does contain a refutation of
certain vaunted theorems of John S Mill on International Trade; and
shows them to be true . . . within very narrow limits' (in Henderson, 1985,
p. 420). Yet in the paper Whewell was careful to avoid allusions to
disagreement between himself and Mill, and the innocent reader would
infer that Whewell had a great respect for the relevant parts of Mill's
Principles. This neglected contribution is examined in detail in Sections 7.2
and 7.3. Whewell's discussion of the gains from trade and the limits within
which Mill's analysis is applicable is then examined in Section 7.4. Finally,
Section 7.5 considers the question of Whewell's possible influence on
Mill's subsequent work.

7.1 Mill's analysis

J. S. Mill produced his pathbreaking analysis of price determination in
international trade as early as 1829, but delayed publication until 1844,
and then included the same piece in his *Principles* (1848). This contribution has been described by Edgeworth as 'stupendous' (1925, II, p. 20) and
by O'Brien as 'one of the greatest performances in the history of economics' (1975, p. 183). The analysis is not of course restricted to foreign
trade, but applies to any exchange situation in which the parties are price-
takers. Mill's contribution is important for, among other things, its use of
the central concept of reciprocal demand in exchange. This is the simple
but powerful idea that the demand for one good carries with it an associated, or reciprocal, supply of another good and is the cornerstone of
general equilibrium analysis. The basic idea was not entirely new, but Mill
was able to indicate its importance much more clearly than other writers
because of his conception of demand as a schedule. Thus 'the demand for

a commodity, that is, the quantity of it which can find a purchaser, varies, as we have before remarked, according to the price' (Mill, 1920, p. 585).

The crucial element of the analysis is the idea that demand depends on *relative prices*. Hence England, which is assumed to have a comparative advantage over Germany in the production of cloth (while Germany has a comparative advantage in linen production), has a demand for linen that depends on the price of linen relative to that of cloth. This relative price can be expressed in terms of an amount of cloth per unit of linen. This is the basis of Mill's argument that 'all trade is in reality barter, money being a mere instrument for exchanging things' (1920, p. 583).

If England demands a certain quantity of linen, there is a reciprocal supply of cloth equal to the amount of linen multiplied by the relative price. The quantity of linen multiplied by the amount of cloth per unit of linen obviously gives an amount of cloth. Mill did not use mathematical notation, preferring to give numerical examples. Neglecting transport costs, equilibrium requires that the post-trade relative price is the same in each country and that the price is such that Germany's demand for cloth precisely matches England's supply (associated with its demand for linen at the corresponding relative price). Following some numerical examples, Mill stated his 'equation of international demand' as follows:

> It may be considered, therefore, as established, that when two countries trade together in two commodities, the exchange value of these commodities relative to each other will adjust itself to the inclinations and circumstances of the customers on both sides, in such manner that the quantities required by each country, of the articles which it imports from its neighbour, shall be exactly sufficient to pay for one another. As the inclinations and circumstances of consumers cannot be reduced to any rule, so neither can the proportions in which the two commodities will be interchanged. (1920, p. 587)

When considering the gains from trade, Mill went on to add that 'the circumstances on which the proportionate share of each country more remotely depends, admit only of a very general indication' (1920, p. 587). It is in Mill's subsequent discussion of the 'general indications' that he made much use of the idea underlying demand elasticity, although he described it with the term 'susceptibility'. Mill effectively argued (1920, pp. 587–8) that if the German demand for cloth is completely inelastic, then all the gains from trade go to Germany. In general, Mill was able to demonstrate that, 'If, therefore, it be asked what country draws to itself the greatest share of the advantage of any trade it carries on, the answer is, the country for whose production there is in other countries the greatest demand, and a demand the most susceptible of increase from additional cheapness' (1920, p. 591). Mill also introduced additional countries, transport costs and additional goods, as well as examining the effects of technological change and shifts in demand.

Mill later added supplementary sections to his international trade chapter to take account of criticisms from unspecified persons. These later sections have generally been poorly received by later critics. Even Marshall stated that, 'the splendid edifice of theory constructed in the first five sections is not improved by the superstructure of later date which forms the latter part of the chapter. This second storey does not carry us much higher' (1925, p. 22). It will be argued below that these supplementary sections add significant insights and that they were probably influenced by Whewell's work.

7.2 Whewell's trade model

It is well known that Marshall's international trade theory was greatly influenced by his early 'translation' into diagrams of J.S. Mill's famous chapter on 'international values'. But Whewell's (1850) paper presented to the Cambridge Philosophical Society has gone almost unnoticed. There are no references to Whewell in any of Marshall's published works, he was ignored by Edgeworth in his survey of trade theory (1925) and his work was only given a cursory treatment by Viner (1955). The general attitude to Whewell's work appears to have been influenced by Jevons's dismissive comments, in particular that he had the 'misfortune' to 'build on sand' (1957, p. xxv). It has been shown in Chapter 2 that Jevons failed to notice Whewell's discovery of the precise nature of the King–Davenant law of demand. While Schumpeter judged Whewell to be an 'Academic leader' and thought Jevons's verdict was too harsh, he nevertheless dismissed his work as not going 'beyond stating in symbols what had already been stated in words and therefore does not really constitute mathematical economics' (1954, p. 448, n. 7).

There is little doubt that the modern reader will find Whewell's analysis rather impenetrable. The discussion is terse and the notation unfamiliar – he was obviously not interested in providing pedagogic help to the reader. A closer examination nevertheless reveals that Whewell's achievement was more significant than has been recognized. It is also suggested that Whewell probably influenced Mill's 'supplementary sections'. In order to make comparisons with the original easier, Whewell's notation will be used throughout.

The basic framework

Following Mill, Whewell considered trade between England and Germany in Cloth (denoted C) and Linen (denoted D). In England before trade, p is the relative price of linen and q is the demand for linen at that price. In Germany before trade, P is the relative price of cloth and Q is the demand for cloth at that price. Hence $1/P$ is the relative price of linen in Germany before trade. This way of setting up the model is far from arbitrary as Whewell assumed that Germany has a comparative advantage in linen; hence $1/P$ is less than p. It is therefore cheaper to purchase linen in Germany than in England, in terms of the cloth that must be exchanged per unit of linen (fewer units of cloth need be given up per unit of linen in Germany). Hence:

$$1/P < p \text{ and } Pp > 1 \tag{7.1}$$

The simplifying implicit assumption was made that units are such that the exchange rate is unity. After trade, when England exports cloth and imports linen, the prices must be equal. Whewell (1850, para. 36) called this requirement the 'equation of uniformity of international prices', represented by:

$$P'p' = 1 \tag{7.2}$$

where P' and p' denotes the post-trade relative price of cloth and linen respectively in 'world markets'.

If England exports Q' of cloth and imports q' of linen from Germany, then for trade to balance it is necessary to have $p'q' = Q'$; remember that p' is the price of linen divided by the price of cloth ($=1/P'$). Similarly, Germany exports q' of linen for Q' of cloth from England, so that trade balance requires $P'Q' = q'$. Thus:

$$p'q' = Q' \tag{7.3}$$

and

$$P'Q' = q' \tag{7.4}$$

Equations (7.3) and (7.4) are equivalent in view of the requirement in (7.2). This result was referred to by Whewell as the 'equation of import and export'. Notice that, just like Mill, Whewell uses the term 'equation' (as in 'equation of supply and demand') to mean *equality*. Hence (7.3) and (7.4) are really accounting identities. But in fact both Mill and Whewell went well beyond stating the obvious accounting relationships since they examined the *process*, via the adjustment of prices and the resulting movements *along* reciprocal demand curves, towards the equilibrium. On this point see the discussion in Viner (1955, pp. 536–7), particularly his quotation from a letter from Mill to Cairnes.

Equilibrium prices
Having set up the condition under which trade takes place and specified the balance of trade equilibrium, Whewell then wished to determine the equilibrium price ratio. This is achieved only by specifying the relevant import demand curves, those of England for linen and of Germany for cloth. Only these demand functions are required in view of the reciprocal demand relationship that applies; England's demand for linen is simultaneously a supply of cloth in exchange. Mill's discussion used specific numerical values for the price elasticity of total revenue, though of course he did not use the expression, but Whewell's specification is very effective and allows a more complete analysis. Whewell's analysis was based on his specification of demand functions, which has been examined in detail in Chapter 3 above.

The problem is to find the extent to which England must reduce the relative price of linen as a result of engaging in trade, and therefore also the extent to which the relative price of cloth in Germany must fall. Since price *reductions* are now relevant, Whewell wrote:

$$p' = p(1 - x) \text{ with } p'q' = pq(1 - mx) \tag{7.5}$$

and

$$p' = P(1 - X) \text{ with } P'Q' = PQ(1 - MX) \tag{7.6}$$

The terms m and M are respectively the 'specific rate of change' of the demand for linen in England and for cloth in Germany; similarly x and X are the proportional reductions in p and P respectively; see Chapter 4 above. Substituting for P' and p' from (7.5) and (7.6) into (7.2), Whewell obtained:

$$P'p = Pp(1 - X)(1 - x) = 1 - k$$

so that

$$\frac{1}{Pp} = (1 - X)(1 - x) = 1 - k \tag{7.7}$$

From the inequality in (7.1) it is clear that $0 < k < 1$; Whewell (1850, para. 38) simply referred to k as 'being a fraction', but it has a fairly straightforward interpretation. It is the proportional difference between the relative price of linen in England and Germany (since $1/Pp$ is the ratio of the relative price of linen in England before trade). Hence, before trade the relative price of linen in Germany is 100k per cent lower than in England. Equation (7.7) can be used to express X in terms of k and x, whence:

$$X = \frac{k - x}{1 - x}$$

(7.8)

Following Whewell's method of writing the demand curve, equations (7.5) and (7.6) give:

$$q' = \frac{q(1 - mx)}{(1 - x)} \quad \text{and} \quad Q' = \frac{Q(1 - MX)}{1 - X}$$

(7.9)

Substituting (7.9) into the 'equation of import and export' given by (7.4) then gives:

$$\frac{q(1 - mx)}{1 - x} = PQ(1 - MX)$$

(7.10)

Using (7.8) to substitute for X, (7.10) can be used to solve for x, whereby:

$$x = \frac{PQ(1 - Mk) - q}{PQ(1 - M) - mq}$$

(7.11)

The derivation of (7.11) shows the considerable simplification obtained by using Whewell's demand functions, rather than the more satisfactory expression derived above in equation (3.13), which would produce an awkward quadratic in x. Hence Whewell's implicit neglect of terms involving x^2 is rather important.

Having solved for x using (7.11), the value of X can obviously be obtained using (7.8). Thus Whewell did not bother to give the symmetrical result, this time starting from (7.3) rather than (7.4) and solving (7.7) for x so that:

$$X = \frac{pq(1 - mk) - Q}{pq(1 - m) - QM}$$

(7.12)

After obtaining the result in (7.11) Whewell went on to define the term, n, using the relation:

$$PQ = nq \qquad (7.13)$$

This allows (7.11) to be rewritten

$$x = \frac{n(1 - Mk) - 1}{n(1 - M) - m} \qquad (7.14)$$

The term n was described by Whewell (1850, para. 39) as, 'the relative value of [cloth] consumed in Germany and of [linen] consumed in England' before trade takes place. Later (1980, para. 53) it was referred to as 'the inequality of mutual demand'. Whewell's description is not, however, strictly accurate since P is a *ratio* of prices in Germany before trade. For completeness, n may be said to measure the ratio of the value of cloth consumed in Germany to that of linen consumed in England, where the latter is valued at its price in Germany, before trade takes place. If, instead, equation (7.12) is used, then:

$$X = \frac{n^* (1 - mk) - 1}{n^*(1 - m) - M} \qquad (7.15)$$

and n^* is the pre-trade ratio of the value of linen consumed in England to that of cloth consumed in Germany, with the latter valued using the English price of cloth.

The result in (7.15) clearly goes beyond Mill in that it establishes the precise extent to which the post-trade relative price of linen is less than its pre-trade relative price in England. It shows exactly how this amount depends on the 'specific rates of change', m and M, the pre-trade proportional difference between the relative price of linen in England and Germany, k, and the pre-trade ratio of the value of cloth consumed in Germany to that of linen consumed in England (measured in German prices), n. A similar interpretation holds for (7.15), although Whewell did not present this result.

Whewell's achievement here may be compared with Mill's summary quoted at the beginning of this chapter. Whewell had shown just what Mill stated could not be expressed. Whewell's contribution is thus much more than a simple restatement of Mill's discussion using mathematical notation. But after presenting his analysis, Whewell concluded rather modestly that he had, 'done little more than put into a general and algebraical form the reasonings which Mr Mill has presented to his readers in numerical examples' (1850, para. 66). Perhaps Schumpeter simply took him at his word when he said that it wasn't real 'mathematical economics'. But it will be seen that Whewell's treatment was really quite sophisticated and provides some useful further insights into the basic model expounded by Mill.

7.3   Numerical examples

After solving for x, Whewell stated that he 'will apply these formulae to the numerical examples given by Mr Mill' (1850, para. 40). Mill's assumptions about pre-trade relative prices imply that $p = 2/3$ and $P = 2$. Hence $Pp = 4/3$ and the inequality in (7.1) is satisfied; substitution into (7.7) then gives $k = 1/4$. Whewell then sets $m = M = 2/3$, without any discussion, giving after substituting in (7.14):

$$x = \frac{6 - 5n}{4 - 2n} \tag{7.16}$$

Supposing n to be 8/7, Whewell found that $x = 1/6$. Hence the relative price of linen in England falls, after trade, by 1/6 and the new price is (2/3) (5/6) = 10/18, which corresponds to the equilibrium price in Mill's example (1920, p. 586). Whewell continued his discussion of this example, with $m = M = 2/3$, for the next two and a half pages. But it can be argued that Whewell's example does not really correspond closely to other aspects of Mill's assumptions. By taking the 'specific rate of change' of both commodities to be positive and less than unity, Whewell implies that they are, according to his classification, 'general necessaries'. Thus a decrease in the price would produce a decrease in total desired expenditure.

In discussing the adjustment from a disequilibrium relative price, Mill (1920, p. 586) supposed that at a relative price of '10 cloth to 17 linen' (that is, $p = 10/17$) the English demand for linen is 13 600 units (which he expresses as 17 times 800 for pedagogic reasons). He then considered a situation in which a change in the relative price to '10 cloth to 18 linen' (that is, a reduction in p to 10/18) would give rise to an English demand for linen of 16200 units. Hence pq changes from 8000 to 9000 and a proportional *reduction* in price of 0.056 leads to a proportional *increase* in total expenditure of 0.125. Thus Mill's example suggests a value of m of about -2.24, which is quite different from Whewell's assumption of 2/3. Mill assumed, more reasonably, that (on Whewell's classification) linen is a 'popular luxury' ($m < 0$).

For convenience, suppose therefore that $m = M = -2$. Substituting into (7.14), along with $k = 1/4$, gives:

$$x = \frac{3n - 2}{6n - 4}$$

In this case, $x = 1/6$, as in Mill's example, if $n = 2/3$. A value of n less than unity is also more sensible than the value needed by Whewell to get Mill's result. The fact that Whewell's numerical examples are not well-chosen does not, of course, imply any criticism of his model.

Further properties of the model may also be noted here. If $m = M = 0$ (linen and cloth are 'articles of fixed expenditure' for both English and German consumers, so that the price elasticity of demand is in each case -1), then (7.14) gives:

$$x = (n - 1)/n \qquad (7.17)$$

Since x must be non-negative, (7.17) only holds for $n \geq 1$, whatever the initial prices, contrasting with the above examples. This now requires the condition that Germany's desired expenditure on cloth exceeds England's desired expenditure on linen, at German pre-trade prices. If, alternatively, only $M = 0$ then:

$$x = (n - 1)/(n - m) \qquad (7.18)$$

and (7.18) shows that n can be less than unity so long as it is less than m and the latter is positive (a reduction in price leads to a reduction in expenditure).

7.4 The gains from trade

Return briefly to Whewell's assumption that $m = M = 2/3$, so that x is given by equation (7.16), where k is assumed (with Mill) to be 1/4. Whewell argued that if $n = 10/9$, the resulting value of x is 1/4 and the relative price of linen after trade is 25 per cent less than its pre-trade price in England. From equation (7.8) it can be seen that this result implies that $X = 0$, and although Whewell did not state this implication explicitly, he argues – by showing that consumption is unchanged – that Germany gains nothing by the trade. The general conclusion is obvious: if $x = 0$ then England gains nothing and if $X = 0$, Germany gains nothing by trade. The higher is x, the greater is England's gain, subject to the condition that $X \geq 0$. This type of reasoning is the basis for Mill's argument that the extent of the gain from trade is measured by the extent of the reduction (from pre- to post-trade) in the relative price of the country's imports relative to its exports. Later commentators referred to this as a 'favourable' change in the 'terms of trade'. It is interesting to consider the following quotation from Mill:

> If, therefore, it be asked what country draws to itself the greatest share of the advantage of any trade it carries on, the answer is, the country for whose

production there is in other countries the greatest demand, and demand the most susceptible of increase from additional cheapness ... it gets its imports cheaper, the greater the intensity of the demand in foreign countries for its exports ... [and] ... the less the extent and intensity of its own demand for them. The market is cheapest to those whose demand is small. (1920, p. 591)

This is a summary of a superb piece of reasoning, but Whewell's result, in equation (7.14), is by no means a mere 'translation' of Mill into mathematical notation. He also investigated the precise limits within which trade would take place.

Whewell's limits

The various parameters of the model must, as Whewell argued, be such that x and X are non-negative (as given by (7.14) and (7.15)). Since Whewell only considered x, the requirement that $X \geq 0$ simply translates, using (7.8), into the condition that $x \leq k$. Whewell wished to use these conditions in order to obtain limits for n according to which the gains would go only to one of the countries. In doing this he has been criticized by Chipman (1965) for making an error, but it will be seen that Whewell's treatment is perfectly correct. His explanation is, however, so terse as to be almost non-existent.

Now, for $x = 0$ (when England gains nothing), the numerator of (7.16) is zero. Hence:

$$n = 1/(1 - Mk) \qquad (7.19)$$

The other limit, from (7.15), is of course given by $n^* \, 1/(1 - mk)$ but Whewell did not take this approach. Now for $x > 0$ there are two possibilities: either the numerator *and* denominator of (7.14) are both positive or they are both negative. Consider first the case where they are positive, that is, when $n > 1/(1 - Mk)$. The requirement that $x < k$ then gives:

$$n(1 - Mk) - 1 < k\{n(1-m) - m\}$$

which gives

$$n > \frac{1 - mk}{1 - k} \qquad (7.20)$$

This is Whewell's condition in (1950, para. 49). Secondly, consider the case where numerator and denominator of (7.14) are negative. Here $n < 1/(1 - Mk)$ and the condition that $x < k$ is given by:

$$1 - n(1 - Mk) < k\{m - n(1 - M)\}$$

so that

$$n > \frac{1 - mk}{1 - k} \tag{7.21}$$

This is Whewell's condition in (1950, para. 47). Whewell went on to introduce additional goods and countries, and to allow for transport costs using, as did Mill, the same basic principles. While these extensions are of interest, they need not be examined here as they raise no new issues.

Whewell's supposed 'slip'
In his major survey of international trade theory, Chipman argued that when Whewell derived an inequality 'for the characterization of solutions with complete specialization; unfortunately a slip entered his argument, and his formulas are therefore valid only for certain values of the para-meters' (1965, p. 492). In a later paper devoted to Whewell's work, Rashid (1977, p. 388) referred to a 'simple algebraic error in his paper on interna-tional values'. But no reference or further details were given and it seems likely that Rashid was just repeating Chipman's point uncritically. It is therefore necessary to examine this argument. Chipman stated that Whewell assumed:

> that $x < k$ implies $tx < tk$, forgetting that this is true only if $t > 0$. . . . Had he possessed an economist's intuition, Whewell might have spotted this error after interpreting the result; except for this slip, Whewell's treatment seems to be quite valid and even ingenious, and one can only lament the fact that, having gone so far, he fell just short of deriving the correct conditions. (1965, p. 492, n. 13)

Several comments are in order here. First, the above discussion has shown that Whewell was fully aware of the trap mentioned by Chipman in dealing with inequalities and his treatment was perfectly correct. Second, it has been said that in this context Mill did not assume zero 'susceptibili-ties' (values of m and M) but assumed that in general they would be negative. Hence price increases reduce total expenditure and vice versa. He only made the provisional assumption of zero values for m and M (unit elasticities) in his supplementary section (1920, pp. 597–601) and quickly relaxed it in the next section. The discussion below will return to this point. Thirdly, Chipman described the context incorrectly. Whewell was concerned with the conditions under which all the gains from trade would go to only one country, not with the conditions for complete specialization, although it is true that a country that does not gain may not specialize fully in the good in which it has a comparative advantage.

7.5 Mill's supplementary sections

Although Mill did not refer to Whewell's analysis when writing his supplementary sections to the great chapter, it is of interest to consider the possibility that he was influenced by the mathematical model. Chipman speculates that 'Mill saw Whewell's memoir and found it of considerable interest, yet did not trouble himself to go through the algebra, and may even (correctly) have suspected it of being faulty' (1965, pp. 492–3). In view of the above argument that Chipman's criticism is misplaced, an alternative hypothesis is that Mill recognized from Whewell's model that the post-trade relative price need not be unique. This is clear once it is recognized that both M and m vary along the respective demand curves. His 'supplementary sections' of 1852 began with the acknowledgement that the equilibrium condition defined earlier need not be associated with a unique price ratio.

The supplementary sections also discuss conditions under which only one of the countries gains from trade. It is suggested that there is a fairly high probability that Mill became conscious of this aspect from Whewell's memoir. Indeed Mill begins with the special case where the elasticities of demand are (minus) unity; that is, where M and m are zero. The implications of Whewell's model for this case are shown in equation (7.15) above, where it is seen that all of the gain goes to England if $n^* = 1$. This is precisely the situation described by Mill as follows:

> Let us therefore assume, that the influence of cheapness on demand conforms to some simple law, common to both countries and to both commodities . . . let us suppose that in both countries any given increase of cheapness produces an exactly proportional increase of consumption; or, in other words, that the value expended in the commodity . . . is always the same . . .
>
> Let us now suppose that England, previous to the trade, required a million yards of linen, which were worth, at the English cost of production, a million yards of cloth . . . Suppose that this is the exact quantity which Germany is accustomed to consume. England can dispose of all this cloth in Germany at the German price. . .thus England would gain the whole benefit of the trade, and Germany nothing. (1920, p. 598)

He then went on (p. 602) to suppose that elasticities are such that $m = 0$ and $M \neq 0$, while in a footnote to p. 603 he assumed non-unit numerical values for the elasticities. It is interesting to observe that Schumpeter (1954, p. 608, n. 7) states that 'Mill never came so close to a grasp of the nature and use of the concept of elasticity of demand. . .as he did in [paragraph] 8 of that chapter'.

It would therefore not be extravagant to argue that Mill's supplementary sections represent an attempt to put Whewell's results in plain English, leading to 'clumsiness and ambiguity of expression that are unavoidable' (Schumpeter, 1954, p. 608, n. 7), and which influenced the later judgements of Edgeworth and Bastable that they are 'laborious and confusing'. Instead of Whewell being judged as simply translating Mill into mathematics, it seems that Mill translated Whewell's extensions back into English (though it is relevant that this is the only place in the *Principles* where Mill felt the need to introduce some mathematical notation). It is rather unfortunate that later attempts to provide mathematical models of Mill's discussion have ignored Whewell so completely.

Whewell certainly took the trouble to circulate privately printed copies of his papers 'to the Economists whom I know, by way of challenge' (quote by Henderson, 1985, p. 421). Mill's failure to acknowledge Whewell's contribution is easily explained by their personal antagonism, although their conflicts mainly concerned moral philosophy and methodology. Mill (1920, p. 586) only gave a vague mention to William Thornton but it is clear that he had other 'intelligent criticism' in mind. It is noteworthy that in the third edition Mill also cut references to the important work of Torrens.

It is also worth stressing that Mill, and following him, Whewell, did not, as sometimes suggested, measure the gains from trade simply by the extent of the difference between the pre- and post-tax relative price (the change in the terms of trade), although a larger value of x was held to imply a larger gain for England. Emphasis was clearly on the allocative efficiency gains allowed by trade. Thus, he argued that 'its advantage consist in a more efficient employment of the productive forces of the world. . .the addition thus made to the produce of the two [countries] combined, constitutes the advantage of the trade' (1920, p. 578). In discussing these efficiency gains, Whewell stressed the need for factors of production to be mobile among industries. He introduced the 'principle of transferable capital' to summarize this requirement. It is also relevant, in considering Whewell's influence, that in his supplementary sections Mill placed much greater emphasis on the domestic transfer of resources.

It has been seen that Whewell's work has suffered considerable neglect and, to make matters worse, he has been accused of making a mathematical error concerning inequalities when in fact he was careful to state (but not explain) the full set of conditions required. Whewell's model has been seen to provide a significant extension to Mill's analysis and to involve genuine mathematical economics rather than a straightforward translation into algebraic notation. Although Whewell's numerical examples were not well chosen, his analytical results stand up to close inspection. It represents a genuine pioneer attempt to produce a general equilibrium model of trade. He concluded, not without justification, that, 'it will have appeared by this mode of dealing with the subject, the limits of the truth of the theorems [and] of the solutions of the problems are much more easily brought into view, at least for the mathematical reader, than in the numerical way' (1850, p. 21).

Notes and further reading

Mill's conception of demand in terms of a schedule is stressed by Robbins (1958, p. 242), O'Brien (1975, p. 183) and Stigler (1965, p. 9). The work of Torrens and Pennington on international trade is of course very important, but Viner (1955, p. 447) stresses the pivotal role of Mill's analysis for future work. Although Pennington refers to the strength of demand when examining the gains from trade, he suggests (1840, pp. 36, 39, 40–1) that the exchange rate will fluctuate between extremes, rather than tend to some determinate value.

A problem of judging later work arises where excessive claims have been made for Mill. Chipman (1965, p. 485) placed considerable emphasis on the case where demand elasticities are unitary. In a pure exchange model this implies utility functions of the form $U = x^\alpha y^\beta$, and Chipman argued that Mill chose the special case of $\alpha = \beta = 1$, which implies that half of expenditure is always devoted to each good. The problem of maximizing $U = xy$, subject to the linear inequalities given by comparative advantage is a problem in homogeneous programming. On examining the solution, Chipman argues that it was 'obtained in all essential respects by Mill' and adds, 'In its astonishing simplicity, it must stand as one of the great achievements of the human intellect; and yet it has passed practically unnoticed for over a hundred years, if only because it was so advanced for its time' (1965, p. 486).

If Mill's achievement was so far ahead of its time, there would indeed be very little for Marshall and others to add. But reality is much more prosaic in this case. Chipman's use of a technique in search of a context has allowed imagination to get the better of judgement, by creating a model out of a highly-restrictive special case. In fact Mill gave only one illustration of unit elasticity, and he certainly did not suggest that the property holds along the complete length of the demand curves. Indeed, Mill argued clearly that demands must be elastic if multiple solutions are to arise. It will be seen in Chapter 8 below that Marshall also wrongly criticized Mill over the use of unit elasticities. Appleyard and Ingram (1979) criticize Chipman's interpretation and provide further references to discussions of Mill's chapter. A linear programming interpretation is also given in Dalal (1979).

There is a useful discussion of Whewell's work in Hutchison (1953, pp. 64–6). It seems that Edgeworth's only reference to Whewell was in his discussion of the role of mathematics in economics (1925, p. 275). Viner referred to Whewell's contribution in one place as an 'uncritical mathematical exposition' of Mill (1955, p. 316, n. 16) and in another as 'primarily a criticism of Mill's doctrines' (1955, p. 450, n. 24). The argument that Whewell influenced Mill's supplementary sections has also been made by Gherity (1988) and Henderson (1989).

8   Diagrammatic treatment of exchange

The previous chapter has shown that Whewell's model, while much more important than has generally been realized, is severely limited by his awkward specification of the demand function, particularly its restriction to small changes. This chapter shows how the approach can be extended. One motivation for this analysis is to consider the precise link between the work of Mill and Marshall, and for this reason much emphasis is given to the diagrammatic treatment of the problem. It is known that Mill provided a great stimulus to Marshall's early work. Marshall himself stated that during the four years after 1870, 'I worked a good deal at the mathematical theory of monopolies, and at the diagrammatic treatment of Mill's problem of international values' (Pigou, ed., 1925, pp. 416–18).

Historians of economic thought have generally suggested that, despite the acknowledged elegance and usefulness of Marshall's international trade diagrams, his contribution amounted largely to clarifying the less transparent analyses of Mill and other writers such as Torrens and Pennington. For example, although Schumpeter was known to be less sympathetic towards Marshall than other commentators, his judgement in this context is not atypical:

> Let us note at once that in this field Marshall did not do more than to polish and develop Mill's meaning. He cast it into an elegant geometrical model . . . that clarified the theory. But he was well aware . . . that his curves 'were set to a definite tune, that called by Mill'. This applies even to the geometrical apparatus: Mill's reads almost like a somewhat clumsy instruction for choosing these curves rather than others. (1954, p. 609)

Viner, the major historian of international trade theory, also remarked that Marshall's treatment 'is in the main an exposition and elaboration in geometrical form of Mill's analysis' (1955, p. 541). This chapter, by considering the genesis of Marshall's diagrams in some detail, will enable the value of these judgements to be assayed. Section 8.1 shows how the Mill/Whewell model can be presented in diagrammatic form using a back-to-back model based on a modification of Cunynghame's version of Cournot's model. This uses the demand functions for the imported goods expressed in terms of relative prices. Section 8.2 then examines the links between the basic form of the model and the offer curve treatment of Marshall. The method of measuring consumers' surplus, derived by Marshall using offer curves, is then considered in Section 8.3. Particular attention is paid to Marshall's numerical example. First, however, it is useful to consider briefly Marshall's attitude to the use of diagrams in economics.

Marshall and the graphical method
Marshall's facility with graphs contrasts with his attitude towards their publication: the word ambivalent is perhaps too weak here. The obvious example is the *Principles*, where all diagrams are relegated to footnotes. But his international trade diagrams were given an even more extreme treatment. Indeed, in the modern atmosphere of 'publish or perish' it is astonishing to realize that Marshall developed his diagrams in the early 1870s, but did not publish them until 50 years later when they were included in an appendix to his *Money, Credit and Commerce* (1923), compiled just before his death. Parts of an early draft were printed for private circulation by Sidgwick in 1879 under the heading of *The Pure Theory of Foreign Trade*, but Marshall, being ill at the time, played no part in their selection. Just as in his treatment of monopolies, Marshall wanted to treat the 'realistic side' extensively before publishing anything.

Despite Marshall's extreme diffidence concerning publication, there seems no reason to dispute Keynes's claim that his diagrammatic exercises 'were of such a character in their grasp, comprehensiveness, and scientific accuracy, and went so far beyond the "bright ideas" of his predecessors, that we may justly claim him as the founder of modern diagrammatic economics' (1972, p. 185). Marshall's reluctance to give his diagrams more prominence has been associated with his puritanical views. For example, Viner has suggested that:

> the formulation and solution of economic problems in mathematical, and especially graphical, terms yielded him so much intellectual and aesthetic delight that it for that reason alone became somewhat suspect to him as a worthy occupation. Mathematics, and especially graphs, were Marshall's flesh-pots, and if he frequently succumbed to their lure it was not without struggle with his conscience. (1958, p. 256)

There is, however, no doubt that Marshall's diagrams have had a firm place in the literature for many years. In the hands of economists such as Edgeworth, and later Meade (1952), they have become extremely powerful techniques of analysis.

8.1   The Mill/Whewell model
The main elements of the Mill/Whewell model are the two demand curves, specified in terms of relative prices, and the equilibrium condition that trade must 'balance'. Denote the English demand for linen as L_d and the

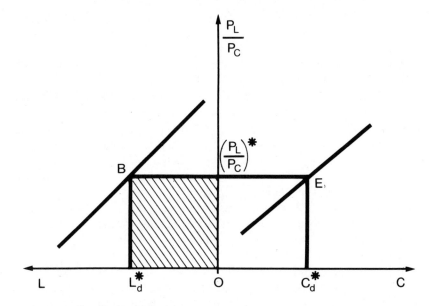

Figure 8.1 The Mill/Whewell model

German demand for cloth as C_d, with prices P_L and P_C respectively. The two demand curves can then be illustrated as in Figure 8.1, which is a simple type of back-to-back diagram. Since C_d is assumed to fall as P_C/P_L rises, the German demand curve in the right-hand side of Figure 8.1 must be upward sloping. Suppose that $(P_L/P_C)^*$ denotes the equilibrium relative price of linen after trade takes place. From the left-hand side of Figure 8.1, the corresponding demand for linen is L_d^*, which carries with it an associated or reciprocal supply of cotton of $L_d^*(P_L/P_C)^*$. This must be equal to the demand for cotton at the same relative price, C_d^*. The equilibrium condition therefore requires the area of the shaded rectangle to be equal to the length OC_d^*. This is equivalent to Whewell's condition $p'q' = Q'$. This kind of operation is extremely simple to state algebraically, but the question arises of how the equilibrium can be found using only graphical methods. A complete diagrammatic treatment of the model should be able to find the equilibrium, given two arbitrarily drawn demand curves.

Extensions of the model

A natural way to proceed would be to derive the English supply curve of cloth from the demand curve for linen. The supply curve, to be placed on the right-hand side of Figure 8.1, necessarily has the property that the abscissa is equal to the corresponding area of the rectangle beneath the demand curve; it would therefore be downward sloping and cut the German demand curve at E. Similarly, the German supply curve of linen would cut the English demand curve at B.

A geometric method of producing the English supply curve of cloth from the demand curve of linen is shown in Figure 8.2. This technique requires the use of a set of rectangular hyperbolas, two of which are shown as H_1 and H_2. The curve H_1 is tangential to the demand curve at E; hence it is known that the elasticity of demand at E is unity and the corresponding supply of cloth is a maximum. If a 45° line is drawn through the origin it is clear that the square with sides $FG = GO$ has the same area as the rectangle with sides EJ and JO. Hence OG is the square root of the required length. The bottom left-hand quadrant of Figure 8.2 has a graph of X^2 plotted against X, so that, combined with the 45° line in the bottom right-hand quadrant, the appropriate abscissa JK can be traced. The diagram also illustrates how the rectangular hyperbola H_2 can be used to plot the points M and N on the 'reciprocal supply' curve. The latter, the locus of such points, can therefore be seen to be backward bending. All that is necessary to trace the supply curve corresponding to a demand curve (and vice versa) is a set of rectangular hyperbolas drawn on transparent paper, along with a graph of X against X^2, as in the two quadrants in the left-hand side of Figure 8.2

Some special cases
Further insight into the diagrams may be obtained by considering the special case where the two demand curves are linear. Suppose that:

$$L_d = a - b(P_L/P_C) \qquad (8.1)$$

and

$$C_d = \alpha - \beta(P_C/P_L) \qquad (8.2)$$

The English supply of cloth, C_s, is thus given by:

$$C_s = L_d(P_L/P_C) = a(P_L/P_C) - b(P_L/P_C)^2 \qquad (8.3)$$

while the German supply of linen, L_s, is given by:

$$L_s = C_d(P_C/P_L) = \alpha(P_L/P_C)^{-1} - \beta(P_L/P_C)^{-2} \qquad (8.4)$$

The relevant curves are shown in Figure 8.3. The German supply of linen is also backward bending, having a maximum when the relative price

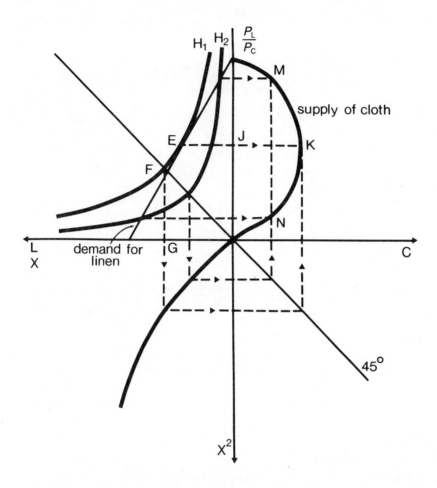

Figure 8.2   Demand and supply curves

of linen is $2\beta/\alpha$ and a point of inflexion where the relative price is $3\beta/\alpha$. The points of unit elasticity of demand for cloth and linen occur respectively when the relative price of linen is $2\beta/\alpha$ and $a/2b$. The corresponding supply elasticities at those prices are thus zero, and the supply curves are vertical. Equilibrium occurs at point E on the left-hand side, corresponding to point E′ on the right-hand side of Figure 8.3. This example shows a single equilibrium value of the relative price of linen, between the two 'extremes' a/b and β/α. However, it can easily be seen that an English demand curve for linen could intersect the German supply curve three

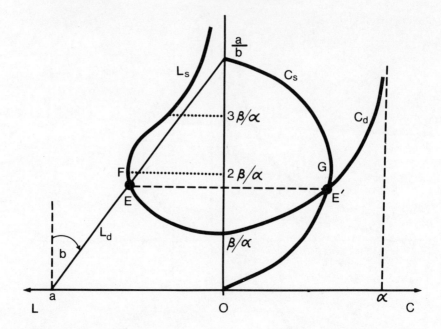

Figure 8.3   Linear demand curves

times; the same is true of the cotton supply and demand curves. Thus linear demand curves do not necessarily generate a unique equilibrium.

Equilibrium requires $C_s = C_d$, so that combining (8.2) and (8.3) gives:

$$\beta - \alpha(P_L/P_C) + a(P_L/P_C)^2 - b(P_L/P_C)^3 = 0 \qquad (8.5)$$

The equilibrium price ratio is therefore the root of the cubic in (8.5), which will in general have three roots though they need not necessarily be real or distinct, as Figure 8.3 shows. Further formal aspects of this possibility of multiple equilibria are examined in Appendix A.

The linear demand curves have the property that the elasticity of demand varies along the whole of their length from infinity to zero. Suppose instead that the demand curves have constant elasticities, so that:

$$C_d = \alpha(P_C/P_L)^{-\beta} \qquad (8.6)$$

and

$$L_d = a(P_L/P_C)^{-b} \qquad (8.7)$$

Setting the English supply of cotton arising from (8.7) equal to the

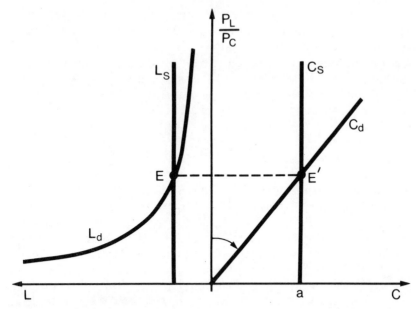

Figure 8.4 Constant elasticities

German demand for cotton, and solving for the price ratio gives the result that:

$$\frac{P_L}{P_C} = \left(\frac{\alpha}{a}\right)^{1/(1-b-\beta)} \tag{8.8}$$

The constant elasticity case therefore yields a unique price ratio. In the special case of constant unit elasticities, with $b=\beta=1$, then the relative price of linen is simply the ratio of a to α. This case is illustrated in Figure 8.4. The graphical derivation of the English supply curve of cotton follows immediately from the fact that the English demand for linen is itself precisely a rectangular hyperbola; with $L_d(P_L/P_C)= a$. From the technique described in Figure 8.2 the supply curve must be vertical.

8.2 From Mill to Marshall

The previous section has explored some geometrical properties of the basic Mill/Whewell framework. The generation of the supply curves from the demand curves can be carried out using a set of rectangular hyperbolas similar to that used by Marshall in his analysis of monopoly. This exercise reveals the possibility, for even quite simple demand curves, of multiple equilibria. It also illustrates the useful point that so long as demand curves are inelastic the corresponding supply curves cannot be backward bending and so only one equilibrium will be possible. The purely diagrammatic approach is capable of avoiding the constraints imposed by the use of specific functional forms, a feature stressed by Marshall. A large variety of comparative static exercises can therefore be carried out, showing the implicit assumptions required for some of Mill's statements to hold. However, the investigation has not yet produced curves corresponding to Marshall's offer curves.

A derivation of the offer curve

Given a demand curve specified in terms of relative prices and the corresponding supply curve, it is possible to combine them to form an offer curve. The procedure is illustrated in Figure 8.5, for England's demand for linen in terms of the offer of cloth. The top two quadrants of Figure 8.5 shows the English supply of cloth and demand for linen curves. The diagram shows how two points H and D on the offer curve may be plotted, using a 45° line in the bottom right-hand quadrant. As seen earlier, point A corresponds to the point of unit elasticity of demand, so that the elasticity of supply is zero at B. Starting from any point on the demand curve, it is only necessary to move around the quadrants in the direction of the arrows. This technique makes it obvious that the point D represents both a turning point of the offer curve and a point where the elasticity of demand for linen is unity. Between O and D the elasticity is numerically less than unity, while between D and L the demand is elastic.

For a linear demand curve, the offer curve of England is easily obtained algebraically as follows. From (8.1), solve for the price ratio to get:

$$P_L/P_C = (L_d - a)/b \tag{8.9}$$

Then substitute for P_L/P_C in (8.3) to give the equation of the offer curve as:

$$C_s = (aL_d - L_d^2)/b \tag{8.10}$$

The offer curve is thus quadratic in L_d. Consider the English offer curve in Figure 8.6. The ordinate represents L_d while the abscissa measures C_s. This has the useful property that the slope of a ray from the origin to any point on the offer curve represents the relative price $C_s = L_d(P_L/P_C)$; hence the slope of the ray equals

$$L_d/C_s = P_C/P_L.$$

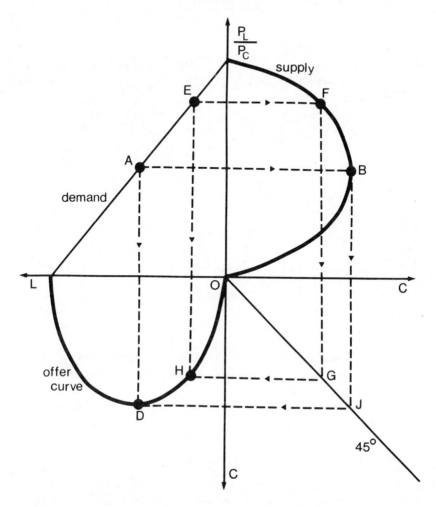

Figure 8.5   The offer curve

On the assumption that the demand curve of Germany is also linear, both offer curves are quadratic. This provides a further illustration of the possibility of more than one equilibrium. Examples are shown in Figure 8.6, where part (a) shows that A,B and C can all be equilibrium points. In part (b) the curves intersect only once at E (other than at the origin, of course). This part of Figure 8.6 also shows that, at E, England has an elastic demand for linen while Germany has an inelastic demand for cloth.

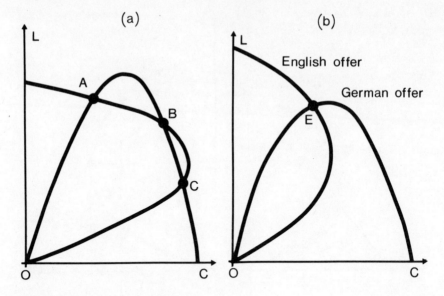

Figure 8.6   Multiple equilibria

The result, which can be seen by returning to Figure 8.5, is that the relative price of linen is much lower than before trade. Thus the majority of the gains from trade go to England.

For the constant elasticity case it can be found that the corresponding offer curve is:

$$C_s = a\left(\frac{a}{L_d}\right)^{(b-1)/b}$$

(8.11)

So that when $b = 1$, $C_s = a$. For the case where $b < 1$, the offer curve is convex to the origin.

It has been shown how offer curves may be derived graphically from basic demand curves, expressed in terms of relative prices, that are implicit in Mill's model; the starting point is the recognition of the reciprocal natural demand and supply. In view of the insights provided by the use of offer curves, particularly concerning the role of demand elasticities and the possibility of multiple solutions, combined with their great potential for comparative static exercises, it seems rather hard on Marshall to describe the development of such valuable analytical tools as merely 'polishing' Mill's meaning. Certainly his starting point was Mill's problem, but Marshall's solution is really a significant advance over that offered by Mill.

To provide a diagrammatic route leading from Mill to Marshall does not, of course, demonstrate that it was necessarily the path taken by Marshall himself, even though the above method uses Marshall's favoured rectangular hyperbolas. It is quite possible that Marshall actually began with the concept of the offer curve, and explored its properties. Although the above approach helps to clarify the structure of the basic model, Marshall's writings do not reveal his own method of discovery. It is certainly of interest to compare Marshall's first 'Essay on International Trade' (1975, I, pp. 260–80) with the 'Pure Theory of Foreign Trade' (1975, II, pp. 117–81), and finally with the published material in *Money, Credit and Commerce* (1923, pp. 330–60). He began in each case with basic offer curves for each country that are inelastic over the whole length shown, and then discussed alternative shapes in terms of elasticities. The earliest essay finds Marshall using the rather clumsy expression 'guidance by the rate' for 'elasticity'. But by 1923 the analysis is clearly stated in terms of elasticities, and includes a footnote giving the now standard geometrical method of finding the elasticity (1923, p.337, n.1).

Multiple equilibria
Marshall's recognition of the circumstances under which multiple equilibria would occur led him to devote much energy to dynamic adjustment problems and the question of which of several equilibria would be stable. Instead of presenting the mathematics of differential equations, Marshall applied, for the first time in economics, the now standard phase-diagram method. After what must have been a great deal of thought on the question, Marshall was sceptical about the use of mathematics to examine dynamic problems. Even if the equations of the offer curves were known precisely, he argued that:

> the methods of mathematical analysis will not be able to afford any considerable assistance in the task of determining the motion of the exchange-index. For a large amount of additional work will have to be done before we can obtain approximate laws for representing the magnitude of the horizontal and vertical forces which will act upon the exchange-index in any position (1975, II, p.163).

It is obviously not possible to examine the details of Marshall's dynamic and comparative static exercises here, and they have been well-rehearsed elsewhere. For example, the standard application of stability analysis shows that, in Figure 8.6(a), the point B represents an unstable equilibrium while A and C are stable. This follows from the simple argument that an excess supply leads to a price fall, while excess demand leads to a price rise.

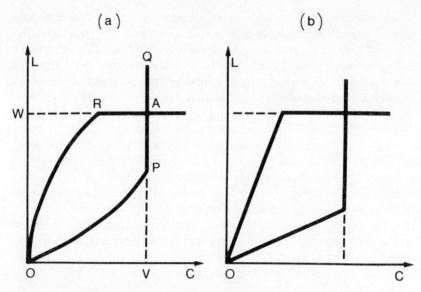

Figure 8.7   Marshall and constant elasticities

This subsection briefly examines Marshall's criticism of Mill's discussion of the possibility of multiple solutions. Marshall argued (1975, II, pp. 148–9; 1923, pp. 354–5, n.3) that when discussing the possibility of multiple equilibria in his supplementary section, Mill (1920, pp. 596–7, para.6) made the special assumption of unit elasticities of demand for cloth and linen. Marshall argued that this would lead the offer curves to 'degenerate' into straight lines. It is therefore clear that on this assumption the offer curves cannot intersect more than once, so that 'there is no problem to be solved' (1923, p. 355). When commenting on Marshall's conclusion, Chipman later argued that 'this conclusion followed from an error in his diagram, which failed to take account of the fact that each country's offer curve would, under Mill's assumptions, start off with a flat segment, and then proceed with a vertical one. This had already been spelled out by Edgeworth in a six page footnote (1894, pp. 609–14) which, it must be concluded, Marshall had never bothered to read!' (1965, p. 491, n.13).

This comment is rather curious. Marshall made it perfectly clear that he was considering the type of situation shown in Figure 8.7. The offer curves do not begin with flat sections, which would be the case in a pure exchange framework, but reflect domestic opportunity costs until after points P and R in Figure 8.7(a), when the offer curves become straight lines. He stated, 'Let VP be the amount of linen which England could make for herself with the expense to which she is put in order to make and export OV cloth, then

PQ is a portion of England's demand [offer] curve' (1975, II, p. 148). The line OP therefore represents part of a 'trade indifference curve' (using Edgeworth's terminology) which reflects a situation of varying costs. The introduction of the 'trade indifference curve' or curve of 'constant advantage' is usually associated with Edgeworth (1925, p. 33), and was later derived from production conditions by Meade (1952).

In addition, Edgeworth, in the long footnote mentioned by Chipman, made it perfectly clear that in the extreme case of unit elasticities the offer curves would not start with a flat section, but would begin (when there are constant costs) with a straight line representing the domestic opportunity cost of producing the import. This case is shown in Figure 8.7(b). Thus the 'constant advantage' curve is linear and no country need accept a zero price for its export good. At the end of the footnote, Edgeworth added, 'I ought to repeat that I have had the advantage of reading Professor Marshall's unpublished papers' (1894, p. 614, n). Edgeworth himself made no claims to originality in his discussion of trade theory. It seems that Chipman was taking too seriously his assumption that the utility function is linear in the logarithms, which would give a price-consumption curve in a pure exchange model of the kind he described. But this is far removed from either Mill or Marshall.

A problem with both Marshall's and Chipman's argument is that a close reading of Mill shows that he did *not* in fact assume unit elasticities. His earlier numerical example involved an equilibrium relative price of 10 units of cloth for 17 units of linen, with Germany exchanging 17 000 yards of linen for 10 000 yards of cloth. Mill suggested that if the price of linen falls such that 10 units of cloth exchange for 18 units of linen, a new equilibrium would exist if England increases its demand for linen to 17 500 yards while Germany simultaneously reduces its demand for cloth to 9722 yards (since the English demand for 17 500 at the new price involves a reciprocal supply or offer of 9722 yards of cloth). A little calculation shows that Mill was assuming that the elasticity of the English demand for linen is 0.52 while that of Germany for cloth is 0.47.

It is also worth noting Marshall's subsequent comment on the gains from trade, with reference to Figure 8.7(a). He suggested, 'If A coincides with P England has to pay for her imported linen the full equivalent of what it would cost her to make it herself; and therefore she derives no benefit from the trade' (1975, II, p.149). This again supports the argument that OP is part of England's 'trade indifference curve' through the origin. Although Marshall is seen to do less than full justice to Mill's discussion of multiple equilibria, his own discussion is therefore valuable in its own right.

It is worth adding here that Marshall came to regard his offer curve apparatus as capable of 'being translated into terms of any sort of bargains between two bodies, neither of whom is subject to any external competition in regard to those particular bargains' (1923, p. 351). A particular context was bargaining between firms and trade unions, but it was left to Edgeworth to extend the analysis to those other areas. This issue is discussed in Chapter 10 below.

Triangular barter

Although it is not known how Marshall arrived at the concept of the offer curve, he can be seen at an early stage struggling with the problem of 'triangular barter'. Some 'pages from a mathematical notebook' are reproduced in Marshall (1975, II, pp. 272–4), where he used demand curves specified in terms of relative prices. Such curves are similar to those considered in Section 8.1 above. Hence at this early stage he did not use offer curves. Marshall examined the situation in which Germany exchanges linen for cloth, England exchanges cloth for fur, while Russia exchanges fur for linen. Marshall's problem is very similar to the three-country case considered by Mill, and the approach can be seen to follow Mill quite closely. Mill suggested that, 'Everything will take place precisely as if the third country had bought German produce with her own goods, and offered that produce to England in exchange for hers' (1920, p. 592).

Marshall proceeded by drawing a German demand curve for cloth in terms of the relative price of cloth (the amount of linen that must be given per unit of cloth), followed by an English supply curve of cloth in terms of the price of cloth relative to fur (the amount of fur that will be obtained per unit of cloth). These two curves were then combined to produce a demand curve for fur in terms of the price of fur relative to linen (the amount of linen that must be given per unit of fur). However, Marshall simply drew a demand curve and gave a numerical example of the properties of one point on the curve. He did not provide a mathematical argument or use a diagrammatic method of construction.

The essence of the problem can however be seen as follows. Suppose the German demand for cloth from England is C_d. The corresponding supply of linen is, following the argument of Section 8.1, $C_d(P_C/P_L)$. With that amount of linen, England can demand an amount of fur given by $C_d(P_C/P_L)(P_L/P_F)$. Here P_F is the price of fur, so that the last term is simply the amount of fur per unit of linen, or the relative price of linen in terms of fur. Then cancelling P_L, the English demand for fur, F_d, is $C_d(P_C/P_F)$. Since the demand for cloth C_d, decreases as P_C/P_L increases and, from the result in the previous sentence, F_d decreases as P_C/P_F decreases, F_d must decrease as the following ratio decreases:

$$P_L/P_F = (P_C/P_F)/(P_C/P_L) \qquad (8.12)$$

Therefore, if the quantity of fur is measured on the vertical axis and the price of fur relative to linen (P_F/P_L) is measured on the horizontal axis, the demand curve is downward sloping to the right.

The final component of the model is the supply curve for fur in terms of the relative price of fur to that of linen, which Marshall drew as upward sloping. The equilibrium position is therefore the intersection of these last two curves. Without providing any discussion Marshall (1975, II, p. 275) simply stated that the conditions for the equilibrium to be stable are:

I.   If England can get more furs she will sell in exchange more cloth.
II.   If Germany can get more cloth she will sell in exchange more linen.
III. If Russia can get more linen she will sell in exchange more furs.

The above discussion might seem to suggest that the second condition should be expressed in terms of the German *demand* for cloth (increasing as the price of cloth relative to linen falls), but the problem is more complex. Section 8.1 has shown that such a downward sloping demand curve can be associated with a backward bending reciprocal supply curve, which is then capable of generating multiple solutions. Indeed, the problem is more clearly examined using Marshall's offer curves, although as already noted he did not use them himself in this context. Consider Figure 8.8, which has the English, German and Russian offer curves in quadrants 1, 2 and 3 respectively, while quadrant 4 simply has a 45° line. The diagram shows how, starting from arbitrarily chosen points A and B on England's offer curve, the points J and G on the 'hybrid' offer curve OD can be plotted. The intersection of this offer curve with Russia's offer curve at E gives the relative price of linen and fur, from which the other relative prices can be obtained by moving to quadrants 1 and 2.

The offer curves in Figure 8.8 have been drawn to reflect Marshall's three conditions given above. It is clear by the method of construction that there can be only one equilibrium. But if the offer curves were instead drawn to reflect elastic demands beyond a certain point, that is if they were backward bending, it can be seen by following the procedure of Figure 8.8 that the hybrid offer curve in quadrant 3 could have a rather unusual shape; viewed from above it would have two humps. Such offer curves that turn back several times are not uncommon in Marshall's *Pure Theory of Foreign Trade* (1879).

It is most unfortunate that so little of Marshall's basic working is not available. What is clear from this example of triangular barter is that Marshall at some stage tried to make use of the types of curve that arise

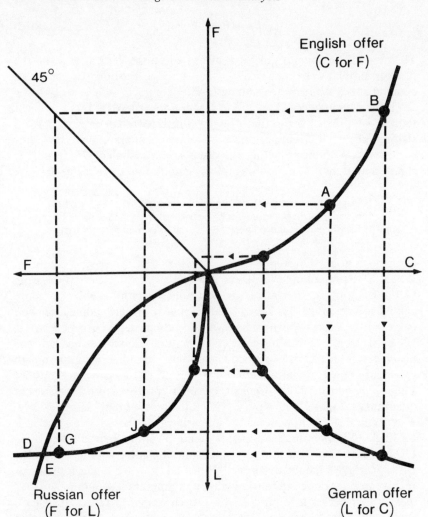

Figure 8.8   Triangular barter

directly from Mill's framework, but found them very awkward when compared with his own offer curves.

Viner's terms of trade diagrams
Mention may briefly be made of the diagrams used by Viner (1955, pp. 362, 468, 539, 544–5), which he refers to as 'terms of trade diagrams'. Viner wrote that they are simply 'a modification of the Marshallian foreign-trade diagrams so as to make the vertical axis represent the linen-

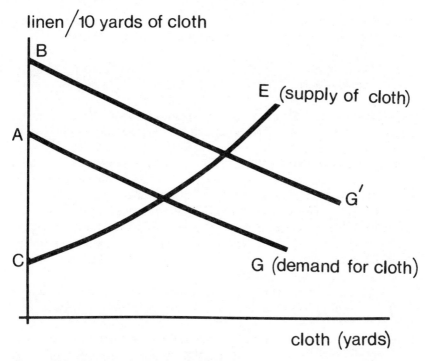

Figure 8.9   Viner's terms of trade diagram

cloth terms of trade instead of the total quantity of linen' (1955, p. 539). An example is shown in Figure 8.9, where Viner stated that A and C respectively represent the German and English domestic cost of producing linen (in terms of cloth). The curve AG represents the German demand for cloth while CE is the 'English demand for linen in terms of cloth' (1955, p. 540), or, more clearly, the English supply of cloth. Viner used the diagram to confirm Mill's suggestion that a reduction in the cost of producing linen in Germany, leading to a shift in the German demand for cloth to BG', implies a movement in the terms of trade away from Germany. The extent of the change depends on the shape of the English supply curve, CE.

Viner has the relative price of cloth on the vertical axis, so that Figure 8.9 compares directly with the mirror image of the left-hand side of Figure 8.3 which deals with the market for linen. However, Viner's criticism of Marshall, that 'the unnecessary complexity of Marshall's diagram seems to have concealed from him the fact that it provided no answers to the questions which he was putting' (1955, p. 545) is misplaced. His criticism concerns Marshall's analysis of the effect of an increase in England's demand for linen and, not surprisingly, the issue turns on the meaning attached to 'increase in demand' rather than the logic of the two different writers.

8.3   Consumers' surplus

The use of offer curves

Although he rejected Cournot's partial equilibrium approach to the analysis of trade, Marshall nevertheless wished to apply the 'surplus' analysis to his own diagrams. But this presented a difficult task and Marshall later told Cunynghame that he 'found all methods of representing the "total benefit" of foreign trade by their special curves very cumbersome' (Pigou, ed., 1925, p. 449). Reference to Figure 8.5 above shows that it is possible to move from any point on the offer curve in the bottom left-hand quadrant to the associated point on the demand curve, shown in the top left-hand quadrant. The area between the demand curve and the horizontal price line would give the appropriate value of the 'surplus', measured in terms of cloth (the export good).

However, Marshall wished to start directly from the offer curve. His method involved 'considerable geometrical ingenuity' (Bhagwati and Johnson, 1960, p. 84) and is shown in Figure 8.10, which is based on Marshall (1923, p. 339). The vertical line DR is placed arbitrarily at point D on the horizontal axis. Consider point A on the English offer curve and draw a ray from O through A, extending to K on DR. The ratio of KD to OD represents the price of linen at A; that is, it is the amount of cloth per unit of linen (when all units are purchased at the same price.) The vertical line through A intersects the horizontal through K at A′. Now consider point P on the offer curve, and draw the ray OPT. The intersection of the vertical line through P with the horizontal line through T is shown as point P′. The locus of points such as P′ traces out a quasi-demand curve for linen, since vertical distances are proportional to prices in terms of the number of units of cloth that must be given per unit of linen. The absolute vertical distances depend of course on the arbitrary position of the line DR. The ray OR is tangential to the offer curve at the origin, so that P′ moves from A′ to U.

The price DK/OD is paid for OB units of linen whereas, for example, consumers would have been willing to pay the higher price of TD/OD for the smaller quantity OM. Since TD/OD = DK/OD + TK/OD, the surplus on the OMth unit of linen is represented by an ODth part of TK units of cloth. The aggregate surplus, when consuming at A, is thus an ODth part of the area UHA′; that is, the area divided by OD, and is measured in terms of cloth. Unlike the standard context where the surplus is measured in money terms, the appropriate area between the 'demand curve' and a

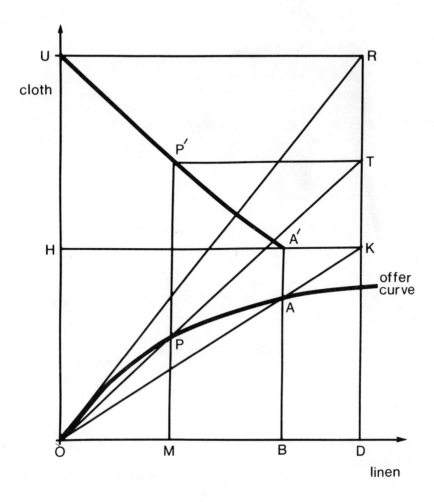

Figure 8.10   Consumers' surplus and offer curves

price line has to be adjusted because of the arbitrary choice of the point D that affects the relative price scale. Of course, it is hardly necessary to add that Marshall's measure here is open to all the usual objections against the concept of consumers' surplus.

Marshall's numerical example
Soon after the publication of Marshall's approach, Allyn Young suggested that 'the great economist appears to have made a perplexing slip'

(1924b, p. 144). However, it is argued here that the method used by Young was incorrect. Marshall considered country E (England) trading with country G (Germany) but instead of using the example of trade in cloth and linen, he simply referred to 'E bales' and 'G bales' as the goods produced and exported by E and G respectively. His hypothetical schedules are reproduced as Table 8.1. It is clear from line nine of the table that the equilibrium price ratio, in terms of a number of G bales per hundred E bales, is equal to 78. Country E's demand for G bales corresponds to G's supply of 70 200 at that price. Marshall stated, without explanation, that:

> Adding up, we find that G gets for 70 200 of her bales a number of E bales for which it would be worth her while to pay 125 300 of her bales rather than forego them. The net benefit of the trade to her therefore is 55 100 unit products of her labour and capital. (1923, p. 163)

The net gain to G, measured in G bales, is thus 55 100. He then stated that the net gain to country E is '80 000 unit products of her labour and capital'.

Young ignored the more detailed treatment described in the previous subsection. In measuring the total gain to country G, Young simply added the nine figures in column four of Table 8.1, giving 230 + 175 + 143 + ... + 78 = 111 950. The net gain was therefore given as 111 950 − 70 200 = 41 750. He then used columns one and three to find the net gain to country E. Young argued that the first 1000 G bales are worth 10 000 E bales, while the next 3000 G bales are worth (20 000/4000) (3000) = 15 000 E bales. The total benefit to country E was therefore calculated by Young as 10 000 + (20 000/4000) (3000) + (30 000/9000) (5000) + (40 000/14 000) (5000) + ... + (90 000/70 200) (15 800). This gives 150 931 rather than the value of 170 000 given by Marshall. Young's figure for E's gain is thus 61 000 E bales, rather than 80 000 given by Marshall.

These differences are of course far from trivial, but evidently did not suggest to Young that he had made an error. Young guessed that 'Marshall, revising his manuscript again and again, altered his tables without changing his text' (1924b, p. 146). But this explanation suggests a degree of carelessness not usually associated with Marshall.

A basic point is that consumers' surplus is associated with an *area*. However, Young quickly dismissed the idea that Marshall had in mind an area beneath a smooth curve on the argument that Marshall used the words 'adding up' rather than 'integrating' and, 'Furthermore, the figures in columns (2) and (4) do not accord with any simple algebraic function of the volume of trade, as very likely would have been the case if the smooth

Table 8.1   Marshall's schedules

	Schedule of terms on which E is willing to trade		Schedule of terms on which G is willing to trade	
(1) Number of E bales	(2) Number of G bales per hundred E bales at which E will part with those in (1)	(3) Total number of G bales for which E is willing to part with those in (1)	(4) Number of G bales per hundred E bales at which G will buy those in (1)	(5) Total number of G bales which G is willing to give for those in (1)
10000	10	1000	230	23000
20000	20	4000	175	35000
30000	30	9000	143	42900
40000	35	14000	122	48800
50000	40	20000	108	54000
60000	46	27600	95	57000
70000	55	38500	86	60200
80000	68	54400	82½	66000
90000	78	70200	78	70200
100000	83	83000	76	76000
110000	86	94600	74½	81950
120000	88½	106200	73¾	88500

Source: Marshall (1923, p.162).

curve had been constructed first and the figures taken off subsequently' (1924b, p.146). Young's first point can quickly be dismissed since Marshall would never have used such an example of mathematical vocabulary as 'integrated'. The second point will be examined below, but it may be asked at this stage why Marshall would have used such awkward numbers if he only had Young's simple computations in mind.

If Marshall's own method, described above, is used, it is found that points such as P′ trace out a smooth curve with coordinates shown in Table 8.2. These values suggest a quadratic relation. Hence, denoting the number of G bales (in 100s) as y and the number of E bales (in 100s) as x, the following ordinary least squares regression result is obtained (with standard errors in parentheses):

Table 8.2   Consumers' surplus in country G

G bales	182000	96000	66000	44000	32000	17500	9000	3500	0
E bales	10000	20000	30000	40000	50000	60000	70000	80000	90000

$$y = 215.083 - 0.570x + 0.00038x^2 \quad R^2 = 0.995$$
$$(18.218) \quad (0.084) \quad (0.000082) \quad F_{2,6} = 64.21$$

The area beneath the curve between $0 < x < 900$ can then be calculated using analytical results for the area under a quadratic. This must then be divided by the horizontal distance OD, to give a value of consumers' surplus of 54 657 G bales, which compares with Marshall's result of 55 100. With this type of calculation, it cannot be expected that Marshall's result could be reproduced precisely. However, this result is remarkably close to Marshall's value given the sensitivity to small changes in the parameters. It might be suggested that Marshall would have used more convenient figures than the point estimates given above. A process of trial and error shows that values of $214.25, -0.55$ and 0.00035, for the coefficients in the quadratic relationship between y and x, give a surplus measure of 55 125. This only needs rounding to three significant figures to produce Marshall's value. It is therefore clear that these results contradict Young's statements that the data do not fit a simple algebraic function and that an arbitrarily high value of the price of E bales would have to be assumed for small volumes of trade.

Further analysis
Figure 8.10 shows the relationship between a quasi-demand curve or what may be called a 'surplus' curve and the offer curve. It is useful to consider the precise relationship between these two curves in further detail. Suppose that the equation of the offer curve is in general $y = f(x)$, where y and x are measured from the origin, O, along ordinate and abscissa respectively. The slope of the straight line OPT is given by:

$$\frac{f(x)}{x} = \frac{TD}{OD} \tag{8.13}$$

hence

$$TD = (OD) f(x)/x \tag{8.14}$$

Denote by y' the vertical distance measured from point H; this is in fact

Table 8.3   Offer curves

Coefficient	G's offer curve	E's offer curve
Constant	112.579	93.768
	(16.526)	(11.397)
x	1.409	2.535
	(0.106)	(0.112)
x^2	−0.00147	−0.0031
	(0.000185)	(0.00026)
x^3	0.000001	.000002
	(0.00000013)	(.00000024)
R^2	0.998	0.999
$F_{3,8}$	1344.54	2093.04

the ordinate of the 'surplus' curve. Since $y' = \text{TD} - \text{KD}$, the equation of the 'surplus' curve is:

$$y' = (\text{OD})\,f(x)/x - (\text{KD}) \qquad (8.15)$$

Thus if the offer curve is a polynomial of degree N, the 'surplus' curve is a polynomial of degree $N-1$. This result suggests that Marshall's offer curve should be approximated by a cubic. Columns one and three of Table 8.1 trace the offer curve of country E, while columns one and five trace the offer curve of country G. Results are presented in Table 8.3 for ordinary least squares estimates of cubic equations, where for convenience the figures in each of columns one, three and five have been divided by 100. The cubic clearly provides a good fit to Marshall's data.

The above result also indicates that Marshall could have constructed a much easier example if he had been prepared to use a quadratic form for the offer curves. The substitution of a quadratic for $f(x)$, where $y = ax - bx^2$, gives a linear 'surplus' curve of the form:

$$y' = \{(\text{OD})a - \text{KD}\} - b(\text{OD})x \qquad (8.16)$$

The term in curly brackets in (8.16) gives the intercept on the vertical axis, that is, the point U. Consumers' surplus, using the well-known result for the area of triangle, is given by:

$$\begin{aligned} \text{surplus} &= 0.5(\text{OD})\,\{(\text{OD})\,a - \text{KD}\}/\text{OD} \\ &= \{a(\text{OD}) - \text{KD}\}/2 \qquad (8.17) \end{aligned}$$

Marshall nevertheless eschewed this simple alternative.

Supply and demand curves
In order to complete the set of inter-relationships involved in Marshall's example, it is necessary to consider the form of the demand curves implied by Table 8.1. Although Young (1924b, p. 144) notes that, 'there are, it will be seen, two demand schedules, of the type which Marshall's *Principles* has made familiar', they actually specify demands in terms of relative prices. The relationship between such demand curves and offer curves has already been examined explicitly above, but it is useful here to approach the problem slightly differently. Consider two goods X and Y, with relative price p_x/p_y and suppose the demand for good X, x_d, is such that:

$$p_x/p_y = a - bx_d + cx_d^2 \tag{8.18}$$

Notice that this demand function has been specified with the price ratio as the dependent variable. The corresponding supply of good Y, s_y, is equal to $(p_x/p_y)x_d$. Using (8.18) for p_x/p_y gives:

$$y_s = ax_d - bx_d^2 + cx_d^3 \tag{8.19}$$

Equation (8.19) is the offer curve specifying the amount of good Y offered in return for given amounts of good X. In view of the finding that the offer curves closely approximate a cubic, the above argument suggests that the demand curves would be expected to take the form shown in equation (8.18). If the demand curve had instead been specified in terms of x_d as a quadratic function of the price ratio, then the offer curve would be much more complex. It would involve the solution for the root of a quadratic.

Returning to Table 8.1, country E's demand curve is given by the relationship between columns two and three. The supposition that the demand for G bales takes a quadratic form similar to equation (8.18) can be tested by regressing the reciprocals of the figures in column two of Table 8.1 with the figures in column three, and their squares. But if these points are first plotted, it seems that the demand curve is divided into two sections each using slightly different quadratics, rather than using the same form for all points. This is supported by the results shown in Table 8.4. A quadratic demand curve fits the first and last six sets of 'observations' well, though the fit to the complete set of data is sufficiently good to be consistent with the cubic offer curve. Marshall's method is therefore rather more complex than may be evident from a cursory examination of the data, but he does appear, contrary to Young's suggestion, to have

Table 8.4 Demand for G-bales – Dependent variable: relative price of G-bales

Coefficient	Observation set		
	1–12	1–6	7–12
Constant	.0642	0.0936	0.0291
	(.00974)	(0.01366)	(0.00121)
Demand	-0.000171	-0.000764	-0.000036
	(0.000052)	(0.000241)	(0.000004)
(demand)^2	0.00000012	0.00000189	0.00000002
	(0.000000049)	(0.00000082)	(0.000000002)
R^2	0.675	0.859	.993
F	9.33	9.11	225.22

based his numerical example on formulae. It is clear that Marshall devoted much thought to his numerical example, and was not prepared simply to use a convenient set of numbers to illustrate 'the possible relations of demand and value' (1923, p. 161).

It may, in conclusion, be argued that it seems to be an injustice to Marshall's work to suggest, with Schumpeter and others, that he 'did not do more than to polish and develop Mill's meaning'. As Edgeworth observed, 'there is more than meets the eye in Professor Marshall's foreign trade curves' (1904, p. 70), and of course this comment could just as appropriately be applied to the vast majority of Marshall's published work. It must be added that Marshall became 'rather tired' of his curves. As he explained to Cunynghame:

> I had followed Mill in taking a yard of cloth as *representative* of England's exports and Germany's imports: which I still think is right. But then I had glided, as he had done, unconsciously into regarding the demand for imports in general as having a similar character to that for a single commodity. And I now think that this is illegitimate, and vitiates a great part of my curves (Pigou, ed., 1925, pp. 449–50).

However, Marshall retained the view that they would be useful to examine bargaining, and this will be examined in a later chapter.

Notes and further reading
On Marshall's early work see also his letter to J.B. Clark in Pigou (ed. 1925, pp. 412–13). The two book-length treatments of Marshall's economics, by Davenport (1935) and Reisman (1987) ignore his contributions to trade theory.

When Schumpeter referred to Marshall's curves as being 'set to a definite tune', he was quoting from a letter from Marshall to Cunynghame. The precise nature of Marshall's offer curves was in fact misunderstood by Cunynghame, who wrongly criticized Marshall's analysis on the grounds that it should deal explicitly with more demand and supply curves (1903, p. 317). When Cunynghame produced the diagrammatic version of Cournot's model discussed in Chapter 6, Marshall commented tersely that, 'As to international trade curves – mine were set to a definite tune, that called by Mill' (Pigou, ed., 1925, p. 451). This was used by Schumpeter and Viner (1955, p. 541) when suggesting that Marshall merely translated Mill into diagrams. But when the quotation is seen in its proper context, rather than being read in isolation, it can be seen that this interpretation is false. Marshall was actually saying that he had good reasons for following the general equilibrium path of Mill rather than the single good model of Cournot when considering international values, not that his diagrams do no more than restate Mill in another language. Marshall also complained to Edgeworth (in 1961, II, pp. 808–11) about Cunynghame's interpretation of his successive cost curves. Cunynghame's book of 1904 was reviewed at length by Edgeworth (1904). The term offer curve was not Marshall's; its first appearance seems to have been in Johnson (1913), and it became more widely used through Bowley (1924).

In discussing Marshall's attitude towards diagrams, Keynes also wrote, 'When his intellect chased diagrams and foreign trade and money there was an evangelical moraliser of an imp somewhat inside him that was so ill-advised as to disapprove' (1972, p. 200). A quotation from Marshall is given in the same page (but with no source), which supports this view. Marshall's attitude is nicely summarized in his advice to Bowley: 'I went more and more on the rules – (1) use mathematics as a shorthand language, rather than as an engine of inquiry. (2) keep to them till you have done. (3) translate into English. (4) then illustrate by examples that are important in real life. (5) burn the mathematics. (6) if you can't succeed in 4, burn 3. This last I often did' (Pigou, ed., 1925, p. 427). See also Marshall (1975, II, p. 4), where in correspondence with Seligman, Marshall refers to some of the work as belonging 'to the economic toy shop rather than practical work shop'. The diagrams became better known through their use by Pantaleoni (1889) and Edgeworth (1894), although Marshall is known to have used diagrams extensively in his teaching; see Keynes (1972, p. 188, n.2).

Viner (1955, pp. 583–6) has some interesting comments on partial and general equilibrium analyses of international trade. Although Viner uses 'terms of trade' diagrams and notes the relationship between supply and demand elasticities (1955, pp. 539–40, n.11), he does not explore the shapes of the curves.

Marshall accepted Jevons's criticism of Mill's measure of the gain – the change in the terms of trade – as confusing marginal with total utility; see Marshall (1975, I, p. 280). Marshall's earlier attempt is reproduced in (1975, I, pp. 280–1) where the diagram is drawn on its side; that is, it has cloth and linen respectively on the horizontal and vertical axes. For further analysis of the gains from trade and Marshall's treatment in particular, see Viner (1955, pp. 570–5), Bhagwati and Johnson (1960, section III), and the references therein. It may also be mentioned that Marshall himself suggested that in the context of barter it is not really appropriate to assume constancy of the marginal utility of one of the goods (which is of course Marshall's assumption in the context where one of the goods is money): see Marshall (1961, I, p. 793; 1961, II, p. 790).

When examining Marshall's example of consumers' surplus in international trade, Young mentioned that the 'discrepancy in Marshall's figures' was pointed out by Taussig, and in a later note (1924a) he called attention to the review of Marshall's book by Achille Loria (1923) who made the same 'correction'. Viner (1955, p. 575, n.2) later referred to Young's note very briefly, without contradicting him. But Viner was mainly concerned to criticize the surplus concept.

Marshall's problem of triangular barter may be examined algebraically for constant elasticities, but rapidly becomes intractable for linear schedules. If the German demand and English supply of cloth are C_d and C_s respectively, with:

$$C_d = \alpha(P_C/P_L)^{-\beta} \text{ and } C_s = a\left(\frac{P_C}{P_F}\right)^b$$

(8.20)

then for $C_d = C_s$ it can be found that:

$$\frac{P_C}{P_F} = \left(\frac{\alpha}{a}\right)^{1/(\beta + b)} \left(\frac{P_F}{P_L}\right)^{-\beta/(\beta + b)}$$

(8.21)

The demand for fur is $C_d(P_C P_F) = C_s(P_C/P_F)$. Substitute for C_s from (8.20) and for (P_C/P_F) from (8.21) to get the demand for fur, F_d, as:

$$F_d = a \left(\frac{\alpha}{a}\right)^{(b + 1)/(\beta + b)} \left(\frac{P_F}{P_L}\right)^{-\beta(b + 1)/(\beta + b)}$$

(8.22)

Finally, if the supply of fur, F_s, is expressed as

$$F_s = \gamma(P_F/P_L)^\delta$$

(8.23)

The equilibrium price of fur relative to linen is given by:

$$\frac{P_F}{P_L} = \left[\frac{a}{\gamma} \left(\frac{\alpha}{a}\right)^{(b + 1)/(\beta + b)}\right]^{(\beta + b)/[\delta(\beta + b) + \beta(b + 1)]}$$

(8.24)

In the special case where the elasticities are unity, the right-hand side of (8.24) reduces simply to the square root of α/γ.

In introducing triangular barter in Marshall (1975, II, p. 272) Whitaker says the notes are included to 'illustrate to perfection the groping, intuitive way in which Marshall often tackled his problems – not at all what one would expect from an erstwhile Second Wrangler'. However, it seems much more likely that, at least here, Marshall is trying to produce a more pedagogic discussion rather than working things out for himself. From Marshall's statement of the conditions for stability it is clear that his understanding extends beyond what is in the basic notes.

9 Exchange with price-taking

It has been seen that progress in the analysis of exchange depended on finding a way of exploiting the simple connection between exchange and reciprocal demand, that the demand for one good carries with it an associated supply of another good. This is of course equally true where one good is money, but significant developments were made when exchange was treated in terms of two goods in a context in which money simply acts as a unit of account and not held for its own sake. In this situation the ratio of prices provides a measure of the rate at which the two goods are exchanged; the price ratio can easily be translated into a statement of the amount of one good which must be given up in order to obtain a unit of the other good.

Chapter 6 showed that Cournot's analysis, as pathbreaking as it was, failed to exploit this basic idea. It is only with hindsight that such fundamental steps seem platitudinous. The partial equilibrium demand curve cannot cope with the general equilibrium problems. However, almost a decade before the publication of Cournot's book, J.S. Mill had made remarkable progress by combining the idea of reciprocal demand with that of demand as a schedule, although his work did not appear in print until much later. Chapter 7 showed how Whewell, exploiting his earlier formulation of the demand schedule in terms of the price elasticity, was able to produce further valuable insights by producing a mathematical analysis of Mill's problem. This involved the specification of demand functions in terms of relative price. Chapter 8 then adapted Whewell's approach by using a less restrictive specification of demand schedules, and found that this provided some useful insights into Marshall's analysis. Marshall, as already noted, explicitly rejected Cournot's approach in favour of that of Mill.

A crucial feature of these contributions that must be stressed is their concentration on the equilibrium properties of models with price-taking behaviour. The absence of price-taking raises difficult problems, some of which are examined in the next chapter. However, a strong result that was clearly perceived is the possibility of multiple equilibria and their associated comparative static implications. In particular, small changes in conditions can lead to large 'jumps' in the relative price from one stable equilibrium to another. Furthermore, it was explicitly recognized that all that is required for the existence of multiple equilibria is a range of prices over which demands are elastic. Although this result was known to Mill (in his supplementary sections), it was most clearly seen in the 'backward bending' offer curves of Marshall.

The present chapter explores further aspects of the development of a basic equilibrium analysis of price-taking. First, Section 9.1 examines Walras's exchange model, which is fundamentally the same as that considered in the previous chapter. It is remarkable that historians of economic analysis, while stressing Walras's pioneering contribution to general equilibrium theory, have so neglected this basic model of exchange. Section 9.2 turns to Jevons's treatment of exchange with price-taking, which so strongly influenced Edgeworth. The magnificent extension and synthesis provided by Edgeworth in his *Mathematical Psychics* (1881) is then discussed in Section 9.3. Section 9.4 examines several 'complex cases' in the theory of exchange which were treated by Jevons, but whose treatment has been neglected by historians of economic analysis. These cases are considered after Edgeworth, so that the famous box diagram can be used to provide further insights.

9.1   Walras on exchange

In Chapter 6 it was shown that Cournot's partial equilibrium approach, while not really applicable to exchange, could be adapted by the simple expedient of writing the *relative* price as the argument of each demand function and suitably modifying the equilibrium condition. This modification produces a basic model of the exchange of two goods that is essentially the same as the later treatments examined in Chapters 7 and 8. It is therefore not surprising that Walras took the same path. His autobiography clearly states that he 'soon perceived' that Cournot's approach could not be applied to exchange and:

> Restricting my attention, therefore to the case of two commodities, I rationally derived from the demand curve of each commodity the supply curve of the other and demonstrated how current equilibrium results from the intersection of the supply and demand curves. Then I proceeded to derive the demand curve itself from the quantities possessed by each individual in the market and from each individual's utility curves for the two commodities considered. (Quoted in Jaffé, 1983, p. 25)

The first part of Walras's analysis is contained in the first three chapters (or 'lessons') of Part II of his *Elements* (1954, pp. 81–114). This treatment, with its 'exuberance of algebraic foliage', shows Walras's transformation of Cournot's model, obtained by adding the insight of the reciprocal demand nature of exchange and the associated interpretation of relative prices. In so doing he retained the use of Cournot's notation.

After making clear that he was dealing with price-taking (1954, p. 86, para. 43), Walras described his framework as follows:

> let us now imagine a market to which some people come holding commodity (A); ready to exchange part of it in order to procure commodity (B); while others come holding commodity (B) . . . let us define *prices* in general as . . . relative values in exchange. (1954, p. 87)

Walras then showed that '*prices, or ratios of values in exchange, are equal to the inverse ratios of the quantities exchanged*' and that '*the price of any one commodity in terms of another is the reciprocal of the price of the second commodity in terms of the first*' (1954, p. 87). He argued that: 'It is of the utmost importance that the invariable reciprocal nature of the relationship between the two prices in any exchange be fully understood, and the use of algebraic symbols is particularly useful in this connection' (1954, p. 88). The crucial ingredient, as seen from Chapter 7, is in Walras's terms the recognition that 'to say that a quantity D_a of (A) is demanded at the price p_a is, *ipso facto*, the same thing as saying that a quantity O_b of (B), equal to $D_a p_a$, is being offered' (1954, p. 88). This implies, of course, that only the two demand curves need to be specified.

Walras then showed how the individual demand curves could be aggregated and suggested that aggregation will result in a continuous total demand curve even if some individuals' curves are step functions (1954, pp. 93–5), and wrote the demand curve as $D_a = F_a(p_a)$. This is the vital step required, with p_a as the *relative* price, to generalize Cournot's model. He then proceeded to show how the supply curve (translated by Jaffé as the *offer curve*) is obtained as an appropriate area beneath a demand curve. These supply curves were drawn as in the left-hand side of Figure 8.2 of the previous chapter, except that Walras placed quantity on the vertical axis and he did not draw the right-hand side.

Walras did not use a specific functional form for the demand curve, but it can be shown that almost any downward sloping demand curve that cuts both axes will take the general shape (in the positive orthant) of the supply curves drawn by Walras. The statement relating to the solution was clearly formulated as follows:

> For the market to be in equilibrium . . . or for the price of either commodity to be stationary in terms of the other, it is necessary and sufficient that the effective demand be equal [to] the effective offer of each commodity. Where this equality does not obtain, . . . the commodity having an effective demand greater than its effective offer must rise in price [and *vice versa*]. (1954, p. 106, the original is in italics)

Walras was thus immediately able to distinguish the possible situations that may arise. There may be no solution giving a positive price. If there are three equilibria Walras distinguished between the stable and unstable solutions using his well-known argument about the adjustment of prices according to excess supply or demand. He also considered the constant elasticity case where, as seen in Chapter 8, the supply is constant. The next two chapters (or 'lessons') then showed how the individual demand curves can be obtained from the pre-trade endowment and utility maximization. The first part of Walras's analysis thus sees him working along the same lines as Marshall in generalizing Cournot's model. The second part of the analysis finds Walras formulating a utility approach to the problem along the same lines as Jevons. The major differences between the approaches is that Jevons's starting point was the treatment of marginal utility as a *function* of the amount consumed (assuming additivity), and therefore exchanged, of each good, and gave equilibrium conditions in terms of marginal utilities. Walras's approach was in terms of demand functions treated as functions of relative prices. The extension of Jevons's approach by Edgeworth and his magnificent synthesis will be examined in the following section, but it is necessary to consider briefly the possibility of any connection between the various contributions.

Walras and his contemporaries
Viewed objectively in terms of first date of publication, Walras can claim priority over Marshall in his analysis of exchange with price-taking, recognition of the possibility of multiple equilibria and an explicit stability analysis that allowed him to identify the unstable equilibrium position. But there is little doubt that their discoveries were entirely independent, as Marshall claimed. Some commentators have argued that Walras and Marshall had different models in mind. However, there seems little doubt that these two major economists were working within precisely the same framework, although their presentations emphasized different aspects.

The 'substantially equivalent' nature of the two analyses was indeed stressed by Hicks (1934) in his brief but penetrating review of Walras. Hicks considered the question of whether the simultaneous development of 'a very new line of thought' was related to the nature of the subject and the quality of the contributors. He suggested that, 'One feels almost obliged to explain it by the intrinsic excellence of the path they followed . . . Yet in fact there is a clear historical reason for it, one decisive influence we know to have been felt by both. Each of them had read Cournot' (1934, p. 346).

It is true that Walras was very familiar with the work of Mill, to which he often referred throughout the *Elements*, but in looking at the genesis of Walras's analysis there is clearly no need to go beyond Cournot. However,

Jaffé (1983, pp. 55–77) has argued that there is a direct line of filiation from Isnard to Walras. Isnard recognized the important point that the price ratio is equivalent to the (inverse) ratio of quantities exchanged, which as stressed above is crucial for the theory of reciprocal demand. He also stressed the mutual interdependence in a general equilibrium system. But Isnard was not alone here, and his discussion is restricted to given quantities; there is no analysis of demand as a function of relative prices. Isnard's analysis is also discussed by Robertson (1949), Schumpeter (1954, p. 217) and Theocharis (1961, pp. 65–9). Given the absence of any direct evidence and the exaggerated claims for Isnard made by Jaffé, the argument is not pursued here. Indeed, it would be easier to make a claim for the influence of Mill.

An objective comparison with Jevons shows, of course, that the formulation of a utility analysis of exchange by Walras was published several years later. But again the independence of these contributions is not seriously questioned. Although it has sometimes been argued that Walras's understanding of the mathematical structure of the analysis of exchange went further than that of Jevons, it is unfortunate that rather misleading comparisons have often been made. For example, Jaffé (1983, pp. 317–18) has argued that Jevons's model 'is, to be sure, a perfect market not unlike that of Walras, but it is not one that could be seen to give rise to multiple equilibrium prices or, indeed, to any equilibrium price at all. Jevons, moreover, did not take systematically into consideration the interactions within a commercially interconnected network of markets'. This statement is remarkably inaccurate, as will be seen when Jevons's analysis is examined in more detail later in this chapter.

Several of the important implications of Marshall's and Walras's analyses of exchange, particularly the possibility of multiple equilibria and the fact that supply curves can be backward bending merely if the associated demand is elastic, have for many years been largely ignored. It is perhaps tempting to attribute this to their styles of presentation. For example, Marshall's polished style tended to conceal the complexities along with his methods of discovery, while Walras's mathematics and notation were extremely clumsy. But such an explanation can carry very little weight.

In the *Principles*, where the major focus of attention was on 'domestic values' rather than international trade, Marshall abandoned his exchange model in favour of a partial equilibrium treatment. The supply of goods was regarded as arising from firms having no demand for the goods being sold, so that the supply and demand sides were treated entirely separately. Yet even here Marshall stressed the possibility of multiple equilibria where there are increasing returns on the production side. Furthermore, his analysis of monopoly focused on the appropriate method of dealing with profit maximization where multiple equilibria are likely; see Creedy and O'Brien (1990). One element in the abandonment of the lessons of Walras's and Marshall's analyses of exchange seems to have been a strong desire to use the simple mathematical methods of constrained optimization and, within that approach, to concentrate on first-order conditions. To face the 'problems' of possible multiple solutions and instability seemed to be a considerable nuisance rather than a challenge.

The supply curve of labour
The neglect of these important contributions is highlighted by the analysis of the supply curve of labour. Walras's and Marshall's treatments show immediately that the supply curve of labour will 'bend backwards' if the demand for income is elastic. This is essentially the approach of Robbins (1930), though it is of interest that Robbins's major influence seems to have been Wicksteed rather than Walras or the foreign trade analysis of Marshall; see O'Brien (1989). Wicksteed's analysis will be examined in detail in Chapter 12 below. The more modern approach, based on indifference curve analysis of income and substitution effects, treats leisure as one of the goods in the individual's utility function. An increase in the wage rate produces an increase in the demand for leisure if the (negative) income effect outweighs the substitution effect. From this point of view, such an effect is typically regarded as being unusual and requiring rather special circumstances. However, the supply curve can bend backwards even without an income effect. This was indeed recognized by Hicks when he noted that 'the elasticity of demand for income must be positive; but this means that the elasticity of individual supply of labour must be either positive or lie between 0 and -1' (1932, p. 98). It is not really surprising, therefore, that the neglect of the Marshallian and Walrasian approach has been described as an example of 'doctrinal retrogression'; see Buchanan (1971).

9.2   Jevons's equation of exchange
Jevons's framework
Jevons's explicitly restricted his exchange analysis to price-taking behaviour, but found it most convenient (along with many other writers) to present his formal analysis in terms of two traders. There is of course a slight tension associated with this type of approach because it can be argued that, with only two traders, there is no reason why prices should be taken as given. Indeed, this point was stressed by Jenkin in correspondence with Jevons, before the publication of *The Theory of Political Economy* (see Black, 1977, pp. 166–78). Jevons's earlier treatment, the

subject of Jenkin's letters, was in terms of exchange between two individuals named Jones and Brown, so that Jenkin's criticism is quite understandable. It may have been in response to these queries that Jevons, wishing to focus on the price-taking equilibrium, invented his rather awkward device of the 'trading body'. This was defined as:

> any body either of buyers or sellers. The trading body may be a single individual in one case; it may be the whole inhabitants of a continent in another; it may be the individuals of a trade diffused through a country in a third. (1871, 5th ed. 1957, p. 88)

Edgeworth later criticized Jevons for not dealing adequately with the role of the number of individuals in the market, but he recognized clearly that Jevons wanted some device for dealing with 'representative' competitors. Thus, Jevons's trading bodies, 'are, I take it, a sort of typical couple, clothed with the properties of "indifference", whose origins in an "open market" are so lucidly described' (1881, p. 109). Edgeworth here was alluding to Jevons's 'law of indifference', by which 'all portions must be exchanged at the same ratio' (Jevons, 1957, p. 91). This again means that attention is restricted to competitive equilibria. In particular, Jevons's law of indifference implies that *'the last increments in an act of exchange must be exchanged in the same ratio as the whole quantities exchange'* (1957, p. 94). Hence if y and x are the amounts exchanged, Jevons stated that the rate of exchange is $dy/dx = y/x$. From the analyses of exchange examined in previous chapters of this part of the present book, it is clear that the idea of an exchange rate in terms of amounts exchanged is quite standard. The rate of exchange is the amount of good Y, y, that must be given up to get x units of good X. This is equivalent to the ratio of the *price* of good X to that of Y. With his law of indifference Jevons simply argued that he was restricting attention to situations in which all exchanges occur at the same price.

Jevons wished to use his equations to solve for the amounts exchanged, x and y, from which the price ratio can then be calculated (examples are given in Section 9.3 below). The decision not to refer explicitly to the price ratio was deliberate, but may have led some later commentators to suggest (incorrectly) that Jevons was not dealing with price-taking behaviour. Jevons had earlier discussed the lack of clarity in the use of the term 'value', stressing that 'value in exchange expresses nothing but a ratio' (1957, p. 78). He indicated that 'when . . . I need to refer to . . . *exchange or exchangeable value*, I shall substitute the wholly unequivocal expression *Ratio of Exchange*, specifying at the same time what are the *two articles* exchanged' (1957, p. 81). Certainly, some writers have confused the role of the expression $dy/dx = y/x$; early examples are provided by the anonymous reviewer in the *Saturday Review* (see Black, 1981, pp. 154–5), and even Marshall in his *Academy* review (see Black, 1981, p. 145).

Jevons was explicit about the fact that if he did not restrict attention to the properties of a static, price-taking, equilibrium, the use of dy/dx to represent the rate of exchange gives rise to 'differential equations, which would have to be integrated' (1957, p. 94). The substitution of y/x for dy/dx in the price-taking equilibrium avoids this difficulty. His discussion of the lever analogy was concerned to stress that the movement of a lever out of equilibrium requires the very difficult treatment of differential equations, but that if attention is restricted to the property of the equilibrium position 'no such process as integration is applicable' (1957, p. 105). Jevons was well aware of the huge difficulties involved in examining the precise dynamics of moving bodies, which had to wait until the computer age before the many approximations, required to produce differential equations capable of being integrated, could be avoided. The relaxation of the 'law of indifference', involving adjustment processes and trading at disequilibrium prices, will be examined in more detail in Chapter 10. In particular, it will be seen that Marshall produced a special case which allowed *some* results of a disequilibrium process to be obtained without the need to integrate any differential equations; his analysis was therefore not dynamic.

Having laid the foundations, Jevons then described the 'keystone' of the theory. This is his result that, *'The ratio of exchange of any two commodities will be the reciprocal of the ratio of the final degrees of utility of the quantities of commodity available for consumption after the exchange is completed'* (1957, p. 95). Jevons's 'final degree of utility', what is now referred to as 'marginal utility', is of course associated with the appropriate partial derivative of the utility function. In giving a formal statement of this result, Jevons described his model as follows:

> Suppose that the first body, A, originally possessed the quantity a of corn, and that the second body, B, possesses the quantity b of beef. As the exchange consists of giving x of corn for y of beef, the state of things after exchange will be as follows:–
>
> A holds $a - x$ of corn, and y of beef
> B holds x of corn, and $b - y$ of beef
> Let $\phi_1 (a - x)$ denote the final degree of utility of corn to A, and $\phi_2 x$ the corresponding function of B. Also let $\psi_1 y$ denote A's final degree of utility for beef, and $\psi_2(b - y)$ B's similar function. (1957, p. 99)

Hence Jevons was able to show that when each individual maximizes utility:

$$\frac{\phi_1(a-x)}{\psi_1 y} = \frac{y}{x} = \frac{\phi_2 x}{\psi_2(b-y)} \tag{9.1}$$

Jevons arrived at this result, or first-order condition, without the formal use of optimization methods. He argued that for any individual attempting to maximize utility, it is necessary to ensure that the rate at which goods can be exchanged in the market is the same as the rate at which utility can be 'exchanged' by substitution in consumption. Unless these rates are equal it is necessary to carry out further substitution; so long as the ratio of the marginal utilities varies continuously, the required equality can be achieved. For two individuals there are thus two equations of this type, but they can be written in the form of (9.1) because both individuals must face the same prices for all units exchanged.

Modern students are typically presented with this result using an argument based on the tangency of an indifference curve (with slope equal to the ratio of marginal utilities) with a budget constraint (with slope equal to the ratio of prices). Alternatively, it is obtained by writing the first-order conditions for constrained utility maximization and then simply eliminating the Lagrange multiplier. When several correspondents, particularly Harald Westergaard, showed Jevons how constrained optimization methods can be used to obtain his result, he preferred to retain, 'a course of argument which is not only fundamentally true, but is clear and convincing to non mathematicians' (1957, p. xiii). Since y/x is equivalent to the price of X divided by the price of Y, equation (9.1) can be rearranged to show that the ratio of the marginal utility of a good to its price must be the same for all goods and individuals. This type of 'equimarginal condition' has attracted much attention in the textbooks.

The two simultaneous equations given by (9.1) are in some ways deceptively simple. Except for some special cases, such as Cobb–Douglas utility functions, the equations are nonlinear and require numerical methods of solution. Furthermore, there may be no solution, or none which satisfies the non-negativity constraints. With such nonlinear equations there is of course always the possibility of multiple equilibria. However, such multiple equilibria are not as immediately clear as the later treatments of Walras or Marshall where intersecting demand curves are evident. The difficulties were recognized by Jevons (as shown below) but he simply added the rather cryptic comment that 'if we had the functions of utility determined, it would be possible to throw them into a form clearly expressing the equivalence of supply and demand' (1957, p. 101). Jevons examined some more complex cases which will be discussed further in Section 9.3 below.

Several later commentators have queried Jevons's failure to draw any standard partial equilibrium demand curves in his *Theory of Political Economy*, and a number of imaginative answers has been provided. Yet there is really no question to be answered; in the context of exchange they are simply not appropriate. It is curious that the same writers do not question the failure of Walras to draw such demand curves. Walras's diagrams show general equilibrium curves in which demand is related to the *relative* price. He did not actually label the axes, but when his translator (Jaffé) later added labels he wrote simply 'price', and perhaps thereby misled casual readers. Jevons's discussion of the King–Davenant law, examined in Chapter 2 above, was really a digression from his main theme. He was well aware of the vast complexity in the link between aggregate demand functions and individual utility functions, even where those functions are very simple (such as displaying constant marginal utility).

9.3   Edgeworth's extension

Walras began his analysis of exchange by taking the relevant demands, as functions of relative prices, as given, and then moved to the utility analysis. Marshall also took his offer curves as the starting point. Jevons, on the other hand, began his treatment directly from the utility functions. It was Edgeworth who, starting from Jevons's framework, provided a complete synthesis of all the approaches and significantly extended the treatment of exchange and the understanding of competition. Edgeworth's analysis, involving his famous 'Edgeworth box', is described briefly in this section.

The contract curve

Edgeworth took Jevons's model and immediately extended it by dropping the assumption of additive utility functions, but using a rather awkward notation. For present purposes it is most convenient to consider goods X and Y (rather than corn and beef respectively), and utility functions $U_A(x,y)$ and $U_B(x,y)$. Notice that, since a and b are constants, it is not strictly necessary to write, for example $U_A(a-x,y)$, but it should be remembered that x and y represent amounts exchanged, 'the *quid* and the *pro quo*'.

Next, Edgeworth began with the problem of barter, rather than price-taking. He raised the question of the equilibrium which may be reached with 'one or both refusing to move further'. In barter, the conditions of exchange must be reached by voluntary agreement, or contract, between the two parties, and of course it is fundamental that no egoist would agree to a contract which would make him worse off than before the exchange. The question thus concerns the nature of the settlement reached by two contracting parties. He immediately answered that 'contract' only supplies part of the answer so that, 'supplementary conditions . . . supplied by competition or ethical motives' will be required, and then wrote the equation of his famous contract curve (1881, pp. 20–1). He then presented three alternative derivations of the equation of the contract curve. The indifference curve, the 'line of indifference', was introduced in the course of the first derivation, although a diagram was not drawn until seven pages later.

Edgeworth considered the utility functions of the two individuals as plotted in a three-dimensional graph, with total utility as the 'ordinate drawn from any point on the plane xy (say the plane of the paper) to the surface' (1881, p. 21). The problem of obtaining the equilibrium values of x and y which, 'cannot be varied without the consent of the parties to it' was clearly stated as follows: 'It is required to find a point (xy) such that, *in whatever direction* we take an infinitely small step, $[U_A]$ and $[U_B]$ do not increase together, but that, while one increases, the other decreases' (1881, p. 21). The locus of such points, 'it is here proposed to call the *contract-curve*'. This is derived as follows. Consider first a movement for person A. The total derivative of U_A is given by

$$dU_A = \frac{\partial U_A}{\partial x}\,dx + \frac{\partial U_A}{\partial y}\,dy \qquad (9.2)$$

and, 'it is evident that [A] will step only on one side of a certain line, the *line of indifference*, as it might be called' (1881, p. 21). This is of course because A will only consider positive values of dU_A; thus the equation of an indifference curve is:

$$\frac{\partial U_A}{\partial x}\,dx + \frac{\partial U_A}{\partial y}\,dy = 0 \qquad (9.3)$$

To obtain the contract curve Edgeworth then asked:

If we enquire in what directions [A] and [B] will consent to move *together*, the answer is, in any direction between their respective lines of indifference, in a direction *positive* as it may be called *for both*. At what point then will they refuse to move at all? When their *lines* of *indifference* are coincident. (1881, p. 22)

Thus the slope of each individual's indifference curve, dy/dx, must be the same, and from (9.3) it can be seen that:

$$-\frac{dy}{dx} = \frac{\partial U_A / \partial x}{\partial U_A / \partial y} = \frac{\partial U_B / \partial x}{\partial U_B / \partial y} \tag{9.4}$$

so that the equation of the contract curve is given by:

$$\frac{\partial U_A}{\partial x} \frac{\partial U_B}{\partial y} - \frac{\partial U_A}{\partial y} \frac{\partial U_B}{\partial x} = 0 \tag{9.5}$$

It is only necessary to assume price-taking, so that $dy/dx = y/x$, and additive utility functions, in order to convert (9.4) into Jevons's famous equation of exchange given by (9.1). The minus sign does not appear in Jevons's formulation because he defined his 'final degrees of ability' such that they were always positive, bearing in mind which goods are being given up.

The important point about the contract curve for the analysis of exchange is of course that the locus of tangencies of indifference curves specifies the 'class of contracts to the variation of which the consent of *both* parties cannot be obtained' (1881, p. 28). The contract curve is shown in Figure 9.1, where each axis measures the amount of the respective good exchanged (not consumed). As person A is assumed to hold all the initial stocks of good X, and none of good Y, the indifference curve which A can reach in isolation is shown as I_A, which passes through O. Similarly, I_B is the indifference curve of person B which passes through O. Without trade they both *consume* at O, but they would obviously agree to any settlement in the area enclosed by I_A and I_B. The locus of efficient exchanges, such that movement would involve at least one party becoming worse off, is the contract curve CC'. Each point along CC' represents a point of tangency, such as between I''_A and I''_B, or between I_A and I'_B which represents the best possible exchange for person B. Since exchange is the focus of attention, there is no need to specify the lengths of the axes in terms of the fixed supplies of the goods. The famous box diagram is obtained simply by specifying these lengths and drawing in the other two sides of the box.

A crucial feature of the contract curve is that, 'the settlements are represented by an *indefinite number of points*' (1881, p. 29). As seen earlier, the rate of exchange at any settlement is simply the amount of one good which is given per unit of the other good, or y/x. It is represented by the slope of a line drawn from the endowment position to the settlement on the contract curve. Hence the rate of exchange is indeterminate. This indeterminacy was, for Edgeworth, extremely important and led to his fundamental contributions regarding the role of numbers in exchange and the nature of utilitarianism; these aspects are discussed in Chapter 11 below.

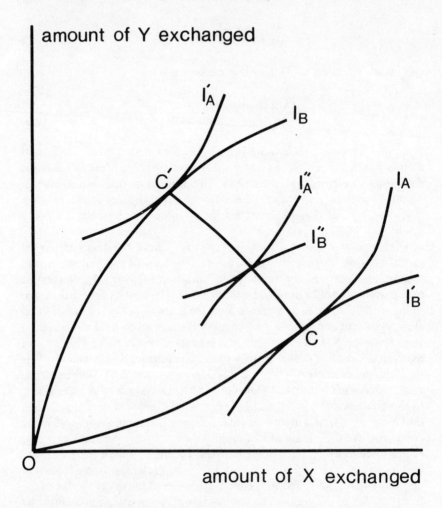

Figure 9.1   Exchange and the contract curve

Price-taking equilibria

Although he concentrated on the implications of indeterminacy, Edgeworth showed how a price-taking equilibrium is represented using his new device of indifference maps, and explained how they could also be used to derive Marshall's offer curves. Edgeworth explained that the offer curve is 'the locus of the point where lines from the origin *touch* curves of indifference' (1881, p. 113). The lines from the origin, the endowment position, represent rates of exchange, of course. A price-taking equilibrium is given by the intersection of offer curves which, by construction, must also be a

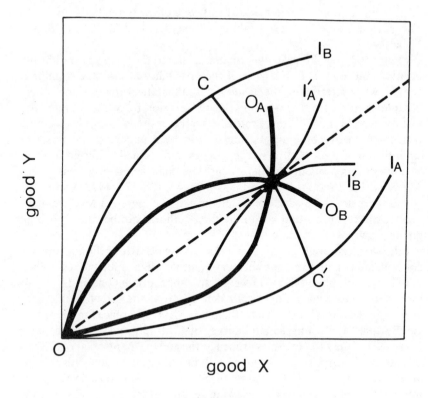

Figure 9.2   The price-taking equilibrium

point on the contract curve. The corresponding equilibrium price ratio is then the slope of the line from the origin to the point of intersection of the offer curves. This point thus also represents a common point of tangency of individuals' indifference curves with the 'price line'; thus if individuals respond independently to that price ratio, there are no excess demands or supplies. This synthesis, for the case where there is a unique equilibrium, is shown in Figure 9.2.

When describing his own results, Jevons had suggested that, 'It is hardly possible to represent this theory completely by means of a diagram' (1957, p. 96). But it has been seen that Edgeworth was able to provide a diagrammatic approach which synthesized and significantly extended the existing results. Although it took a long time for Edgeworth's approach to become widely adopted, it is now probably the most widely used device in economics. The result that the price-taking equilibrium is a point on the contract curve demonstrates that it is efficient, in the sense that a movement from the point would make at least one of the individuals worse off. The efficiency aspects of price-taking will be discussed further in Chapter 11 below.

Figure 9.2, like Edgeworth's diagram, illustrates a single equilibrium position, but he was fully aware of the possibility of multiple equilibria. Indeed, when referring to the 'beauty of mathematical analysis', he added, 'I cannot refrain from illustrating this proposition by one more reference to Principal Marshall's and Professor Walras's similar – doubtless independent – theory of multiple intersection of demand curves, unstable equilibrium of trade' (1881, p. 125). Edgeworth actually referred to these 'doubtless independent' results on no less than seven occasions in his *Mathematical Psychics* (1881, pp. 5, 26, 38, 46, 105, 125, 147). A situation where there are three equilibria is illustrated in Figure 9.3 More modern analyses have shown that such multiple equilibria can be ruled out if all goods are gross substitutes.

Edgeworth showed that without price-taking behaviour the appropriate concept is that of the contract curve, rather than offer curves. When individuals are price-takers, however, the appropriate concept is that of the offer curve, which Edgeworth derived from the set of indifference curves. In dealing with exchange, there is of course no place for the partial equilibrium supply and demand curves of Cournot, Jenkin and the later Marshall (of the *Principles*), as argued at the end of Chapter 6 above. Thus it is not really surprising that Edgeworth in 1881, in common with Jevons, Walras and Wicksell (1893), did not use 'standard' demand curves. It is of interest that Marshall, when reviewing Jevons's *Theory* in 1872 and criticizing his use of mathematics, alluded to Jenkin in stating his preference for 'the language of diagrams', despite the fact that Jenkin's diagrams were not appropriate.

9.4   Jevons's 'complex cases' of exchange

It has been seen that when Jevons first presented his theory of exchange, he used the example of two trading bodies holding stocks of corn and beef. But he was eager to show how the basic results could be applied to a variety of situations. After considering the relatively simple introduction of transport costs, Jevons added three subsections (1957, pp. 111–19) which clearly demonstrated his confident handling of his approach. Despite Marshall's critical comments on Jevons's handling of mathematics, these examples show a clear and succinct statement of their mathematical structure. These more 'complex cases' have been largely neglected and are therefore examined closely in this section. It is also shown that Edgeworth's box diagram apparatus can usefully be employed to throw some light on these problems.

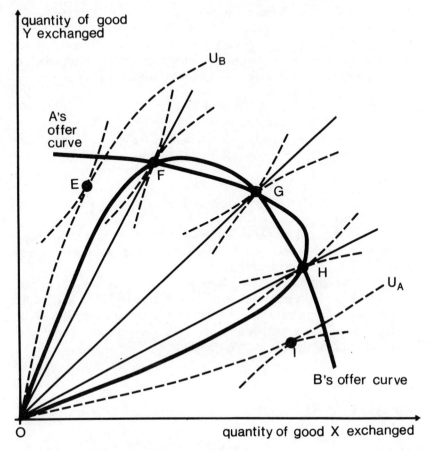

Figure 9.3   Multiple equilibria

Large and small traders

Jevons stated quite clearly that in less simple cases, 'the principles will be exactly the same, but the particular conditions may be subject to variation' (1957, p. 112). His first example was of a very large trader, A, holding stocks of goods X and Y of a and b respectively, dealing with person C who holds a small quantity, c, of good Y. Jevons argued that since the amounts traded are very small in relation to the initial holdings a and b, it is reasonable to treat A as having constant marginal utilities. (This type of argument was later used by Marshall to justify the assumption of constant marginal utility.) Hence A's utility, after exchange, is given by:

$$U_A = \alpha(a-x) + \beta(b+y) \tag{9.6}$$

The slope of A's indifference curves is thus constant at $dy/dx = \alpha/\beta$. Jevons argued that this ratio fixes the rate of exchange, y/x, so that $y = (\alpha/\beta)x$ and the set of two equations in (9.1) can very easily be reduced to one equation in one unknown. Jevons did not specify a utility function for C, but suppose that C's utility function takes the form:

$$U_C = x^\delta + (c-y)^\theta \tag{9.7}$$

Substitution of the appropriate partial derivatives into (9.1), along with the earlier result that y is proportional to x, gives:

$$\frac{\theta}{\delta}\frac{\alpha}{\beta} = \frac{x^{\delta-1}}{\{c - (\alpha/\beta)x\}^{\theta-1}} \tag{9.8}$$

so that x is the root of (9.8). In this example, numerical methods are therefore required to solve the 'equation of exchange' in order to obtain the equilibrium amounts traded.

Jevons did point out that 'for a large part of our purchases . . . we may suppose that y . . . is a very small part of c' (1957, p. 113). This implies that C's marginal utility of y is also constant, but Jevons did not examine the implications of this assumption in detail. In terms of the example used earlier, this means that U_C in (9.7) becomes:

$$U_C = x^\delta + \gamma(c-y) \tag{9.9}$$

and it can be shown that substitution into (9.1) gives the result that:

$$x = \left(\frac{\gamma\alpha}{\delta\beta}\right)^{1/(\delta-1)} \tag{9.10}$$

The above approach indicates two important aspects of Jevons's model. First, trader A obtains no gains from trade as the price ratio coincides with the indifference curve that passes through the endowment point. Second, the solution in (9.10) contains no reference to the stocks available, whereas the inequality constraint $y \leq c$ must hold. Hence a corner solution is in fact the most likely outcome, unless individuals A and C have similar tastes; that is, they both prefer good X to Y, or vice versa. The situation is illustrated in the Edgeworth box diagram of Figure 9.4 The endowment point is at E and A's pre-trade indifference curve is the line FE, which has a slope of α/β. Unless there is an interior solution, shown by the indifference curve U_c', there will be a corner solution either at E (where C consumes only good Y) or at F (where C consumes only

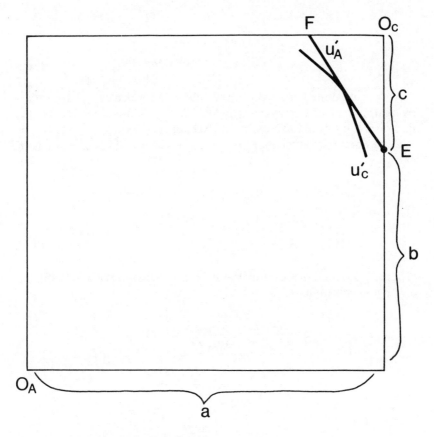

Figure 9.4   Large and small traders

good X, given by the amount $c\beta/\alpha$). Jevons did, however, discuss the general possibility of corner solutions in his later section on 'failure of the equations of exchange' (1957, p. 119). He explained the situation where the ratios of marginal utilities are such that 'no benefit can arise from exchange' or where 'the whole quantities of commodity possessed are exchanged, and yet the equations fail'.

Three traders and three goods
The next case Jevons examined was that of exchange between three individuals A, B and C who hold stocks a, b and c respectively of goods X, Y and Z. If amounts exchanged are denoted, as before, by lower case letters, the exchanges can be described as follows:

A gives x_1 for y_1, and x_2 for z_1

B gives y_1 for x_1, and y_2 for z_2

C gives z_1 for x_2, and z_2 for y_2

As Jevons pointed out, there are six unknowns which can be determined by treating each of the trades as 'independent exchanges; each body must be satisfied in regard to each of its exchanges' (1957, p. 115). Using the modern notation, rather than that of Jevons, the utilities after exchange are:

$$U_A = U_A(a - x_1 - x_2, y_1, z_1)$$
$$U_B = U_B(x_1, b - y_1 - y_2, z_2)$$
$$U_c = U_c(x_2, y_2, c - z_1 - z_2) \qquad (9.11)$$

and the six simultaneous equations from the first-order conditions for utility maximization are:

$$\frac{\partial U_A/\partial x}{\partial U_A/\partial y} = \frac{\partial U_B/\partial x}{\partial U_B/\partial y} = -\frac{y_1}{x_1}$$

$$\frac{\partial U_A/\partial x}{\partial U_A/\partial z} = \frac{\partial U_C/\partial x}{\partial U_C/\partial z} = -\frac{z_1}{x_2}$$

$$\frac{\partial U_B/\partial x}{\partial U_B/\partial z} = \frac{\partial U_C/\partial x}{-\partial U_C/\partial z} = \frac{z_2}{y_2} \qquad (9.12)$$

The minus signs are not of course required with Jevons's own notation which, as explained earlier, takes absolute values of marginal utilities. Jevons's statement that the trades described above may be treated as 'independent exchanges' is not, however, strictly accurate. It has been implicitly assumed that the conditions (tastes and endowments) are such as to rule out any arbitrage possibilities from indirect trades. For example, consider trader A, who for each unit of good X sold obtains (y_1/x_1) units of Y from person B. Given the price ratio established in the trade between B and C, person A could sell each unit of y in exchange for (z_2/y_2) of good Z from C. This indirect route would imply a price of X relative to Z such that each unit of X sold gives A $(y_1/x_1)(z_2/y_2)$ of good Z. But the direct trade with C means that each unit of X can be sold for (z_1/x_2) units of Z. Hence the absence of arbitrage possibilities requires that:

$$\frac{z_1}{x_2} > \left(\frac{y_1}{x_1}\right)\left(\frac{z_2}{y_2}\right) \tag{9.13}$$

Jevons did not examine any functional forms, but the six equations of (9.12) will in general be nonlinear. He was certainly well aware of the fact that his exchange equations cannot usually be solved explicitly. When discussing the 'limits of scientific method' in *The Principles of Science*, he alluded to this very problem, as follows:

> as soon as we attempt to draw out the equations expressing the laws of demand and supply, we discover that they have a complexity entirely surpassing our powers of mathematical treatment. We may lay down the general form of the equations, expressing the demand and supply for two or three commodities among two or three trading bodies, but all the functions involved are so complicated in character that there is not much fear of scientific method making rapid progress in this direction. (1909, 2nd ed., pp. 759–60)

Jevons was, however, optimistic that 'we may rely upon it that immense, and to us inconceivable, advances will be made by the human intellect, in the absence of any catastrophe to the species or the globe' (1909, p. 758). It was indeed many years before even the conditions were established under which a general equilibrium system (adding production to the exchange equations) has a feasible solution. Those who discussed general equilibrium models, including Marshall, Fisher (1925) and Bowley (1924, pp. 47–54), were content, like Jevons and Walras, to count unknowns and equations. Nonlinear sets of equations can now be solved relatively quickly using iterative methods with electronic computers. Nevertheless, Jevons had done sufficient to show how 'the exchanges in the most complicated case may thus always be decomposed into simple exchanges, and every exchange will give rise to two equations sufficient to determine the quantities involved' (1957, p. 117).

Jevons's equations may, however, be solved explicitly for one special case, that of the well-known Cobb–Douglas utility functions. Suppose that the exponents on the amounts consumed of X, Y and Z are respectively α, β and γ for person A, α_1, β_1 and γ_1 for person B, and α_2, β_2 and γ_2 for person C. The Cobb–Douglas case is mathematically highly tractable and generates interior solutions. Substitution of appropriate derivatives into equations (9.12) gives, after much manipulation, the result that:

$$x_1 = a\{\beta/(\alpha + \beta + \gamma)\} \qquad x_2 = a\{\gamma/(\alpha + \beta + \gamma)\}$$
$$y_1 = b\{\alpha_1/(\alpha_1 + \beta_1 + \gamma_1)\} \qquad y_2 = b\{\gamma_1/(\alpha_1 + \beta_1 + \gamma_1)\}$$
$$z_1 = c\{\alpha_2/(\alpha_2 + \beta_2 + \gamma_2)\} \qquad z_2 = c\{\beta_2/(\alpha_2 + \beta_2 + \gamma_2)\} \tag{9.14}$$

Table 9.1   *Utility functions: three traders and three goods*

Person	Exponents on good:		
	X	Y	Z
A	.3	.4	.2
B	.5	.3	.5
C	.2	.3	.5

Suppose that $a = b = c = 1$ and the parameters of the utility functions are as shown in Table 9.1. These values can be found to give the solution: $x_1 = .444$; $x_2 = .222$; $y_1 = y_2 = .385$; $z_1 = .2$; $z_2 = .3$. Substitution into (9.13) shows that $0.9 > (0.865)(0.78)$, so that indirect trades are not profitable. Any other set of utility functions must be solved using numerical procedures.

Competition between two traders
Jevons's next case was regarded as 'of considerable importance, and arises when two parties compete together in supplying a third party with a certain commodity' (1957, p. 117). He then specified a situation in which trader A holds a of good X while B and C hold b and c respectively of good Y. The trades are such that:

A gives x_1 of a to B and x_2 to C

B gives y_1 of b to A

C gives y_2 of c to A.

Jevons pointed out immediately that since the goods are homogeneous 'the rate of exchange must be the same in one case as in the other' so that:

$$\frac{y_1}{x_1} = \frac{y_2}{x_2} \tag{9.15}$$

Furthermore, A 'does not care whence it [his supply of Y] comes, so that we do not, in his equation, distinguish the source or destination of the quantities; he simply gives $x_1 + x_2$, and receives in exchange $y_1 + y_2$' (1957, p. 118). Hence:

$$\frac{y_1 + y_2}{x_1 + x_2} = \frac{y_1}{x_1} \tag{9.16}$$

The three further equations necessary to determine the four quantities are the two required for the trade between persons A and B, given by:

$$\frac{\partial U_A/\partial x}{\partial U_A/\partial y} = -\frac{y_1}{x_1} = \frac{\partial U_B/\partial x}{\partial U_B/\partial y} \qquad (9.17)$$

along with the equation describing C's price-taking equilibrium, given by:

$$\frac{\partial U_C/\partial x}{\partial U_C/\partial y} = -\frac{y_2}{x_2} \qquad (9.18)$$

Again, Jevons did not pursue this further, but remarked only that 'Various suppositions might be made as to the comparative magnitudes of the quantities *b* and *c*, or the character of the functions concerned ... The general result would be, that the smaller holder must more or less conform to the prices of the larger holder' (1957, p. 118). However, the last statement in this quotation is not entirely clear, although it would seem to suggest that the relative price of the goods, given by equation (9.16), is dominated by whichever of B and C has the largest stock of good Y before trade. But this is an oversimplification.

Consider Figure 9.5, which shows the equilibrium situation using two juxtaposed Edgeworth boxes. Trade between A and B is shown in the lower box, while that between A and C is shown in the upper box. The ray from the endowment point, the price-taking equilibrium price, in each box must have the same slope. Notice that the dimensions of the upper box depend on the equilibrium position in the lower box. If one of the traders, say B, has a large stock of Y relative to person C, then the upper box of Figure 9.5 will look more like the situation shown in Figure 9.4. The possibility of a corner solution is thus again more likely. If trader A is regarded as having extremely large stocks of good X, then it may appear that A, rather than B or C, is the 'larger holder'. What is clear is that Jevons's statement has no clear meaning. Given the equilibrium shown in Figure 9.5, there must be no potential for further gains from trade between B and C. That this indeed is the case is illustrated in Figure 9.6. The price line (parallel with those in Figure 9.5) must 'separate' the two traders at their (post-trade) endowment point.

This problem may be examined further using the case of Cobb-Douglas utility functions, which are so tractable in such contexts. The utility functions may be written:

$$U_A = (a - x_1 - x_2)^\alpha (y_1 + y_2)^\beta \qquad (9.19)$$

$$U_B = x_1^\gamma (b - y_1)^\delta \qquad (9.20)$$

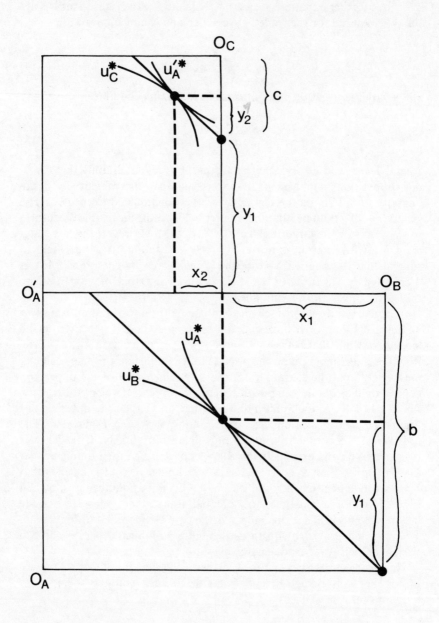

Figure 9.5   Competition in exchange

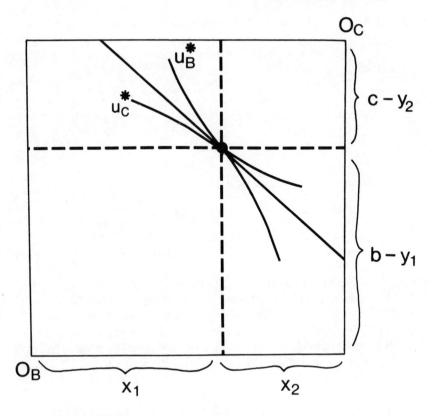

Figure 9.6   No trade between competitors

$$U_C = x_2^\epsilon (c - y_2)^\theta \qquad (9.21)$$

Appropriate differentiation of (9.20), and substitution, into the equation on the right of (9.17) gives, after rearrangement:

$$y_1 = b(1 + \delta/\gamma)^{-1} \qquad (9.22)$$

Similarly, using (9.21) with (9.18) gives:

$$y_2 = c(1 + \theta/\epsilon)^{-1} \qquad (9.23)$$

Then setting $(\partial U_A/\partial x)/(\partial U_A/\partial_y)$ equal to $(y_1 + y_2)/(x_1 + x_2)$ gives, after rearranging:

$$x_1 + x_2 = a(1 + \alpha/\beta)^{-1} \qquad (9.24)$$

Table 9.2   Utility functions: three traders and two goods

| Person | Exponents on good: | |
	X	Y
A	.3	.4
B	.3	.5
C	.4	.2

Combining these results with (9.16) gives:

$$x_1 = \frac{a(1 + \alpha/\beta)^{-1}}{1 + \frac{c}{b}\left(\frac{1 + \delta/\gamma}{1 + \theta/\epsilon}\right)} \tag{9.25}$$

Suppose the tastes are as shown in Table 9.2, and $a=1$, with $b=0.7$ and $c=0.3$. It can be found by direct substitution into (9.22) to (9.25) that: $x_1 = .324$; $x_2 = .247$; $y_1 = .263$; $y_2 = .2$. These values imply a price of X relative to that of Y, $(y_1/x_1 = y_2/x_2)$, equal to 0.809. In this example both A and B have a relatively stronger preference for good Y. If the value of b and c are changed to 0.8 and 0.2 respectively, then more of good Y is in the hands of the trader with a lower preference for good X; hence the relative price of X to Y is found to fall, to 0.758.

There is no problem with corner solutions in this example because of the assumption of Cobb-Douglas utility functions. But suppose that the marginal utility of one of the goods is constant and that the utility functions take the form:

$$U_A = (a - x_1 - x_2)^\alpha + \beta(y_1 + y_2) \tag{9.26}$$

$$U_B = x_1^\gamma + \delta(b - y_1) \tag{9.27}$$

$$U_C = x_2^\epsilon + \theta(b - y_2) \tag{9.28}$$

The appropriate differentiation and substitution into (9.16) to (9.18) gives rise to nonlinear equations whose solutions will not necessarily satisfy the inequality constraints: $y_1 \le b$, $y_2 \le c$, and $x_1 + x_2 \le a$, along with the non-negativity constraints on the x and y values. Suppose that the preferences are given by those in Table 9.3. If $a=1$, $b=0.7$ and $c=0.3$, numerical methods of solution can be used to obtain the following values: $x_1 = .204$; $x_2 = .253$; $y_1 = .243$; $y_2 = .30$. Hence there is a corner solution with

Table 9.3   Utility functions with constant marginal utility of Y

| Person | Exponents on good: | |
	X	Y
A	.3	.5
B	.2	.6
C	.4	.4

person C trading all his stock of good Y. The ratio x_1/y_1 is in this situation not quite the same as the ratio $(x_1 + x_2)/(y_1 + y_2)$; person C would prefer to consume more of good X. Experiments with alternative parameter values show that the existence of corner solutions is the rule rather than the exception with this model, if the endowments of B and C differ substantially. These special cases appear to have been neglected by historians of economic analysis, but they demonstrate that Jevons was in full control of his technical apparatus and provided a succinct and substantially accurate treatment.

Notes and further reading

The suggestion that the neglect of Walras and Marshall on backward bending supply curves is 'doctrinal retrogression' was made by Buchanan (1971). Hicks (1934, p. 346) stated that, 'there is, I think, no question that Marshall's analysis is quite independent of Walras'. The identity of the two approaches, and particularly the stability conditions, is also stressed by Samuelson (1947, p. 264, n. 9). Jaffé (in his translator's notes to Walras, 1874) continued to argue that the approaches were different, and incorrectly reported Samuelson's position. For brief summaries of Walras's model by Schumpeter see (1952, p. 77) and (1954, pp. 1003–4). The basic features of Walras's exchange model were presented in works by Launhardt (1885) and Wicksell (1893, pp. 82–92; 1934, pp. 55–60), though only Wicksell's books have been translated into English. As usual, Wicksell discussed the major implications with great clarity and presented diagrams (closely following Launhardt) which are much easier to follow than those of Walras. Several pages from Launhardt are translated in Baumol and Goldfeld (1968, pp. 28–30). This relates to Launhardt's argument that the level of freight rates which maximizes total welfare (the sum of producers' and consumers' surplus) requires price to equal average cost. This result (rather than the marginal cost rule) holds only for Launhardt's linear functions; for analysis of this question in the context of Marshall's monopoly analysis, see Creedy and O'Brien (1991). Walras does not seem to have been influenced by Whewell, since in 1875 Jevons, in replying to a query, advised Walras that the memoirs were only available in the expensive volumes of the transactions of the Cambridge Philosophical Society. Jevons added that he thought they were not 'of much value', but advised Walras to write to Todhunter, the editor of Whewell's papers (see Jaffé, ed., 1965, I, letter 328). Todhunter's subsequent reply to Walras, in 1877, suggests that the latter was not aware of the memoir on Mill's trade theory (examined in Chapter 7 above), which Todhunter rates as the best (see Jaffé, ed., 1965, I, letter 375). A section from Isnard's analysis is reproduced in Baumol and Goldfeld (1968, pp. 255–7), who suggest that the judgement of Schumpeter and Theocharis is 'somewhat over-enthusiastic' (1968, p. 253).

While discussing Jevons's contribution, Young (1927, p. 201) accurately referred to the 'elimination of money as an essential part of the mechanism of the market', since it operates merely as a unit of account. Young (1927, pp. 229–30) argued that *The Theory of Political Economy* is 'mathematical only in a superficial way', and referred to the awkwardness of mathematical processes, but this type of criticism is not really warranted. In his 'brief account' of his theory of 1862 (reprinted in 1957, pp. 303–14), Jevons was explicit about the indeterminacy that results in the absence of price-taking. He stated that, 'the ratio of the increments of the commodities [that is, the price ratio], however, would be indeterminate but for the existence of a law that all quantities of the same commodities, being uniform in kind, must be exchanged at the same rate' (1957, p. 309). He was also clear about the nature of the gains from trade, stating, 'there cannot be equality in the whole utilities gained and lost, which are found by integrating the functions of utility of the respective commodities before and after exchange. The balance is the gain of utility, and from the nature of exchange there must be gain in one side at least' (1957, p. 311). The treatment of Jevons has sometimes been rather shoddy as, for example, by Schumpeter (1954, p. 911, n. 7). Stigler (1965, p. 91) gratuitously refers to Jevons's 'inability to translate any but simple thoughts into mathematics', and even suggested that the use of the equation of exchange to determine amounts traded is 'illicit on his own view that utilities of different individuals are not comparable' (1965, p. 91). But of course comparability is not required. Interpersonal comparisons are needed only when examining the gains from trade or when deriving the arrangement that maximizes total utility (discussed in the next chapter). Jaffé (1983, pp. 294–5) repeatedly criticizes Jevons, and quotes dismissive comments of others on Jevons, without any substantive argument. Jaffé's failure to appreciate Jevons's analysis is also exemplified by his argument that Walras obtained substantial advice from Paul Piccard (Professor of Mechanics at Lausanne); but Jaffé does not recognize that Piccard's analysis is (independently) the same as that of Jevons (1983, pp. 303–4).

A faithful treatment of Jevons's analysis is given by Fisher (1925, pp. 11–19), whose purpose was to extend Jevons's treatment to the many good, many person case. Fisher, following Jevons so closely, was explicit about the difference between his approach and that of Walras, saying 'the only fundamental differences are that I use marginal utility throughout and treat it as a function of the quantities of commodity, whereas Prof. Walras makes the quantity of each commodity a function of the prices' (1925, p. vi). It is really not surprising that, given their common starting point, both Edgeworth and Fisher independently produced the concepts of indifference curves and the contract curve. But Fisher gave a more extensive treatment of the types of simultaneous equation sets produced by the case of many goods and traders, examining the possibility of solving these equations by counting equations and unknowns (as did Jevons and Walras). It is unfortunate that Fisher's masterly contribution has been ignored by subsequent critics of Jevons, and noteworthy that Fisher, with his extensive mathematical training, did not find fault with Jevons.

For further analysis of Edgeworth's contribution, see Creedy (1986). Edgeworth showed that in the many good, many person case the equation of the contract curve is given by setting the determinant of the matrix with (i,j)th element $\partial U_i/\partial x_j$ equal to zero. For an example of utility functions giving rise to multiple equilibria, see Shapley and Shubik (1977). Edgeworth's discussion of Walras's *tatonnement* process is worth mentioning here. He argued that Walras 'describes *a* way rather than *the* way by which economic equilibrium is reached. For we have no general *dynamical* theory determining the path of the economic system from any point assigned at random to a position of equilibrium' (1925, II, p. 311). He added that only the static properties are known, and referred to Jevons's lever analogy discussed above. Edgeworth suggested that 'Walras's laboured description set up or "cried" in the market is calculated to divert attention from a sort of higgling which may be regarded as more fundamental than his conception' (1925, II, p. 311). The higgling he had in mind was of course his own recontracting process which is described in Chapter 11 below. Edgeworth also suggested that in a complex market, 'it is no longer a straightforward problem in algebra or geometry, given the natures of all the parties, to find the terms to which they will come' (1925, II, p. 281).

10 Exchange without price-taking

The three previous chapters in this part of the book have concentrated on the analysis of exchange in the context of price-taking behaviour. Edgeworth's emphasis on the problem of indeterminacy was, however, stressed in Chapter 9. The purpose of the present chapter is therefore to begin the examination of several issues that arise when individuals do not take prices as given, or as being outside their control. Marshall emphasized the potential usefulness of his offer curve apparatus to the analysis of bargaining between firms and trade unions, and Edgeworth argued that this context is precisely one where indeterminacy plays a significant role. The subject of wage bargaining is therefore discussed in Section 10.1.

In his desire to avoid the problems raised by indeterminacy in typical markets, Marshall used a special case involving the assumptions of independent utilities and constant marginal utility of one of the goods. The nature of this special case is examined in Section 10.2, when it is seen that, as Edgeworth argued, the indeterminacy is not all removed. An interesting feature of Marshall's analysis is that he allowed for trade to take place at non-equilibrium prices, resulting in changes in individuals' endowments during the process of adjustment towards the equilibrium price. His special assumptions ensure that the equilibrium price is independent of the path taken to reach the equilibrium. Such adjustment processes are examined in Section 9.3.

10.1 Wage bargaining
Marshall and Edgeworth
Marshall at a very early stage of his career hinted at the application of international trade analysis to wage bargaining. This appeared in his 1876 paper on J. S. Mill's theory of value (see Pigou, ed., 1925, pp. 132–3). He delayed the formal publication of his trade diagrams for 50 years, and felt unhappy about the implicit assumption that the demand for imports in general has similar characteristics to that for a single commodity, but he always thought that the diagrams could be applied to wage bargaining. For example, he made the point quite clearly in a letter to Edgeworth of 1891:

> I believe I told you that the first chapter of that part of my original MSS (printed by Sidgwick) was given to arguing that the

$$x = \text{amount} \Big\}$$
$$y = \text{amount} \Big\}$$

curves had perhaps more real applications to industrial groups and employer–employee-questions than to foreign Trade. I have always intended to reproduce that in my vol.II and that is one reason why I have not discussed Trades Unions in vol.I. (1975, II, p.112)

Marshall here was referring to the never-completed sequel to his *Principles*, but the Marshalls' *Economics of Industry* of 1879 also influenced Edgeworth directly. The relevance of the latter 'seemingly simple textbook' to wage bargaining can be traced without difficulty. When discussing Thornton's comments on the difference between Dutch and English auctions, Edgeworth (1881, p. 48, n.1) referred not to the original source but to Marshall and Marshall (1879, p. 200, n.1). This reference by the Marshalls appears, significantly, in their chapter on the influence of trade unions on wages. On the same page, they suggest that, 'If then the labourers enter into local trade combinations, and refuse to sell their labour except at a reserve price, it is quite possible that they may increase their share of the Wages-and-Profits fund, and raise wages at the expense of profits'.

It is no surprise that Edgeworth placed considerable stress on the indeterminacy that arises in wage bargaining and saw clearly that the growth of unions would increase the need for peaceful arbitration. As Edgeworth stressed, rather less prosaically, 'The whole creation groans and yearns, desiderating a principle of arbitration, an end of strifes' (1881, p. 51). It is in this area also that Edgeworth took his utilitarianism further than Marshall. Whereas the latter was prepared to arbitrate on the basis of what the corresponding competitive wage would have been, Edgeworth argued that this could be improved upon by choosing the point that maximizes the total utility of the contracting parties. (The difference between these two arrangements will be clarified in Chapter 11 below.)

Edgeworth argued that the same basic analysis of exchange can be applied to many contexts. But he did not develop the special features of wage bargaining at any length. It was implicitly assumed that the axes of the Edgeworth box measure the wage bill and the level of employment, but the special characteristics of the two sets of indifference curves were not explored. What Edgeworth did make clear, however, was the result that although settlements would generally be expected to be on the contract curve, if bargaining is over wages *only*, then settlements will be along the demand curve for labour. This demand curve is the employer's offer curve of wages for employment. Edgeworth wrote:

the property of *indeterminateness, plurality of final settlements*, will abide. Only the final settlements will now be by way of demand-curve, not contract-curve. If, for instance, powerful trade unions did not seek to fix the *quid pro quo*, the *amounts* of labour exchanged . . . but only the *rate of exchange*, it being left to each capitalist to purchase as much labour as he might demand at that rate, there would still be that sort of *indeterminateness favourable to unionists* above described. (1881, p. 48; see also pp. 137–8)

Later developments

The subject was later examined in a little-known book by Pigou (1905). He may be said to have taken a Marshallian position that bargaining will only concern the rate of wages and consequently 'settlement between the parties is determined by way of demand and not by way of contract curve' (1905, p. 210). In this case the relevant position on the contract curve is the point of intersection of the two offer curves; Pigou implicitly ruled out multiple equilibria.

The typical bargaining framework in the context of exchange of two goods between individuals or groups was later described by Bowley (1924, p. 8), who achieved something that hardly seems possible – his book was even more terse than *Mathematical Psychics*. Consider Figure 10.1, which shows the position of 'A-type' traders holding stocks of good X, dealing with 'B-type' traders who hold good Y. The competitive equilibrium is the point E at the intersection of the offer curves. If the A-type individuals form themselves into a monopoly and are therefore able to set the price, the best they can reach is point V on the offer curve of the Bs. Similarly, V' represents the best position that a monopoly of the Bs could reach. The points V and V' can be seen to correspond to points reached by the imposition of 'optimum' tariffs in the international trade context. Bowley stated that 'the double curve [VEV'] is called the bargaining locus' (1924, p. 8), but argued that E will be reached with 'equal bargaining strength'. Bowley did not, however, develop the analysis further and in particular did not examine the special circumstances of bargains between a union and employers.

The view taken by Edgeworth was that bargaining over only wages is inefficient, since it is not on the contract curve, so that CC' is really the bargaining locus, with both employment and wages subject to negotiation. Except for a brief comparison of Marshall and Edgeworth on wage bargaining by Hicks (1930), the most important subsequent developments seem to be that of Dunlop (1944, although some of this book had been published earlier in articles). Dunlop devoted much attention to the nature of the union's utility function and made explicit what the previous writers had left implicit, that the vertical axis (in a diagram such as Figure 10.1) represents the total wage bill, while the length of the other axis

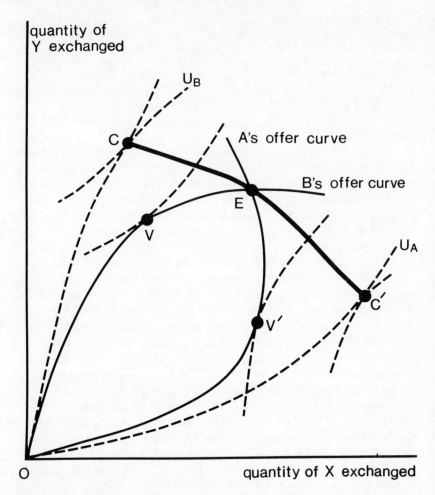

Figure 10.1   Bowley and bargaining

measures employment. A ray drawn from the origin therefore represents a
price line whose slope equals the wage. Trader A represents the union and
trader B is a firm or group of firms. The indifference curves of the firm
must represent *iso-profit* lines, which therefore depend on the role of
labour in production and the nature of the market in which the good is
sold.

A qualification to the argument that efficiency requires contracts to be
on the contract curve rather than the demand, or offer, curve was made by
Leontief (1946). He argued that if employment exceeds the size of the
union, efficient contracts are in fact on the demand curve for labour.

Several years later Fellner (1949) extended the analysis by producing diagrams which have the wage rate, rather than the wage bill, on the vertical axis. He compared situations in which unions are prepared to trade employment for wage gains, that is where indifference curves are downward sloping in the usual way, with those where unions are not concerned with the level of employment and therefore have horizontal indifference curves. In the latter case, Fellner (1949, p. 276) pointed out that the demand curve for labour is the contract curve and that 'neither the firm nor the union would gain from an employment guarantee'. This ties in with Leontief's point, since indifference curves will become horizontal after all the union's members are employed, even if they are downward sloping for lower employment levels.

These contributions did not form the basis of a continuous literature, and in fact the next 30 years saw few economic analyses along the lines originated by Edgeworth and Marshall. The next important step, marking the beginning of a large resurgence of interest in these issues, was made in ignorance of the details of the earlier literature. Precisely 100 years after the appearance of *Mathematical Psychics*, McDonald and Solow (1981) considered the union's indifference curves and a firm's iso-profit curves in detail. They produced the contract curve of efficient bargains between limits specified by zero profits and the opportunity cost of working, and showed that the Nash bargaining equilibrium produces a wage equal to the average of the marginal and average product of labour. A comparison of the Nash equilibrium with other solutions is made, for the case of exchange, in Appendix B.

10.2 Marshall's special case
Indeterminacy in exchange
It has been seen that Edgeworth placed great stress on what he believed to be the widespread existence of indeterminacy in exchange, leading to the need for a principle of arbitration. Indeterminacy means that the contract curve, rather than the offer curve, is the appropriate analytical device for the analysis of exchange. Marshall took a rather different position and in his review of *Mathematical Psychics* argued that, 'the greater part of economic theory can be dealt with most easily' by the use of supply and demand curves; see Marshall (1975, I, p. 267). This was also the position taken by Marshall throughout his *Principles*. Not surprisingly, when Edgeworth in turn reviewed Marshall's book, he criticized Marshall for not dealing sufficiently with the problem of indeterminacy. On first seeing the review, which was published in an Italian journal, Marshall did not fully recognize the criticism. He wrote to Edgeworth saying that 'it would never do for me to substitute your argument for mine – since it is so put as

to be of little use for my purpose' (1961, II, p. 793), adding that he intended to use Edgeworth's diagram and to refer to the contract curve in his Appendix on barter. (This diagram will be discussed in the next section.) He also mentioned the relevance of his foreign trade diagrams to wage determination, though ignoring the indeterminacy that was so important to Edgeworth. It seems that the full force of Edgeworth's criticism did not become clear until he asked Arthur Berry, a mathematician with a good knowledge of Italian, to look at Edgeworth's paper. After discussing the article with Berry, Marshall sent a long and deeply-felt reply to Edgeworth. A sample of this letter is as follows:

> I now throw myself on your kind and generous forbearance, and ask you to listen without anger ... What I want to say is that I do not think you at all appreciate the deadly and enduring injury that A does to B, if he reads rapidly a piece of hard argument on what B has spent an immense amount of work; and then believing that argument to be wrong, writes an article full of the most polite phrases, in which a caricature of that argument is held up to the most refined, but deadly scorn. I fancy you think that the polite phrases diminish the mischief ... Their effect ... is that of a white flag under which the ship approaches close to another and rams or torpedoes it ... There! I feel so much better. I am like a person who has held his mouth full of air under water for a minute (1961, II, pp. 796–8).

The essential analytical point behind Marshall's indignation was that he believed he had avoided the problem of indeterminacy by assuming that the utility function is additive and that the marginal utility of one good is constant. Marshall's assumptions can be examined in Edgeworth's framework as follows. As before, suppose that individuals A and B have initial endowments of goods X and Y equal to a and b respectively. Person A exchanges x of X in return for y of Y from person B. Their utilities after exchange takes place, U_A and U_B, are given by:

$$U_A = U_1(a-x) + \alpha y \qquad (10.1)$$

and

$$U_B = U_2(x) + \beta(b-y) \qquad (10.2)$$

Hence differentiation and substitution into the equation of the contract curve gives

$$\frac{\partial U_1/\partial x}{\partial U_2/\partial x} = -\frac{\alpha}{\beta} \qquad (10.3)$$

Equation (10.3) shows that $-\alpha/\beta$ is a function of x only, so it implies that the contract curve is a straight line parallel to the y axis. It is true that the value of x is determinate in this special case, but there still remains a range of values of y. Edgeworth himself made this point in his original review, reprinted in (1925, II, p. 37, n.1). Bowley was clearly familiar with this debate when writing the *Groundwork* (1924), though he did not allude to any of it. He went through the algebra very quickly and showed that 'the equation of the contract curve . . . only involves x and represents therefore a line (or conceivably lines) parallel to OY' (1924, p. 13). Bowley's point in parentheses is a useful qualification, since the equation may not necessarily have a unique root.

Consider a further special case in which $U_1(a-x) = (a-x)^\gamma$ and $U_2(x) = x^\sigma$. Substituting the appropriate partial derivatives into (10.3) gives:

$$x^{\sigma-1}(a-x)^{1-\gamma} = \gamma\beta/\alpha\sigma \tag{10.4}$$

which can be solved for x. However, in general the solution can only be found using numerical methods. In the simple case where $\sigma = \gamma$, and writing the right-hand side of (10.4) as k, the value of x can be obtained directly as:

$$x = a\{1 + k^{1/(1-\sigma)}\}^{-1} \tag{10.5}$$

It is of interest to compare this general context of exchange with the wage and employment bargaining framework discussed earlier. If the members of the union are assumed to be risk neutral, such that the marginal utility of the wage *rate* is constant, then it can be shown that the contract curve (in a diagram with the wage rate on the vertical axis and employment in the horizontal axis) is also vertical. The implication is that the level of employment is determinate, but that the wage rate is indeterminate.

10.3 Trading at 'false' prices
The rate of exchange
There is a further aspect of the debate between Marshall and Edgeworth on indeterminacy which is worth considering. Marshall's analysis, contained in his chapter on the 'temporary equilibrium of demand and supply' (1961, pp. 331–6), explicitly assumed that some trading could take place at disequilibrium prices. These were later called 'false' prices by Hicks (1939). This assumption is very different indeed from Edgeworth's recontracting process (examined in more detail in Chapter 11 below) in which provisional bargains are made, but can be broken costlessly following subsequent negotiations. Even with small numbers, Edgeworth's

traders find their way to the point on the contract curve which represents a *final settlement*, without actually trading. At the final settlement no trader can be made better off without another being worse off, so recontracting comes to an end. All trading takes place at the final settlement and the associated rate of exchange is measured by the slope of a line drawn from the initial endowment point to the appropriate point on the contract curve. Edgeworth's argument was that without price-taking behaviour and with only a small number of traders, the rate of exchange reflected in the final settlement is indeterminate, since all points on the contract curve qualify as final settlements.

As so often is the case with Marshall, he concealed the detail of his argument from the reader. What he appears to have had in mind is a process in which traders attempt to sell as much as possible of their stock of goods at high prices. Purchasers are effectively price-takers and initial trades are made at what is now referred to as the 'short end' of the market, that is, the minimum of demand and supply (in this case demand). The price is gradually reduced until a price-taking equilibrium is found where demand and supply are equal. Hence there is a sequence of trades, giving rise to changes in individuals' endowments. In Edgeworth's framework, the endowment point therefore moves from a corner of the Edgeworth box to a point on the contract curve. The path taken depends on the sequence of prices, depending, as Marshall put it, on who 'gets the better in the "higgling and bargaining" of the market' (1961, I, p. 333).

In the general case, the final rate of exchange which produces a price-taking equilibrium, equal to the common marginal rate of substitution of individuals at the relevant point on the contract curve, will not equal that which would generate a price-taking equilibrium given the initial endowments. Marshall refers to the latter as the 'true equilibrium price: because if it were fixed on at the beginning, and adhered to throughout, it would exactly equate demand and supply' (1961, I, p. 333).

Marshall's special assumptions produce, however, the result that the final exchange rate is always the same as the 'true equilibrium price', irrespective of the sequence of trades and thus the path of the endowment point. This result can be obtained as follows. From equations (10.1) and (10.2) it can be seen that the slope of each individual's indifference curve, $-(\partial U/\partial x)/(\partial U/\partial y)$, is independent of y since it depends only on the value of x. Since x is constant all along the contract curve, it follows that the indifference curves have the same slope at all points on the contract curve. Hence the final price resulting from Marshall's sequence of disequilibrium prices must be the same at all points on the contract curve. The only thing that varies is the total amount of good Y traded. In a letter to Edgeworth, Berry described the result as follows:

Although the position on the contract curve is indeterminate, yet the quantity x, of one commodity, and the rate of exchange dy/dx are determinate; the only thing which is indeterminate being y.

i.e. in the case of money, the volume of commodity sold and final price are determinate, but the total amount of money which changes hands is indeterminate. (Marshall, 1961, II, p. 794)

This statement by Berry is much more explicit than anything in Marshall's chapter, but Edgeworth had already recognized these results in his review, while at the same time arguing that it is not appropriate to describe the model as 'determinate'. It is an indication of the relationship between these two economists that Edgeworth did not press his point, even though he was strictly correct in his view that Marshall's special assumptions did not remove indeterminacy. Soon after Marshall died, Edgeworth prepared a translation of his Italian review for inclusion in his *Papers Relating to Political Economy*. In his introduction, Edgeworth suggested that 'the term "determinate" is used by Marshall in a somewhat different sense from that which I have adopted. Apropos, it may be remarked that there is a certain indeterminateness about the use of the term "determinate" by economists' (1925, II, p. 313). He was therefore able to have the last word.

The 'Edgeworth' process
In the review of Marshall's book mentioned above, Edgeworth produced a diagrammatic presentation of the process of moving from the initial endowment point to a point on the contract curve, where trading at 'false' prices is allowed. He argued that the process must end at a point on the contract curve, but that the point depends on the precise path taken. Marshall reproduced the diagram in his appendix on barter, but perhaps surprisingly he did not adapt it to his special assumptions. Edgeworth's description of the process has led some later commentators to argue incorrectly that his own recontracting process allowed for trade to take place before the final settlement is reached. Neither Edgeworth with his recontracting, nor Walras with his *tatonnement* process, allowed trade to take place before the final settlement. The characterization of Marshall's process by Edgeworth has nevertheless come to be known as the 'Edgeworth process', though it is obviously a misnomer. In fact the details of the process were stated much more clearly in a neglected paper by Johnson (1913), who did not bother to refer to any other authors. He described the sequence as follows:

If the two parties make a succession of contracts with one another *on alterable terms*, a crooked price-line will represent their transactions, in which the conclusion of each contract is represented by the point where the price-line . . . drawn from the point representing the conclusion of the previous contract *touches* a utility curve of *one* of the two parties earlier than one of the *other*.

> Further, as long as the next section lies *between* the two utility curves, further exchanges are made, since they add to the utility of both parties; but, when finally the new section of the price-line touches both the utility curves simultaneously, exchange ceases ... The construction of the ordinary supply or demand curves is based on the assumption that the whole exchange is transacted on *unaltered* terms. (1913, p. 100)

An important feature of this process is therefore that each stage or iteration of the sequence involves Pareto improvements. Johnson was careful not only to explain this aspect, but he also explicitly described the use of trading at the 'short end' of the market. He did not attempt to justify this feature, but it obviously arises from the impossibility of forcing any individual either to buy or sell more than desired at any price. Johnson's diagram, unlike Edgeworth's, showed parts of the appropriate indifference curves at each intermediate trade, but unfortunately it was not well drawn and shows curves that will intersect.

An example of two disequilibrium trades is shown in Figure 10.2, where the endowment moves from E to E_1, and then to E_2. With a price line represented by EP, there is an excess supply of good X and trade takes place at E_1. The price of X must be lowered in order to induce person B to purchase more. At a price represented by the line E_1P_1 through the new endowment point, the excess supply is lower than formerly and trade takes place at E_2, It is clear that person A is better off, the slower is the fall in the price of X relative to Y at each stage.

The combination of Pareto-efficient moves at each stage, combined with an excess supply leading to a price reduction, and vice versa, produces a stable process that converges to an equilibrium on the contract curve. However, it is important to recognize that an arbitrarily imposed price change may not produce an equilibrium; the process must allow for sufficiently small changes in the price in the region of equilibrium to avoid continual oscillations either side of the equilibrium.

Some examples
The above discussion has suggested that the range of final settlements on the contract curve depends significantly on the initial price at which disequilibrium trading begins and the extent to which the price changes in response to an excess supply. The orders of magnitude involved can only be obtained using a numerical procedure. Consider Marshall's assumptions combined with the forms for U_1 and U_2 used to derive equation (10.4), giving the solution for x. Allowing for changes in endowments as a result of trading at 'false' prices requires the utility functions to be written as:

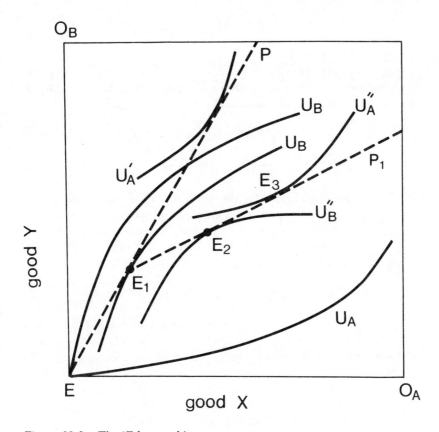

Figure 10.2   The 'Edgeworth' process

$$U_A = (a_A - x)^\gamma + \alpha(y + b_A) \tag{10.6}$$

and

$$U_B = (x + a_B)^\sigma + \beta(b_B - y) \tag{10.7}$$

In these equations, a_A and b_A represent the stocks of X and Y respectively held by person A at each stage in the process, and similarly for person B, with initial values given by $b_A = a_B = 0$ and $a_A = a, b_B = b$. The slopes of the indifference curves are given by:

$$\frac{-\partial U_A/\partial_x}{\partial U_A/\partial_y} = \frac{\gamma}{\alpha}(a_A - x)^{\gamma-1} \tag{10.8}$$

$$\frac{-\partial U_B/\partial_x}{\partial U_B/\partial_y} = \frac{\sigma}{\beta}(x + a_B)^{\sigma-1}$$

(10.9)

So that if the price of good X relative to good Y is denoted by p, the respective demands for good X are obtained by setting the price equal to the slope of the indifference curve and rearranging to get

$$x_A = a_A - (\alpha p/\gamma)^{1/(\gamma-1)}$$

(10.10)

$$x_B = (\beta p/\sigma)^{1/(\sigma-1)} - a_B$$

(10.11)

Starting with an initial value of p, the smallest of x_A and x_B determines the amount traded and then p is increased if $x_A < x_B$ and vice versa. New values of x_A and x_B are then obtained for adjusted endowments a_A and a_B. The amount of good Y traded is given simply by $y = px$ where x is the amount of x traded. An equilibrium is obtained when $x_A = x_B$, whence:

$$a = (\alpha p/\gamma)^{1/(\gamma-1)} + (\beta p/\sigma)^{1/(\gamma-1)}$$

(10.12)

with $a = a_A + a_B$. The equilibrium price is thus the root of (10.12). It is clear from this equation that, although even in this simple model p cannot be solved explicitly, its value is independent of the endowments of the individuals.

Consider also the pre-trade indifference curves of each individual, given that person A begins with all the stocks of X and B has all the initial stocks of good Y. The equations of the indifference curves are thus:

$$\text{for A: } y = \{a - (a - x)^\gamma\}/\alpha$$

(10.13)

$$\text{for B: } y = x^\sigma/\beta$$

(10.14)

Hence the limits of the contract curve between the pre-trade indifference curves can be obtained by substituting the root of (10.4), which gives the constant value of x along the vertical contract curve, into (10.13) and (10.14).

Suppose that γ, α, σ, β take the values of 0.5, 0.8, 0.3 and 0.9 respectively, and that $a = b = 1$. It is found that the equilibrium price, irrespective of the sequence of trades, is equal to 0.752 and that the amount of good X traded in total is 0.31. The limits of the contract curve are given by $y = 0.211$ and $y = 0.781$. If the price of 0.752 were imposed at the outset, then an amount equal to $(.752)(.31) = 0.233$ of good Y would be traded. This case is illustrated in Figure 10.3.

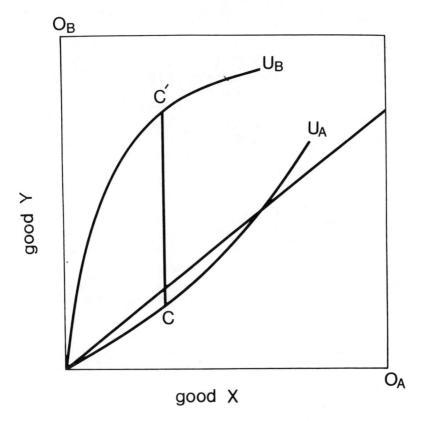

Figure 10.3   Marshall's special case

It might be thought that the restriction to Pareto improvements at each iteration of the process would reduce the range of indeterminacy in the amount of good Y traded in total. The following question thus arises: Starting with the highest price possible for good X, given B's willingness to trade at all, would the process of gradually dropping the price, until the contract curve is reached, eliminate the highest point of the contract curve in Figure 10.3 from the range of feasible trades? Given an assumption of continuity, allowing for 'very small' amounts traded at each iteration and 'very small' price reductions, it is found that in fact the previous limits cannot be ruled out.

The final trading position moves closer to the price-taking equilibrium, where $p = .752$ is imposed right at the beginning, the quicker the price adjusts and the closer to the equilibrium it begins. While these statements are quite obvious, is it found that in this model there is an asymmetric effect of taking different starting prices. For very small price adjustments, if the price starts advantageously for B, at 0.05, the final settlement is virtually at the limit of the contract curve so that B obtains nearly all the gains from trade. With the starting price of good Y lower, so that p is initially 0.2, person A still ends up holding only 0.212 of good Y. But if the price begins advantageously for person A, at 20, then A ends up with 0.649 of good Y, which is some way in from the upper limit of the contract curve. When the starting value of p is set at 10 and 5 respectively, the final amount of y held by A is reduced to 0.603 and 0.539 respectively. To get to the upper limit of the contract curve requires an extremely high initial price of good X. The reason for this asymmetric effect can be seen by considering the shapes of the no-trade indifference curves of each individual. It is a characteristic of Marshall's special assumptions.

This so-called 'Edgeworth process' in which adjustments at each iteration are restricted to being Pareto improvements, is not the only type of procedure that may be envisaged. It is possible to consider processes in which an individual may be prepared to engage in a trade which reduces utility in the 'short run', with the prospect of securing a better position in subsequent trades. This type of analysis is, however, beyond the scope of the present volume.

Notes and further reading

In considering Marshall's influence on Edgeworth's interest in the application of his analysis to trade unions, Edgeworth's copy of Marshall and Marshall (1879), now held by the University of Kansas library as part of the magnificent collection assembled by R.S. Howey, is of interest. A reference to this copy was made by Howey (1960, p. 239. n.29). The word 'indeterminate' is written in the margin on p. 210, where the effects of unions on wages is discussed. But it cannot be claimed with certainty that it is Edgeworth's handwriting, and the book was in the circulating section of the Kansas Library for nearly 30 years before being placed in the Special Collections' closed stack. Edgeworth also referred to Marshall and Marshall (1879) in *Mathematical Psychics* (1881, pp. 136–7). Edgeworth's stress on the widespread importance of indeterminacy and the applicability of his own analysis was stated as follows. He suggested that the analysis of contract provided, 'a sort of unification likely to be distasteful to those excellent persons who are always dividing the one into the many, but do not appear very ready to subsume the many under the one' (1881, p. 146). Here he is seen to be using the Platonic motto of *Industry and Trade* 38 years before Marshall. It is surprising that, with respect to Edgeworth's stress on the indeterminacy of wages in union and employer bargaining, Hicks (1932, p. 26, n.2) wrote, 'Edgeworth did not himself imagine that his proposition was very important in practice'. The wage bargaining situation corresponds more closely to that of bilateral monopoly (a monopolist in a goods market buying inputs from a monopolistic supplier), which Bowley examined in some detail.

Leontief's (1946) paper on union bargaining is rather curious as in virtually all its essential arguments it did not go beyond the position reached by Edgeworth in 1881. Furthermore, Leontief did not refer to a single book or article, yet Dunlop (1944, p. viii) mentioned that several of his chapters had been read by Leontief. The main purpose of Leontief's paper was to make the point that both wage and employment must be subject to negotiation if bargains are to be efficient. This was not original, but more recent writers on union bargaining have emphasized this contribution to the neglect of the earlier literature.

For a further example of Marshall's ability to write rather strong letters, see his treatment of Sidgwick in Sidgwick and Sidgwick (1906, pp. 394–5), which was perhaps even more harsh than his letter to Edgeworth. This is despite the fact that Marshall at one time described Sidgwick as his 'spiritual father and mother'. The debate is also examined in Newman (1990), who is very unsympathetic to both Marshall and Edgeworth. On Marshall's model see also Samuelson (1942) and Walker (1967).

Hicks (1939, pp. 127–9) provides a useful brief discussion of Marshall's treatment of price determination. He points out that trading at false prices involves 'wealth effects', which are ruled out by the assumption of constant marginal utility. Marshall regarded his assumption of constant marginal utility of income as being 'in accordance with the actual conditions of most markets' (1961, I, p. 334) and 'justifiable with regard to most of the market dealings with which we are practically concerned' (1961, I, p. 335). The exception he discussed was the labour market. He seemed to believe that the assumption was justified because 'when a person buys anything for his own consumption, he generally spends on it a small part of his total resources'.

Suppose that instead of Marshall's assumptions, the utility functions are of the Cobb–Douglas form:

$$U_A = (a_A - x)^\gamma (y + b_A)^\alpha \tag{10.15}$$

$$U_B = (x + a_B)^\sigma (b_B - y)^\beta \tag{10.16}$$

where initially person A holds the majority of good X and person B holds the majority of good Y, with $a_A + a_B = a$ and $b_A + b_B = b$. In this case it can be found that the equilibrium price, p, is proportional to the ratio of the amounts of the goods available and is given by:

$$p = \frac{a\alpha(\beta + \sigma)}{b\sigma(\alpha + \gamma)} \tag{10.17}$$

and the equation of the contract curve is:

$$y = b\{1 + k\,(a/x - 1)^{-1}\}^{-1} \tag{10.18}$$

At each stage of the process of trading at false prices, the demands for X are given by:

$$x_A = a_A - \frac{\gamma(pa_A + b_A)}{p(\alpha + \gamma)} \tag{10.19}$$

$$x_B = \frac{\sigma(pa_B + b_B)}{p(\beta + \sigma)} - a_B \tag{10.20}$$

The amount traded at each iteration is equal to the minimum of x_A and x_B. If the parameters γ, α, σ, and β take the values 0.3, 0.5, 0.6 and 0.4 respectively, and if $a = b = 1$, with $a_A = 0.9$ and $b_A = 0.1$, it can be found that the price-taking equilibrium relative price of X to that of Y is equal to 0.959. Unlike Marshall's special case, the result of trading at 'false' prices is to produce a different price ratio, depending on the adjustment path taken towards equilibrium. Examples are shown in Figure 10.4 for alternative initial price ratios. In each case the price adjustment at each stage was specified to be an arbitrarily small amount, in order to ensure convergence. When, for example, the initial price ratio is set at 10, the final equilibrium price is equal to 0.744. At the other extreme, when the price begins at 0.1, the equilibrium becomes 1.225. The result of taking alternative starting prices, favourable to either person A or B, can be seen to be more symmetric than in Marshall's special case. There is an extensive literature on alternative adjustment process and their convergence properties. Useful starting points are papers in Eatwell, Milgate and Newman (1989).

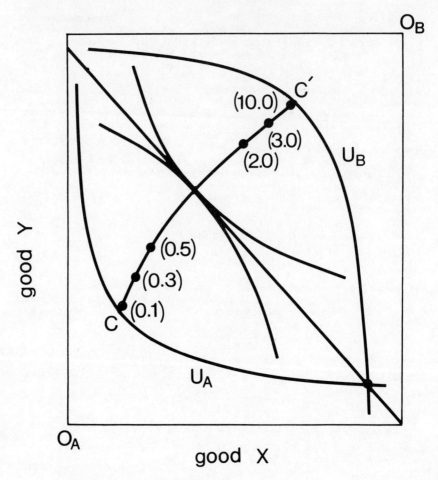

Figure 10.4   Cobb–Douglas utility functions

11 Competition and efficiency

When individuals do not regard prices as being outside their control, that is when they are not price-takers; the typical situation is one in which the rate of exchange is indeterminate. This is particularly evident in the context of trade or barter between two individuals. Many writers before Edgeworth were well aware of this aspect of barter, but concentrated on the nature of price-taking equilibria in a static framework. It has been shown in Chapter 10 that Marshall, who wished both to avoid indeterminacy and allow for the dynamic adjustment of prices with disequilibrium trading at the 'short end' of the market, produced an ingenious special case in which the equilibrium price is independent of the adjustment path and the total amount of one good traded is determinate. But he could not remove the indeterminacy in the total amount of the other good traded, which depends on the precise path of price adjustments towards equilibrium. The central question which Edgeworth tried to resolve in the second part of *Mathematical Psychics* was that of the conditions necessary to remove this type of indeterminacy. However, Edgeworth restricted his attention to a model in which no trade takes place out of equilibrium; that is, before a 'final settlement' is reached. The question naturally arises as to the extent to which this indeterminacy is the result of the absence of competition in the simple two-person market. Edgeworth thus quickly moved on to the introduction of further traders. His analysis of this problem, completed in just a few pages, is not easy to follow. Section 11.1 therefore provides a simplified exposition of the role of the number of traders.

The existence of indeterminacy gives rise to a need for arbitration. Jevons had made this point quite explicitly when he suggested, 'it may be that indeterminate bargains of this kind are best arranged by an arbitrator or third party' (1957, p. 125). While some economists, such as Marshall, suggested that the process of arbitration should attempt to replicate a competitive outcome, Edgeworth gave special emphasis to the application of the utilitarian principle of maximizing the sum of individual utilities. This is the subject of Section 11.2. By showing that competitive equilibria are on the contract curve, Edgeworth provided a more rigorous basis for the idea that competition is in some sense efficient, though of course there are infinitely many other efficient allocations. He was also able to provide a rationale for the acceptance by individuals of the use of utilitarian principle, thereby resolving a long-standing problem of utilitarianism.

Subsequent literature was not always clear on this issue, as shown in Section 11.3.

11.1 The role of numbers
The recontracting process
Edgeworth began his analysis by introducing his stylized description of the process of barter, the famous recontracting process. Edgeworth did not assume that individuals begin with perfect knowledge. This contrasts with Jevons's treatment, which explicitly assumed complete knowledge and product divisibility. Edgeworth continued to assume divisibility but instead of assuming initial perfect knowledge he supposed that, 'There is free communication throughout a *normal* competitive field. You might suppose that constituent individuals collected at a point, or connected by telephones – an ideal supposition, but suficiently approximate to existence or tendency for the purposes of abstract science' (1881, p. 18). The knowledge of the other traders' dispositions and resources could then be obtained by the formation of tentative contracts which are not assumed to involve actual transfers, and can be broken when further information is obtained. Edgeworth introduced this in typical style:

> 'Is it peace or war?' asks the lover of 'Maud', of economic *competition*, and answers hastily: it is both, *pax* or *pact* between contractors during contract, *war*, when some of the contractors *without the consent of others recontract*. (1881, p. 17)

(The allusion here is to Alfred Tennyson's poem 'Maud; a Monodrama', part I, verse VII.) An important role of the recontracting process is thus to disseminate information among traders. It allows individuals who initially agree to a contract, which is not on the contract curve, to discover that an opportunity exists for making an improved contract whereby at least one person can gain without another suffering. Edgeworth's stylized process does not direct attention to the role of information, or other well-known market imperfections, but provides a mechanism by which traders eventually reach a point on the contract curve. Edgeworth's process is therefore not really dynamic at all, in the sense that no exchanges take place out of equilibrium. It shares this characteristic with Walras's *tatonnement* process, which provides a different type of *deus ex machina* for the determination of a set of equilibrium prices in a price-taking context. But Edgeworth's process is broader and provides more insight into the properties of competitive equilibria.

A very important and innovative feature of the recontracting process is the fact that it makes it possible to analyse the use of collusion among some of the traders. Several individuals are thus allowed to form coalitions in order to improve bargaining strength and thereby improve each individual's gain from exchange. Recontracting enables the coalitions to be broken up by outsiders who may attract members of a group with more favourable terms of exchange. Edgeworth's procedure was clearly stated as follows:

> It is not necessary to resolve analytically the composite mechanism of a *competitive field*. It will suffice to proceed synthetically, observing in a simple typical case the effect of continually introducing into the field additional competitors. (1881, p. 34)

The remarkable result then follows, as seen below, that the process of bargaining by forming and breaking coalitions will lead, if there is a sufficiently large number of individuals, to a settlement in which each person behaves as if he is responding *independently* to a specified rate of exchange. *The bargaining solution turns out to be equivalent to the price-taking equilibrium.*

Two pairs of traders
Edgeworth began by introducing a second person A and a second person B, where the new traders are assumed to be exact replicas of the initial pair, having the same tastes and endowments. This simplification is very useful because it enables the same diagram to be used as when only two traders are considered. Two basic points can be stated immediately. The first is that in the final settlement all individuals will be at a common point in the Edgeworth box. The second basic point is that the settlement must be on the contract curve. These two results were clearly stated by Edgeworth as follows:

> It is evident that there cannot be equilibrium unless (1) all the field is collected at one point; (2) that point is on the *contract curve*. For (1) if possible let one couple be at one point, and another couple at another point. It will generally be the interest of the [A] of one couple and the [B] of the other to rush together, leaving their partners in the lurch. And (2) if the common point is not on the contract-curve, it will be the interest of all parties to descend to the contract-curve. (1881, p. 35)

The question at issue is whether the range of indeterminacy is reduced by the addition of these additional traders. Consider Figure 11.1 and suppose that when A_1 and B_1 are trading independently of A_2 and B_2, trader B_1 has all the bargaining power and is able to appropriate all the gains from trade by pushing A_1 to the limit of the contract curve at point C. Suppose also that the same applies to A_2 and B_2. If the two pairs of traders are then able to communicate with each other, the question arises

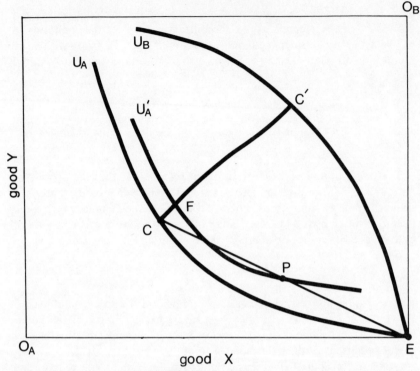

Figure 11.1   Two pairs of traders

of whether it is still possible for the Bs to push the As to the extreme of the contract curve.

With A_1 and B_1 at C, it can be seen that A_2 can now simply refuse to trade with B_2 at C. With no transaction costs, A_2 was previously indifferent between trading at C and consuming at the endowment position, E. This endowment position was effectively the 'threat point' of the As: it is the position in which they would find themselves if the bargaining process broke down. But A_2 can now trade with A_1, after A_1 has traded with B_1 and has therefore obtained some of good Y, rather than remain in isolation. Many different trades are of course possible; indeed, it would be possible to produce a separate Edgeworth box to describe the trades between A_1 and A_2. But consider situations in which the two As share their stocks of X and Y equally. In view of the assumption that they have identical tastes, such an equal division maximizes their total utility and at the same time places the two As at a point on their own contract curve, not shown in Figure 11.1. (This result is clarified in the next section and the notes at the end of this chapter.)

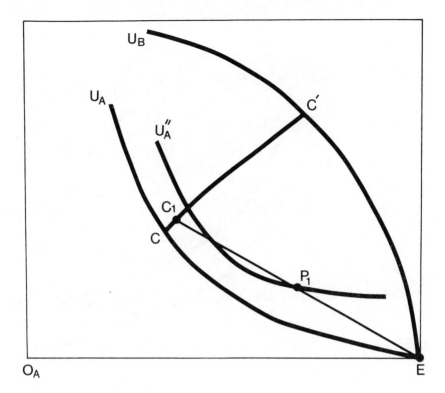

Figure 11.2   A new contract

The two As can thus share their resources and consume at point P in Figure 11.1, which is half way between C and the initial endowment point E. The convexity of the indifference curves implies that they are both better off than anywhere on the no-trade indifference curve. Trader B_2 who has been 'left out in the cold' cannot prevent such a bargain. Thus B_1 is at C, both As are at P and B_2 is at E. In this situation B_1 has no incentive to change, but B_2 has a strong incentive to offer a better deal to one of the As than that obtained by trader B_1. So long as B_2 offers one of the As, say A_2, a trade on the contract curve which allows A_2 to reach a higher indifference curve than U'_A, then the initial agreement with B_1 will be broken and recontracting will take place.

A new set of contracts is shown in Figure 11.2 whereby B_2 and A_2 deal at C_1. The two As then share their stocks in order to consume at point P_1 (which is half way between C_1 and E), allowing them to reach the higher indifference curve U''_A. Notice that C_1 does not need to be to the right of point F in Figure 11.1; all that is required is that the point C_1 (in Figure

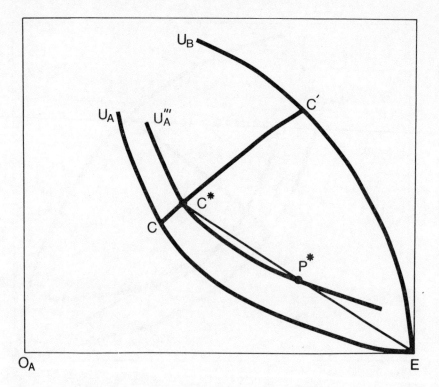

Figure 11.3   The new limit to the contract curve

11.2) is such that U''_A is higher than U'_A. Trader B_1 is now left out in the cold at point E. The ability of the As to turn to someone else, rather than deal with a single trader, means that the Bs now compete against each other. Trader B_1, who cannot prevent the recontracting, will then make a better offer, so that the iterative process continues.

The above stylized process will produce a final settlement at the point C* in Figure 11.3. This has the property that the indifference curve U'''_A passes through C* and P*, where P* is half way between C* and E. This means that the two As are indifferent between C* and P*, and since they cannot reach any point between C* and P* along C*E, they are unable to improve on C*. Hence there is no need to leave one of the Bs 'in the cold', and the two Bs will trade with the two As at point C*; any A can trade separately with one of the Bs at that point.

This argument has shown that at the final settlement all traders are at a common point on the contract curve and the limit has moved inwards along the old contract curve. The analysis can of course be repeated by

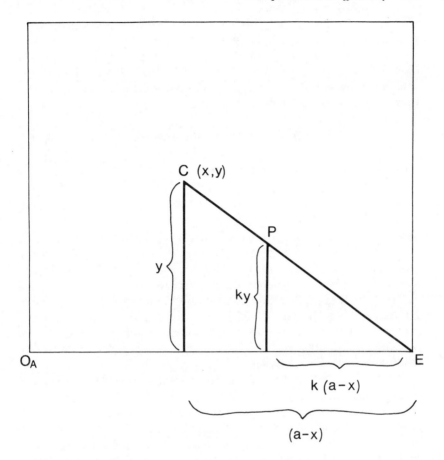

Figure 11.4   Many traders

starting with an alternative situation whereby the As initially appropriate all the gains from trade. The point C′ would then no longer qualify as a point on the new contract curve.

Many pairs of traders
The extent to which the contract curve shrinks is influenced by the fact that the As cannot get further than half way along a ray from a point on the contract curve to the endowment position. What if there are additional pairs of trades? Suppose that in Figure 11.4 there are N pairs of traders and $(N-1)$ Bs deal with $(N-1)$ As at the point C, which has coordinates (x,y). The Nth A leaves the Nth B in isolation at E and shares with the

$(N-1)$ As who have traded with the other Bs. The As can now get to point P, which is a proportion, k, along the ray from E to C.

The As thus consume a total amount of good Y equal to Nky. The $(N-1)$ Bs consume $(N-1)(b-y)$ of good Y, since they each give up y, while the remaining B consumes the initial endowment, b. Total consumption must equal the total amount available, so that:

$$Nb = (N-1)(b-y) + b + Nky \qquad (11.1)$$

This can be used to solve for k, whereby:

$$k = (N-1)/N \qquad (11.2)$$

Thus when $N=2$, $k=1/2$ as earlier; when $N=3$, $k=2/3$, and so on. As N increases, the value of k approaches unity. This means that the As can reach all the way from E to the contract curve and the final settlement must therefore be such that the indifference curve must be tangential to the ray from the origin. The condition shown in Figure 11.3 corresponding to very large N is such that C* and P* coincide at a point on the contract curve. The final settlement is therefore shown in Figure 11.5. The effect of 'working in' from the point C' would lead to an equivalent result for an indifference curve of the Bs.

The result is that the final settlement, with a large number of pairs of traders, looks just like a price-taking equilibrium. The result that a recontracting process with many traders leads to a price-taking equilibrium has some interesting implications about the use of prices in large economies. First, it shows that a price-taking equilibrium cannot be 'blocked' by a coalition of traders. In this sense the competitive equilibrium may be said to be stable (using the word in a different sense from that used when discussing price dynamics). Second, the use of an equilibrium set of prices provides a considerable reduction in the amount of information required by traders. Individuals only need to know the prices, whereas in the recontracting process they have to learn a considerable amount of information about other individuals' preferences and endowments.

Earlier discussions
Edgeworth's analysis of the role of numbers in competition was a remarkable step in the development of economic theory. Many earlier economists had of course noted the indeterminacy which results from barter between two individuals. Furthermore, on an intuitive level the idea that a single individual in a very large market can have no noticeable impact on the

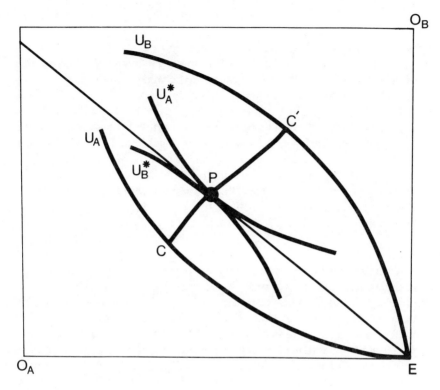

Figure 11.5 The final settlement with many traders

total supply and demand was readily accepted. Indeed, an early statement can be found in Cantillon's discussion of markets, where he says:

> Suppose that Butchers on one side and the Buyers on the other. The price of Meat will be settled after some altercations, and a pound of Beef will be in value to a piece of silver pretty nearly as the whole Beef offered for sale in the Market is to all the silver brought here to buy Beef.
> The proportion is come at by bargaining. The Butcher keeps up his Price according to the number of Buyers he sees; the buyers, on their side, offer less according as they think the Butcher will have less sale: the Price set by some is usually followed by others. Though this method of fixing market prices has no exact or geometric foundation . . . it does not seem that it could be done in any more convenient way. (1955, p. 117)

Useful discussions of barter also appear in the works of Beccaria, Turgot, Isnard, Gossen, Courcelle-Seneuil, Thornton and Menger. Although Edgeworth was familiar with some of these authors, the influence of Jevons and Marshall is clearly the most important in tracing a direct line of filiation. Gossen and Beccaria are only mentioned (in 1881) in the context of the greatest happiness principle.

More important is Courcelle-Seneuil, who Edgeworth quoted approvingly (1881, p. 30) in the context of determinacy in large markets, referring to his example of indeterminate exchange between a hunter and a woodman. In his later brief discussion of barter in Palgrave's *Dictionary of Political Economy*, Edgeworth praised Courcelle-Seneuil's discussion of additional traders. Courcelle-Seneuil in turn praised the work of Turgot, whose brilliant analysis was not, however, mentioned in *Mathematical Psychics*. Turgot's discussion, partly reproduced in Meek (1973, pp. 77–100), is without doubt of a very high quality in many respects, but its analysis of the role of numbers is highly suggestive rather than conclusive. Cournot's (1927) analysis, involving the introduction of additional firms into a monopoly until a competitive market is reached, was actually criticized by Edgeworth (1881, p. 47) for not allowing for indeterminacy when numbers are small.

A very interesting, though much maligned, contribution to the analysis of price determination was made by Canard (1801). The lower limit to the price is determined by the price of 'necessary labour' used in production, while for non-necessities Canard argued that the maximum price is that for which total revenue is a maximum. Between these limits is a 'latitude of price', with the actual price depending on the relative 'forces' of buyers and sellers. The force in turn is inversely proportional to the respective 'needs' to buy or sell and the extent of competition among buyers and sellers. With a monopoly the price is at the upper limit while competition among sellers reduces the price to its lower limit. Edgeworth did not refer to Canard in 1881, and in his brief entry in *Palgrave's Dictionary*, he simply quoted Cournot's (1927, p. 2) comment that Canard's 'pretended principles are so radically at fault and the application of them is so erroneous'.

Although the subject of indeterminacy had often been discussed before Edgeworth, along with the general idea that competition would reduce the range of indeterminacy, there is really nothing that comes close to Edgeworth in terms both of rigour and clarity of purpose.

11.2   Utility maximization

Edgeworth argued that in the absence of competition there is an urgent need for a principle of justice or arbitration in the 'universal sigh for articles of peace' (1881, p. 51). It is in this context that he explored the use of utilitarianism, where explicit interpersonal comparisons are required. Thus:

For moral calculus a further dimension is required; to compare the happiness of one person with the happiness of another, and generally the happiness of groups of different members and different average happiness. (1881, p. 7)

His attitude was that 'such comparisons can no longer be shirked' (1881, p. 7), since they are so often required in the consideration of practical problems. Questions of distribution were never far from Edgeworth's mind, and indeed this applies to many of his contemporaries who had approached economics via moral philosophy. To be nihilistic, as many later economists were to become, about distributional outcomes would have been unthinkable to Edgeworth. A similar view was taken by Marshall, who observed that:

It is useless to say that various gains and losses are incommensurable, and cannot be weighed against one another. For they must be, and in fact they are, weighed against one another before any deliberate decision is or can be reached on any issue. (Pigou, ed. 1925, p. 302)

Edgeworth did not minimize the problems involved in making such comparisons, though he often stressed the importance of 'sympathy' as the means by which individuals make inferences about the well-being of others. The importance of the utilitarian method of arbitration is that it results in a position on the contract curve, and is therefore efficient. This contrasts with a principle such as equal division, which is typically not efficient. Edgeworth's argument can be shown as follows.

Total utility and efficiency
Return to the context of a single pair of individuals where the total amounts of good X and Y available are denoted a and b respectively. It is convenient to define x and y as the amounts of the two goods consumed by the first individual, leaving $a-x$ and $b-y$ available to the second person. The allocation of goods that maximizes total utility, W, is given by:

$$W = U_1(x,y) + U_2(a-x, b-y) \qquad (11.3)$$

The first-order conditions require:

$$\partial W/\partial x = \partial U_1/\partial x + \partial U_2/\partial x = 0 \qquad (11.4)$$

$$\partial W/\partial y = \partial U_1/\partial y + \partial U_2/\partial y = 0 \qquad (11.5)$$

Multiply (11.4) by $\partial U_1/\partial y$ and (11.5) by $\partial U_1/\partial x$, subtract the resulting equations and rearrange to get:

$$\frac{\partial U_1/\partial x}{\partial U_1/\partial y} = \frac{\partial U_2/\partial x}{\partial U_2/\partial y} \tag{11.6}$$

This is of course the equation of the contract curve, so that the solution to (11.6) must therefore be a point on the contract curve. The importance of this result to Edgeworth cannot be exaggerated. As he said:

> It is a circumstance of momentous interest that one of the in general indefinitely numerous settlements between contractors is the utilitarian arrangement . . . the contract tending to the greatest possible total utility of the contractors. (1881, p. 53)

He had of course also demonstrated that the competitive, price-taking, equilibrium is on the contract curve. Thus competition might be viewed as a kind of impersonal arbitrator, simultaneously setting the rate of exchange and the distribution of the gains from exchange. The utilitarian position will not coincide with the price-taking equilibrium; in general there is no reason why the two approaches should yield the same position on the contract curve. A further analysis of the difference between these alternative positions, including a comparison with Nash bargaining equilibria, is given in Appendix B.

Edgeworth (1881, p. 53, n.1) pointed out that the argument demonstrating that the utilitarian solution is somewhere on the contract curve is not affected by the existence of sympathy. If the contractors are not entirely egoistic, but actuated 'by a sympathy for each other's interests' then the range of indeterminacy will also be reduced, although the rest of the contract curve remains as before. This may be seen by setting the first person's objective at $U_1 + \lambda U_2$ and that of the second person at $U_2 + \mu U_1$. It can be shown that in this case the contract curve is given by

$$\frac{\partial U_1/\partial x + \lambda \partial U_2/\partial x}{\partial U_1/\partial y + \lambda \partial U_2/\partial y} = \frac{\partial U_2/\partial x + \mu \partial U_1/\partial x}{\partial U_2/\partial y + \lambda \partial U_1/\partial y} \tag{11.7}$$

which can be rearranged to give the same result as in the standard case. Thus sympathy simply reduces the range of indeterminacy, along the same contract curve as in the case of egoism. Thus Edgeworth's main argument covers the whole range of impure (egoistic) to pure (universalistic) hedonism. However, in discussing the utilitarian solution as a principle of arbitration in indeterminate contract, Edgeworth did not clearly indicate in 1881 that the utilitarian solution of maximum total utility could specify a position which makes one of the parties worse off than in the no-trade situation. This was nevertheless later made explicit when, after proposing arbitration along utilitarian lines, he added, '. . . subject to the condition that neither should lose by the contract' (1925, II, p. 102). This possibility of course depends largely on the initial endowments of the individuals.

Justification of utilitarianism

Edgeworth recognized that although it could be shown that the utilitarian solution is on the contract curve, this result was not sufficient to justify the use of utilitarianism as a principle of arbitration. The contract curve defines a *range* of positions. It is only a necessary condition of a principle of arbitration that it should place the parties on the contract curve. If they are not on the contract curve, then of course at least one party can gain without the other losing and the arbitration would not be stable. Edgeworth's justification for utilitarianism as a principle of justice, comparing points along the contract curve, was as follows:

> Now these positions lie in a *reverse order of desirability* for each party; and it may seem to each that as he cannot have his own way, in the absence of any definite principle of selection, he has about as good a chance of one of the arrangements as another . . . both parties may agree to commute their chance of any of the arrangements for . . . the utilitarian arrangement. (1881, p. 55)

The important point to stress about this statement is that Edgeworth clearly viewed distributive justice in terms of choice under uncertainty. He argued that the contractors, faced with uncertainty about their prospects, would choose to accept an arrangement along utilitarian lines. A crucial component of this argument, also clearly stated by Edgeworth in this quotation, is the use of equal a priori probabilities; this is the suggestion that 'each party . . . has about as good a chance of one of the arrangements as another'. Edgeworth was extremely conscious about the wide gulf between theory and practice, but the importance to him of this new justification of utilitarianism cannot be exaggerated. Indeed the whole of *Mathematical Psychics* seems to be imbued with a feeling of excitement generated by his discovery of a justification based on a 'social contract'.

Edgeworth clearly believed that he had provided an answer to an age-old question that had defeated so many earlier utilitarians. Thus he stated that, 'by what mechanism the force of self-love can be applied so as to support the structure of utilitarian politics, neither Helvetius, nor Bentham, nor any deductive egoist has made clear' (1881, p. 128). This feature was, however, ignored for many years. It was even overlooked when, following the development of the von Neumann–Morgenstern approach to choice under uncertainty, major restatements of utilitarianism along the same lines were made by Harsanyi (1953) and Vickrey (1960). This approach is now usually described as 'contractarian neo-utilitarianism'.

11.3   Later analyses

It has been seen that Edgeworth, having defined the contract curve as a locus of efficient exchanges, showed that each competitive equilibrium is one of the points along the contract curve. He went on to argue that this point does not necessarily coincide with the arrangement that maximizes the sum of individual utilities, although the latter is also on the contract curve (ignoring, as Edgeworth did for most of his discussion, the possibility that one of the parties may be made worse off relative to the no-trade position, depending on the distribution of initial endowments).

The modern textbook treatments of welfare economics now usually concentrate on the first statement above, where it is said that each competitive equilibrium is one of an infinite number of 'Pareto efficient' allocations (defined to include the complete set of allocations, rather than only efficient *exchanges*). Interpersonal comparisons of welfare are now the responsibility of a social welfare function, which specifies the appropriate point on a utility possibility curve for the achievement of maximum social welfare. These issues have now been clarified and are included in any serious training in economics. It is, however, of some interest to see that the general clarification of these points in the literature did not follow in quite so straightforward a manner; indeed, there was much confusion and Edgeworth's contribution was neglected even by those who admired his work. The main figures are Walras, Launhardt, Pareto and Wicksell, and as in many economic debates it is not a straightforward matter to distinguish the problems of logic from those of logomachy.

Walras, Launhardt and Wicksell

The debate was often framed in terms of the question of whether or not government intervention could improve upon the competitive equilibrium, but it was often confused by the lack of a clear distinction among types of gain. It was not always clear whether the discussion concerned the relative maximum utility of each individual constrained by facing fixed prices, the total gains from trade, or the total utility resulting from the final allocation of goods. Walras (in the second edition of the *Elements*) criticized Gossen essentially for confusing the competitive equilibrium with the utilitarian maximum. However, the difficulty and often the lack of clarity of Walras's writing seems to have led Launhardt (1885) to accuse Walras of wrongly suggesting that the competitive equilibrium maximizes total utility after exchange. Wicksell also accused Walras of giving 'in several passages . . . a wrong or at least misleading formulation' (1893, p. 19), and went on to say that, 'it would indeed be the remarkable attribute of free exchange to call forth the greatest possible economic gain or total satisfaction' (1893, p. 13). However, Wicksell later defended Walras against such an accusation, and it does indeed seem that Walras had only constrained, or relative, utility maximization in mind. This view is indeed supported by the (above mentioned) note on Gossen where Walras said that the position of maximum total utility 'is not the relative maximum utility of free competition' (1874, p. 205). Interpretation of Walras is of course complicated by the fact that, as Robbins suggested, 'no one would contend that the exposition of the [*Elements*] . . . is a model of expository clarity' (in Wicksell, 1934, Introduction, p. xi).

Wicksell was, however, less generous to Launhardt. Wicksell (1893, p. 67) gave a numerical example where the gains from exchange, for two price-taking individuals in equilibrium, are equal. He noted that Launhardt gave a similar example, recognizing that he was dealing with a special case. But Wicksell later accused Launhardt of arguing that competition actually maximizes total utility (see 1893, p. 76, n.2; 1934, p. 81, n.1). Wicksell's inconsistency is difficult to explain, especially as Launhardt's purpose was precisely to show that maximum total utility is only attained in competition under very special circumstances (see Hutchison, 1953, pp. 187–8). The point was recognized quite clearly by Pantaleoni (1889, p. 161, n.1) who cited Launhardt and Marshall as providing caution, 'against the mistake of inferring . . . that [the competitive equilibrium] coincides necessarily with that which realises the maximum of general happiness'.

Pareto and Wicksell
Wicksell was more consistent in his criticisms of Pareto's *Cours*. He argued that, 'throughout the book [Pareto] reasons as if the gain from exchange were at an absolute maximum under free competition, and that, moreover, it is so for each trading subject (which actually involves a mathematical absurdity)' (1958, p. 143). Wicksell justified his argument using the same kind of mathematical analysis as in the *Lectures* (1934, p. 81), and also criticized Pareto for not having read Marshall's *Principles* sufficiently carefully (especially the latter's analysis of decreasing cost industries). In reviewing the *Manuel*, Wicksell later criticized Pareto's now famous criterion, according to which welfare is maximized, and argued that Pareto had not clearly recognized that it is satisfied at an infinite number of points, one of which is actually a welfare minimum rather than a maximum (1958, p. 168). Wicksell's criticism was of course quite valid, and it is worth noting that what is now called the Pareto criterion of efficiency was initially proposed by Pareto as his definition of what he thought of as a unique maximum social welfare; to say that 'the contract curve is a locus of Pareto efficient allocations' therefore distorts historical perspective somewhat. Pareto's errors arose partly, Wicksell argued, because of his failure to give sufficient emphasis to indeterminacy in

exchange. Thus Edgeworth's contribution in this area marks a significant improvement that was not noticeably extended for many years.

Notes and further reading

It has been stated that neither Edgeworth nor Walras allowed trade to take place out of equilibrium, but it should be acknowledged that there is a long (and rather confused) literature debating this issue. For a flavour of this, see Jaffé (1983) and Menard (1990) along with the associated commentary.

In considering the effects of introducing additional pairs of traders, in section 11.1 above, equal division between identical As was assumed. Thus, with two pairs of As and Bs and after A_1 had traded with B_1, the trade between A_1 and A_2 was assumed to result in an equal sharing of their total endowment. Suppose that two individuals have utility functions $x^{\beta_1} y^{\gamma_1}$ and $x^{\beta_2} y^{\gamma_2}$ and that amounts a and b of goods X and Y are available. With the axes representing consumption, rather than amounts exchanged, the consumption of x and y by the first person leaves $a - x$ and $b - y$ for the second person to consume. The equation of the contract curve is given by $(\partial U_1/\partial x)/(\partial U_1/\partial y) = (\partial U_2/\partial x)/(\partial U_2/\partial y)$, which for the above utility functions becomes:

$$\frac{\beta_1 y}{\gamma_1 x} = \frac{\beta_2(b-y)}{\gamma_2(a-x)} \tag{11.8}$$

and if $k = \beta_1\gamma_2/\gamma_1\beta_2$, the equation of the contract curve, between appropriate limits, is then:

$$y = b\{1 + k(a/x - 1)\}^{-1} \tag{11.9}$$

Hence, if the individuals have identical tastes, $k = 1$ and the contract curve reduces to the straight line:

$$y = (b/a)x \tag{11.10}$$

Thus it is easily seen that if $x = a/2$, $y = b/2$. This implies that for individuals with the same tastes, but different endowments, equal division of the stocks produces a point on the contract curve. In this situation the sharing of their resources by the As is efficient. It can also be seen, by appropriate substitution into equations (11.4) and (11.5), that the maximization of total utility for identical individuals also involves equal division. The second section above has shown that in general the 'utilitarian arrangement' is efficient (that is, it is on the contract curve), which of course provides a more general demonstration that equal division is efficient for identical individuals.

A valuable detailed summary of Canard's contribution is given by Theocharis (1961, pp. 72–88), who also traces the considerable injustice done to Canard by a long line of leading authors. A small sample of Canard's work is translated in Baumol and Goldfeld (1968, pp. 157–60).

The earliest rigorous analysis of Edgeworth's analysis of the role of numbers in competition, in terms of recently developed theories of co-operative games, was by Shubik (1959). For more extensive treatments and bibliographies, see Hildebrand and Kirman (1976). It is perhaps surprising that Edgeworth did not mention Jenkin (1870, reprinted 1931, pp. 82–7). Jenkin discussed auctions, mentioned Thorton's case of Dutch and English auctions, and even used the example of horse trading. Also of significance is his statement that, 'in simple transactions between man and man for one object . . . neither demand nor supply curves can be drawn' (1870, p. 86).

On the question of competition and efficiency Samuelson (1947) is still useful. However, citing only Wicksell's *Lectures*, he actually 'credits' Launhardt with being, 'the only economist who attempted to give rigorous proof' of the theorem that competition maximizes total utility (1947, p. 205). Samuelson went on to say that, 'we can learn more from his unambiguous failure than from many pages of fuzzy literary effusion'. Jaffé (1983, p. 91) is also grossly unfair to Launhardt. More interesting, however, is the fact that neither Wicksell, Pantaleoni nor Samuelson mention Edgeworth's analysis in *Mathematical Psychics*. Of course Wicksell and Pantaleoni may have experienced difficulty in obtaining a copy of the privately printed book. When Wicksell discussed indeterminacy (1934, p. 51) he referred to Edgeworth indirectly, giving the source as Marshall's *Principles*, and when he accused Pareto and Marshall of paying it insufficient attention, he referred to Edgeworth's review of Marshall's *Principles* in the *Giornale Degli Economisti* of 1895 discussed in Chapter 10 above. Fisher (1892, in 1925, pp. 97–100) gives a good discussion of individual (constrained) utility maximization relative to the maximization of total utility, and refers to Launhardt.

12 The role of stocks in supply and demand

The previous chapters in this part of the book have explored the development of the theory of exchange, which was given so much emphasis by the neoclassical economists. Instead of taking the partial equilibrium approach of Cournot, these economists examined what may be called a 'catallactic community'. It has been seen that Marshall (with his foreign trade analysis) and Walras arrived at essentially similar treatments, and examined the stability properties of models which can easily give rise to multiple equilibria. This 'research programme' may be said to have reached a high point with the contribution of Edgeworth, which took Jevons as the starting point. The work of these economists provided the foundation for the later, technically more demanding, work in general equilibrium theory.

It is therefore somewhat surprising to find Wicksteed, in 1910, strongly criticizing the partial equilibrium treatment of demand and supply. What is surprising is not that he was critical, but that he chose to ignore the exchange analyses of Jevons, Walras, Marshall and Edgeworth, while using the same context of exchange. In criticizing one partial equilibrium technique, he attempted to replace it with an inappropriate partial technique, rather than simply using the available general equilibrium methods.

Wicksteed's analysis was concentrated on his criticism that the partial equilibrium supply and demand curves do not pay adequate attention to the role of stocks of goods. The purpose of this chapter is therefore to examine Wicksteed's analysis in some detail. It will be seen that although the emphasis on the role of stocks in the treatment of exchange is valuable, Wicksteed's technical analysis is deficient in several important respects. Section 12.1 provides a brief summary of Wicksteed's argument. Section 12.2 then considers two simple algebraic formulations of the approach. The first is based on Walras's treatment of exchange, and the second uses the approach pioneered by Edgeworth, both of which have been examined in earlier chapters. The wider implication of Wicksteed's treatment, beyond the technical analysis, is that it emphasizes the importance of the concept of 'opportunity cost'. This aspect, with its 'Austrian' connections, is discussed briefly in section 12.3. First, however, it is necessary to consider the precise nature of Wicksteed's complaint.

Wicksteed's criticism of supply and demand

Wicksteed is perhaps best known for his contribution to the marginal productivity theory of production and distribution. But he also attached great importance to his criticism of the partial equilibrium analysis of supply and demand. His major criticism was directed at the concept of the partial equilibrium supply curve. Wicksteed even went so far as to describe the standard diagrammatic analysis as 'profoundly misleading' (1910, reprinted in 1933, II, p. 785) and actually stated that there is 'no such thing' as a supply curve. He argued that although it is useful to separate the supply and demand sides of the market in considering the *process* of adjustment by which an equilibrium price may be reached, it is of dubious value when considering the precise determinants of that price. Wicksteed suggested that:

> the cross curves of demand and supply, so often employed by economists, are really no more than two sections of the true collective curve of demand, separated out from each other, and read, for convenience, in reverse directions. This separation is irrelevant to the determination of the equilibrating price. These cross curves, then, as usually presented, confuse the methods by which the equilibrating price is arrived at with the conditions that determine what it is. (1933, II, pp. 797–8)

The basis of Wicksteed's criticism was the argument that when the usual set of demand and supply curves are drawn there is an implicit assumption about the fixed stock of the good available for consumption. The situation he had in mind was not of firms producing only for sale but, along with other major neoclassical economists, of exchange. He envisaged the standard exchange situation in which individuals hold stocks of a good which are brought to a market. His examples include the results of a harvest, or the 'catch' of a fishing fleet (1933, II, p. 787). Those who hold stocks of the good also consume the good and therefore have a demand for it comparable with that of individuals who do not hold stocks. This context is therefore the same as that of Mill, Jevons, Walras, Marshall and Edgeworth, but he took a quite independent position.

Wicksteed lost no opportunity to stress his argument that supply curves represent merely a part of the total demand curve for the good, placed in 'reverse'. A broad treatment is given in the *Common Sense* (1933, I, pp. 229–34), but the most substantial exploration is in his 1913 presidential address to section F of the British Association, reprinted in (1933, II, pp. 772–96). The argument is repeated briefly in his *Palgrave's Dictionary* article on 'Final Utility', and in his review of Davenport's book on the *Economics of Enterprise*. The last two pieces were also reprinted by Robbins with the 1933 edition of the *Common Sense* (1933, II, pp. 797–800 and 822–6, respectively).

The fact that Robbins chose to include these pieces in his edition of the *Common Sense* is an indication of the great importance he attached to this part of Wicksteed's work. Indeed, in his introduction to the new edition, Robbins gave this aspect of Wicksteed's work special emphasis. The views of such a major historian of economic analysis, with a strong sympathy for abstract theory, are worth considering. He wrote:

> A second contribution which must always be associated with his name is his famous demonstration of the reversibility of the market supply curve. The general proposition that the reservation prices of sellers are, in the ultimate analysis, demands, was one which he continually reiterated with varying shades of emphasis . . .
> It is safe to say that no one who has followed through his beautiful diagrammatic analysis of this proposition, and realised its wider implications . . . will deny that the whole of the analysis of economic equilibrium has received thereby a transforming elucidation. (in Wicksteed, 1933, I, p.xx)

In view of the importance attached to this argument by Robbins, a detailed analysis of Wicksteed's treatment seems warranted, although the technical aspects have been rather neglected by historians of economic analysis. Brief discussions usually emphasize the associated approach to the concept of cost.

12.1 Wicksteed's approach
The total demand curve
The basic framework of analysis is, as mentioned earlier, of exchange where individuals possess fixed stocks. Wicksteed's diagrammatic approach is shown in Figure 12.1, which is based on (1933, II, pp. 787–8). Figure 12.1(a) shows the total demand curve of the 'possessors' of a single good as SS' and the demand curve of the 'non-possessors' as DD'. For the latter, demand is measured from the origin, O, but for the former it is measured in a leftward direction from the vertical line at the distance S_x. The distance OS therefore measures the total stock of the good available. Of course, this figure looks like the conventional representation of intersecting curves, with the equilibrium price given by p. But with the stocks introduced explicitly, an alternative statement of the equilibrium condition is that the total demand, of possessors and non-possessors combined, must equal the total stock. Wicksteed prefers to call the curve SS', the conventional supply curve when quantities are measured from the origin, O, a 'reversed' demand curve. He argues:

> But what about the 'supply curve' that usually figures as a determinant of price,

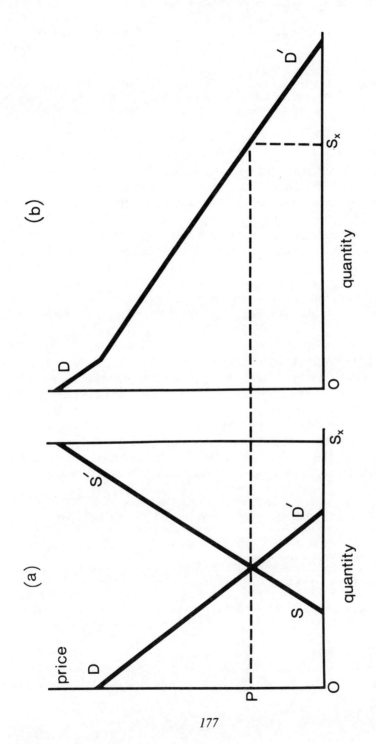

Figure 12.1   Wicksteed's approach

co-ordinate with the demand curve? I say it boldly and baldly: There is no such thing. When we are speaking of a marketable commodity, what is usually called the supply curve is in reality the demand curve of those who possess the commodity. The so-called supply curve, therefore, is simply a part of the total demand curve. The separating out of this portion of the demand curve and reversing it in the diagram is a process which has its meaning and its legitimate function, but is wholly irrelevant to the determination of the price. (1933, II, p. 785).

Changes in stocks

Wicksteed's preferred representation is shown in Figure 12.1(b) where the total demand of possessors and non-possessors is shown as DD'. The equilibrium price is obtained as the intersection of the demand curve with a vertical line at S_x, representing the amount of the good held in stock. Wicksteed's preference for the presentation in part (b) of Figure 12.1 arose because it makes explicit the fact that the holders of the good have a demand for it which is precisely comparable with that of the non-possessors. In addition, the stocks of the good are seen to represent a more fundamental measure of the supply of the good available for consumption. But of course sections (a) and (b) show precisely the same information.

Wicksteed also believed his presentation was superior because it allowed him to develop the analysis to make two further points. First, he suggests that the effect of an increase in the stock of the good is simply to shift the point S_x in Figure 12.1(b). An increase in the stock is therefore seen to decrease unambiguously the equilibrium price of the good. Second, he argues that a redistribution of a fixed stock among individuals, including possessors and non-possessors, will have no effect on the equilibrium price. This is because both the total demand curve and the points remain unchanged. His most comprehensive summary is as follows:

> It will be found in a careful analysis that the construction of a diagram of intersecting demand and 'supply' curves always involves, but never reveals, a definite assumption as to the amount of the total supply possessed by the supposed buyers and the supposed sellers taken together as a single homogeneous body, and that if this total is changed the emerging price changes too; whereas a change in its initial distribution (if the collective curve is unaffected, while the component or intersecting curves change) will have no effect on the market, or equilibrating price itself, which will come out exactly the same. Naturally, for neither the one curve nor the one quantity which determine the price has been changed. (1933, II, pp. 785–6)

It will be argued in the following section that both of these results are open to question. In fact, it is easily seen that the second result was not actually derived by Wicksteed, but was simply assumed. This involves his comment, in parentheses in the above quotation, that the 'component' curves change while leaving the 'collective' curve unchanged. Wicksteed did not examine the precise conditions under which this condition could be expected to hold.

A fundamental problem with Wicksteed's approach is that he criticizes the partial equilibrium diagram for failing to emphasize that supply is really 'reverse demand' and that an *exchange* analysis is really needed. But he simply replaces one partial equilibrium presentation with another. The context essentially requires a general equilibrium treatment of exchange. It will be seen that, by eschewing these general equilibrium treatments, Wicksteed's conclusions were incorrect.

12.2 Further analysis
A two-good model
Wicksteed's approach took the demand curves as given, in that he did not derive them from basic utility theory. It has been seen that Whewell, Marshall and Walras independently developed an exchange model in which demands were written as functions of the relative price of the two goods. It is instructive to consider Wicksteed's problem using the simple exchange model examined in more detail in Chapter 8. Suppose person (or persons) A holds stocks of good X while person (or persons) B holds stocks of good Y. The prices of goods X and Y respectively are denoted p_x and p_y. Person B is assumed to have a demand, x_d for good X given by:

$$x_d = a - b\,(p_x/p_y) \tag{12.1}$$

Person A, who holds stocks of good X, is assumed to have a demand for good Y, y_d given by:

$$y_d = \alpha - \beta(p_y/p_x)$$

$$= \alpha - \beta\,(p_x/p_y)^{-1} \tag{12.2}$$

The demand must be associated with a reciprocal supply of good X by A. If A demands y_d of Y at a relative price of p_y/p_x, the corresponding supply of good X is simply $y_d(p_y/p_x)$. Hence the supply, x_s, is given by:

$$x_s = \alpha\,(p_x/p_y)^{-1} - \beta(p_x/p_y)^{-2} \tag{12.3}$$

If the stock of good X held by A is denoted S_x, then (12.3) implies that the demand for X by A is given by $S_x - x_s$. The total demand, x_D, corresponding to Wicksteed's total demand curve, is thus given by:

$$x_D = x_d + (S_x - x_s)$$

$$= S_x + a - b\left(\frac{p_x}{p_y}\right) - \alpha\left(\frac{p_x}{p_y}\right)^{-1} + \beta\left(\frac{p_x}{p_y}\right)^{-2} \tag{12.4}$$

The equilibrium price ratio is therefore obtained by setting x_D equal to S_x, which gives rise to the cubic:

$$a\left(\frac{p_x}{p_y}\right)^2 - b\left(\frac{p_x}{p_y}\right)^3 - \alpha\left(\frac{p_x}{p_y}\right) + \beta = 0 \tag{12.5}$$

Equation (12.5) therefore shows, as seen earlier, that there may be three distinct roots. The relevant curves no longer take the simple shape depicted by Wicksteed, but are shown in Figure 12.2. Figure 12.2(a) shows only one point of intersection, but it is clear from the shape of the supply curve that the curves may intersect three times. Part (b) of the figure shows that Wicksteed's type of total demand curve does not simply fall from left to right, so that it too may intersect a vertical line, repesenting the total stock, three times. All that is required for the supply curve to bend backwards is that there is a range of the demand curve where the elasticity of demand is numerically greater than unity.

A cursory look at equation (12.4), the total demand curve, and (12.5), the condition for an equilibrium price ratio, might suggest that a change in the total stock of good X held by person A, S_x, would have no effect on the equilibrium price. It seems as if the total demand curve simply shifts by the same extent of the change in the stock. This would give Wicksteed's first statement mentioned above. But this fails to recognize that the parameters of A's demand curve for good Y (and consequently of A's demand for X, obtained as a residual) would be expected to change as a direct result of the change in stocks. By beginning with a statement of the demand curve, it is simply not possible to deal with the effects of changing the stocks of goods available without making arbitrary assumptions. Only a basic inequality concerning the parameters of the demand curves is available. Thus, from equation (12.3), person A's supply of good X reaches a maximum when $p_y/p_x = \alpha/2\beta$. Hence the maximum amount A is prepared to supply is $\alpha^2/4\beta$, which must be no greater than S_x. Thus it is necessary to have:

$$\alpha < 2\sqrt{\beta S_x} \tag{12.6}$$

This condition is insufficient for comparative static exercises. By simply drawing the demand curves of the traders as basic 'data'. Wicksteed failed to recognize that his assumption that a reallocation of fixed stocks would

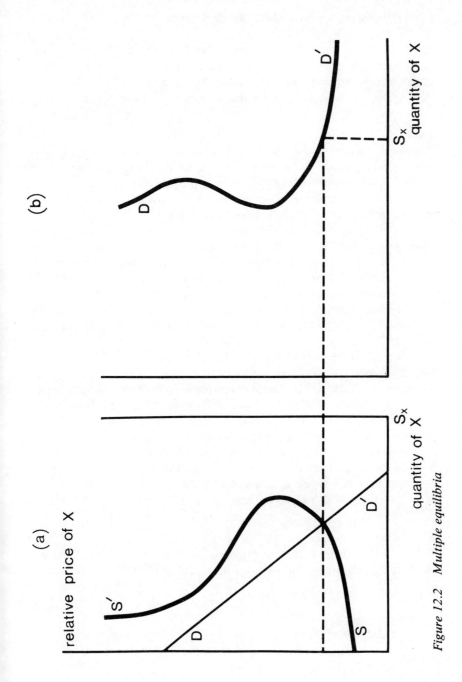

Figure 12.2 Multiple equilibria

leave the total demand curve, and therefore the equilibrium price, unchanged, was in fact a very special case. His accusation that the conventional supply and demand curves leaves the role of stocks implicit, and may consequently be misleading, applies equally to his own approach.

Prices and distribution

A method of handling the role of stocks in the determination of prices was already available to Wicksteed in the form of Edgeworth's extension of Jevons's exchange model. In this framework the demand functions are derived from the basic utility functions, in which the initial stocks held by each person appear explicitly. Consider Figure 12.3, which uses Edgeworth's exchange diagram. In Figure 12.3(a), the initial endowment position is at point R, where person A initially holds all the stock of good X and B holds all of good Y. The equilibrium price ratio is given by the slope of the line RP and exchange takes place at point E on the contract curve. A redistribution of the initial stocks such that the endowment point is R_1 leads to a new equilibrium at E_1 along the price line R_1P_1. Contrary to Wicksteed's assumption, there is no a priori reason to believe that the slopes of RP and R_1P_1 will be the same.

Figure 12.3 (b) illustrates the situation where the initial stock of good X held by person A increases, with the amount of good Y held by B remaining unchanged. The initial endowment point therefore shifts from R to R_1 and the equilibrium price line shifts from RP to R_1P_1. Person A is better off as a result of the increase in stocks. It is, however, possible to produce a result corresponding to 'immiserising growth', whereby person A becomes worse off as a result of the large reduction in the price of good X when the stock increases. This is illustrated in Figure 12.3(c). In this situation, person A would of course throw back some of his catch of fish, or destroy some of the wheat harvest.

A special case

The role of stocks can be seen explicitly using a simple Cobb–Douglas utility function for each individual, so that person A has utility function:

$$U = x^\beta y^\gamma \tag{12.7}$$

While B has utility function:

$$U_1 = x^{\beta_1} y^{\gamma_1} \tag{12.8}$$

It is well-known that this form of the utility function implies that Engel

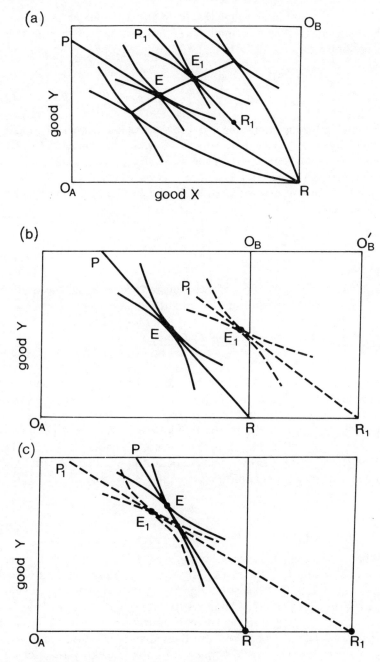

Figure 12.3   Changes in stocks

curves are straight lines through the origin and demand curves are rectangular hyperbolas. If M represents A's endowment in money units, then it can be shown that:

$$x = \frac{M}{p_x}\frac{\beta}{\gamma+\beta} \quad \text{and} \quad y = \frac{M}{p_y}\frac{\gamma}{\gamma+\beta} \tag{12.9}$$

Following Jevons's notation, suppose that the initial stock of good X is denoted by a, and is held by person A, while the amount of good Y initially held by B is denoted b. Then with prices p_x and p_y this means that A's budget is $M = ap_x$ and B's budget is bp_y. Person A will therefore demand an amount of good X equal to $a\beta/(\gamma+\beta)$ and B will demand an amount equal to:

$$b\frac{p_y}{p_x}\frac{\beta_1}{\gamma_1+\beta_1} \tag{12.10}$$

For equilibrium, the sum of two demands must equal the available stock, a, so that the equilibrium price ratio is unique and is given by:

$$\frac{p_x}{p_y} = \frac{b\beta_1(\gamma+\beta)}{a\gamma(\gamma_1+\beta_1)} \tag{12.11}$$

This gives the simple result that the relative price of good X is inversely related to the ratio of the stock of X to that of Y. In the more general case, the stocks may be divided between the two traders. Suppose that A initially holds x^* of x while person B holds $a - x^*$; further, A holds $b - y^*$ of good Y while B holds y^* of Y. Person A's money budget is thus $x^*p_x + (b - y^*)p_y$ for prices p_x and p_y. Following the above procedure, it can be found that the equilibrium price ratio is given by:

$$\frac{p_x}{P_y} = \frac{b}{a}\frac{S}{(1-R)} \tag{12.12}$$

Where R is a weighted average of $\beta/(\gamma+\beta)$ and $\beta_1/(\gamma_1+\beta_1)$, with weights equal to x^*/a and $1 - x^*/a$ respectively. The term S is a weighted average of $\beta/(\gamma+\beta)$ and $\beta_1/(\gamma_1+\beta_1)$ with weights $1 - y^*/b$ and y^*/b respectively. It can easily be seen that (12.12) reduces to (12.11) if $x^* = a$ and $y^* = b$. This result shows explicitly how the equilibrium price ratio will change as the distribution of fixed stocks between the individual changes, contrary to Wicksteed's argument. Less simple forms for the utility functions are unfortunately considerably less tractable.

12.3 The opportunity cost concept

The previous section has examined Wicksteed's construction of a total demand curve obtained by 'reversing' the conventional supply curve, given the stock of the good available. It has been argued that Wicksteed, by considering the demand curves as basic 'data' and simply producing a minor variation of the standard partial equilibrium diagram, was incorrect in his argument that the price of a good is independent of the distribution of the initial stocks. Thus Robbins's statement that 'Wicksteed demonstrated to the British Association the true nature of the supply curve. To-day the majority of economists would accept his demonstration as irrefutable' (in Wicksteed, 1933, I, p. xv), must be substantially qualified.

In order to appreciate Robbin's attitude towards this aspect of Wicksteed's work, it is necessary to consider the wider implications of Wicksteed's approach, beyond the technical detail of his diagrams. The vehemence of Wicksteed's criticism of the standard partial equilibrium model is difficult to understand if attention is restricted only to the technical aspects. The basic reason for his insistence on the concept of supply as 'reverse' demand and his emphasis on the role of fixed stocks is usually associated with the 'Austrian' elements of his work. In particular, it concerns the view that all productive resources are ultimately fixed in 'supply' and that cost must be seen in terms of opportunity cost. Wicksteed extended his argument to cover cases of continuous production (in addition to his examples from commodity markets). As Hutchison suggested, 'This enabled him to consider, in the Austrian manner, the treatment of cost of production as a separate element in determining market transactions in addition to demand, as ultimately misleading and unnecessary' (1953, p. 104).

It was precisely this stress on the concept of cost in terms of foregone alternatives that appealed to Robbins, who summarized the argument by stating that '*all* psychological variables can be exhibited as phenomena of demand acting on fixed stocks' (Wicksteed, 1933, I, p.xx). This approach necessarily leads to attention being concentrated on the question of labour supply, so it is not surprising that Robbins was interested in the nature of the labour supply function.

The subject of the Austrian approach to cost is much too large to be discussed in detail here. However, it is worth recognizing that Wicksteed's stress on the idea of foregone alternatives and his emphasis on choice and exchange as underlying all economic phenomena does not really depend on his technical treatment of supply and demand curves. His diagrammatic approach can be seen as an inappropriate attempt to remedy the problem of the partial equilibrium 'cross', using a partial equilibrium variant. From the point of view of the filiation of ideas, the model of exchange of (the 'Austrian') Jevons and his disciple Edgeworth provides precisely the approach that would have fitted Wicksteed's needs most closely, as shown above, though he made no use of it. As stressed by Fraser (1937, p. 104), the view of costs in terms of foregone alternatives is 'merely the extension of the exchange relationships to the whole range of economic life'. It is therefore rather curious that Wicksteed should have chosen unsuccessfully to construct a technique based on a minor modification of apparatus that he explicitly criticized, rather than use the readily available models of exchange.

Notes and further reading
Brief discussions of Wicksteed's analysis, concentrating on his 'Austrian' opportunity cost approach, can be found in Fraser (1937), Hutchison (1953) and Blaug (1968). A valuable brief statement of Robbin's position on opportunity cost is given by O'Brien (1988a, pp. 89–95). An attempt to apply Wicksteed's approach to the supply of and demand for money was made by Thirlby (1948), whose interest was probably associated with Robbins and the cost controversy; of relevance here is Buchanan and Thirlby (1973). In this context, Knight's (1956) review of Wicksteed (1933) is of much interest, in view of his own 'Austrian' connections. Knight (1956, p. 116) was actually critical of the assumption of fixed labour stocks, arguing that the dominating factor is labour mobility, rather than variations in amounts supplied.

The failure of Wicksteed to use the work of Jevons and Edgeworth is curious in view of the fact that Jevons had a decisive influence in directing Wicksteed (along with Edgeworth) towards the serious study of economics. He had also corresponded with Walras at length. The context of exchange is also similar to that of Böhm–Bawerk's model of horse trading. But Wicksteed only made indirect use of this, through discussion of it by Hobson (1900).

The focus on the role of stocks also raises the issue of the manipulation of the price-taking or competitive equilibrium by traders who conceal some of their stocks. The analysis in the second section has shown that, with 'immiserising growth' effects, traders may sometimes prefer to destroy stocks. But consider the incentive to conceal stocks which are subsequently consumed by the holder. For the case of Cobb–Douglas utility functions, used in the second section above, suppose that $a = b = 1$, so that the relative price, from equation (12.11) is equal to k, where:

$$k = \frac{\beta_1(\gamma + \beta)}{\gamma(\gamma_1 + \beta_1)} \tag{12.13}$$

Trader A's demand for good X (which he holds) is then equal to $\beta/(\gamma + \beta)$, whatever the price, and the associated demand for good Y is $k\beta/(\gamma + \beta)$, since in equilibrium the amount spent on good Y must equal the amount raised from the sale of good X. A's utility after trade takes place is thus given by:

$$U_A = \left(\frac{\beta}{\gamma + \beta}\right)^\beta \left(\frac{k\beta}{\gamma + \beta}\right)^\gamma \tag{12.14}$$

Suppose that, instead of revealing all the stocks ($a = 1$) held, A decides to claim only to have an amount δ. This gives rise to the utility, after trade, of U^*_A, given by

$$U^*_A = \left\{(1 - \delta) + \frac{\delta\beta}{\gamma + \beta}\right\}^\beta \left(\frac{k\delta\beta}{\delta(\gamma + \beta)}\right)^\gamma \tag{12.15}$$

Notice that this is not defined for $\delta = 0$. Person A is better off as a result of concealing part of the stock of good X if $U^*_A > U_A$, that is, if:

$$1 - \delta + \frac{\delta\beta}{\gamma + \beta} > \frac{\beta}{\gamma + \beta} \tag{12.16}$$

This easily reduces to the condition that $(\gamma + \beta)/\beta$ is greater than unity. Hence in this special case there is always an incentive for traders to attempt to manipulate the trades (so long as the other trader is not doing the same thing). This result is essentially generated in this special case by the fact that each trader offers a fixed proportion of his stocks, so long as the price is positive (the offer curves are 'L' shaped). Hence person A will always get the same offer of good Y from person B, whatever A decides to reveal. There is therefore an incentive to reveal only enough to induce B to trade. The Cobb–Douglas case thus produces this rather extreme incentive to cheat. Furthermore, the manipulation of stocks can be directly translated into an equivalent misrepresentation of A's preferences. For a general treatment of this issue, see Postlewaite (1979). The incentive to cheat clearly falls as the size of the economy increases and A's stock becomes so small that any concealment does not significantly affect the price ratio.

Appendix A: Multiple equilibria in a Walras/Marshall model

For the simple exchange model considered in Chapter 8, it was demonstrated that alternative parameter configurations could change the number of equilibria and that a necessary but not sufficient condition for three equilibria is that the demand schedule is elastic. This appendix establishes more formal conditions needed for multiple equilibria. The equilibrium values of the relative price, p, are given by the roots of the polynomial in equation (8.4). This can be written as:

$$p^3 - (a/b)p^2 + (\alpha/b)p - (\beta/b) = 0 \tag{A1}$$

It is convenient to transform (A1) in order to reduce the number of parameters from three to two. This is achieved by using a simple transformation of the relative price which preserves the qualitative properties of the solution. Define w as the adjusted relative price, where:

$$w = p - a/3b \tag{A2}$$

The term $-a/3b$ is simply the coefficient on p^2, in (A1), divided by three. Substituting for p gives, after rearrangement:

$$w^3 + \tau_1 w + \tau_0 = 0 \tag{A3}$$

where $\tau_1 = \alpha/b - a^2/3b^2$, and

$$\tau_0 = -\beta/b - 2a^3/27b^3 + a\alpha/3b^2$$

The model's parameters are now summarized by τ_0 and τ_1. It is useful to consider the relationship between w and τ_0, for alternative values of τ_1. Taking the total differential of (A3) while holding τ_1 constant gives:

$$(3w^2 + \tau_1)dw + d\tau_0 = 0$$

The slope of the relationship between w and τ_0 is thus:

$$dw/d\tau_0 = -(3w^2 + \tau_1)^{-1} \tag{A4}$$

Three separate cases can be distinguished according to whether τ_1 is

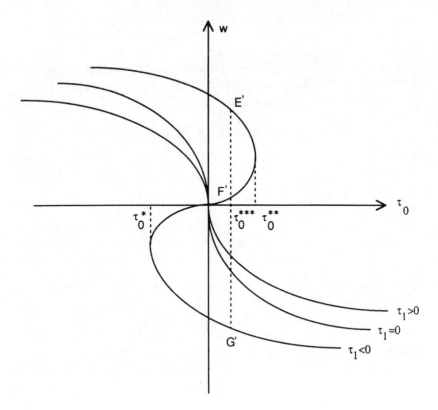

Figure A1 Relationship between τ_0 and w

negative, zero or positive. These are illustrated in Figure A1. First, when $\tau_1 > 0$, $dw/d\tau_0 < 0$ and a unique inverse relationship between w and τ_0 exists. The explanation for this relationship is that a shift in the demand schedule for good Y, caused for example by a decrease in β, leads to an increase in the price of Y and therefore a fall in the relative price p. The decrease in β involves an increase in τ_0, while the fall in p is associated with a fall in w. Hence an increase in τ_0 is associated with a reduction in w.

Second, when $\tau_1 = 0$, equation (A4) reduces to:

$$dw/d\tau_0 = -(3w^2)^{-1} \tag{A5}$$

As with the case where $\tau_1 > 0$, there is an inverse relationship between w and τ_0 except at the point $w = 0$, in which case the slope approaches (minus) infinity. This property is also demonstrated in Figure A1.

The two cases discussed above show that for $\tau_1 \geq 0$, the model has a unique equilibrium. The more interesting case is when $\tau_1 < 0$, since multiple equilibria may now arise. The relationship between w and τ_0 when $\tau_1 < 0$ is depicted in Figure A1 by the inverted S-shaped schedule. The two points τ_0^* and τ_0^{**} are referred to as the threshold points and correspond to the points when the slope of the line approaches (minus) infinity. From (A4), this occurs when

$$w = \pm(-\tau_1/3)^{\frac{1}{2}} \tag{A6}$$

For $\tau_0^* > \tau_0 > \tau_0^{**}$, there is a unique inverse relationship between w and τ_0 and as with the cases discussed above, the model has a unique equilibrium. However, for $\tau_0^* < \tau_0 < \tau_0^{**}$, there is no unique relationship between w and τ_0, as the slope of the line given by (A4) can be negative ($w^2 > -\tau_1/3$) as well as positive ($w^2 < -\tau_1/3$). This is the zone of multiple equilibria where the stable equilibria are given by the upper and lower schedules in Figure A1 and the unstable equilibrium points are given by the interior schedule. Thus, the point $\tau_0 = \tau_0^{**}$ yields three equilibrium points, E', F' and G'. For values of τ_0 at the threshold points, there are two stable equilibria, one stable and one unstable.

It is helpful to state the conditions of the equilibrium properties of the model more formally by looking at the relationship between τ_0 and τ_1. Consider the case of two equilibrium points when, for a particular (negative) value of τ_1, τ_0 is at one of the threshold points. From (A6):

$$\tau_1 = -3w^2 \tag{A7}$$

Substituting (A7) into (A3) and rearranging gives:

$$\tau_0 = 2w^2 \tag{A8}$$

Solving both (A7) and (A8) or w, and equating yields:

$$(-\tau_1/3)^{\frac{1}{2}} = (\tau_0/2)^{\frac{1}{3}} \tag{A9}$$

Rearranging this expression yields the following relationship between τ_0 and τ_1, which holds when there are *two* equilibria:

$$27\tau_0^2 + 4\tau_1^3 = 0 \tag{A10}$$

This relationship is shown in Figure A2, which gives the combinations of τ_0 and τ_1 resulting in the model having two equilibrium points. These lines can be derived from Figure A1 by mapping the threshold points for different (negative) values of τ_1 on to the (τ_0, τ_1) surface in Figure A2.

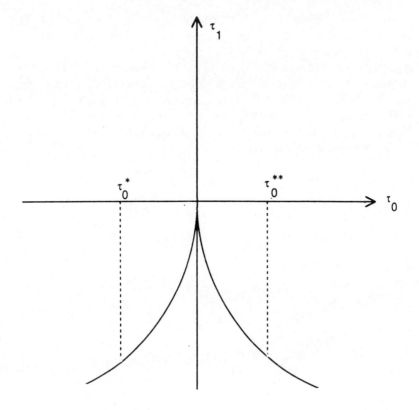

Figure A2   Relationship between τ_0 and τ_1

To see how the number of equilibria change for different combinations of τ_0 and τ_1, consider Figure A1. If τ_0 increases above the threshold point τ_0^{**}, while holding τ_1 constant, the number of equilibria reduces from two to one. Comparing this result with equation (A10), this implies that the model has a *unique* equilibrium when:

$$27\tau_0^2 + 4\tau_1^3 > 0 \qquad \qquad \text{(A11)}$$

Similarly, if τ_0 is decreased below τ_0^{**}, such that $\tau_0^* < \tau_0 < \tau_0^{**}$, there are three equilibria. Again, comparing this result with (A10) implies that for *three* equilibria:

$$27\tau_0^2 + 4\tau_1^3 < 0 \qquad \qquad \text{(A12)}$$

The equilibrium properties of the model can be summarized as follows. A necessary condition for multiple equilibria is that $\tau_1 < 0$. A necessary and sufficient condition for multiple equilibria is that $27\tau_0^2 + 4\tau_1^3 \leq 0$. The necessary condition has a simple interpretation in terms of the demand and supply curves. For $\tau_1 < 0$ it is seen that $\alpha < a^2/3b$. Now α is the asymptotic value to which the demand for Y approaches as the price ratio increases. The elasticity of the demand for X is unity when the price ratio is $a/2b$, which implies that the maximum supply of good Y is equal to $a^2/4b$. Hence the necessary condition for two or more equilibria to occur requires that the maximum demand for good Y is less than one and one third times the maximum supply of good Y.

Appendix B: Barter and Nash equilibria

The general case

In many bargaining contexts, modern theorists use the concept of a Nash equilibrium or set of equilibria. The purpose of this appendix is to examine Nash equilibria in the context of exchange, and to compare outcomes with price-taking equilibria and the 'utilitarian arbitration' position suggested by Edgeworth.

The Nash equilibrium involves the use of each traders' 'threat point', which is the worst situation possible; in the trading context it is the utility obtained from the pre-trade endowment of goods. The 'payoff' to each individual is defined as the utility in the bargained outcome less the threat point; it thus reflects the net gain from trade. The approach allows for the relative bargaining power of each trader, though the sources of such power are not usually examined.   The Nash equilibrium is the outcome which maximizes the weighted geometric mean of the payoffs, with weights equal to the respective power parameters.

Consider traders A and B exchanging goods X and Y. The pre-trade stocks are as follows:

person A holds a_A and b_A of X and Y respectively
person B holds a_B and b_B of X and Y respectively.

These stocks are such that A holds most of X, and B holds most of Y, so that trade involves A giving up x of X in exchange for y of Y from B. After trade:

person A's utility $= U_A (a_A - x, b_A + y)$
person B's utility $= U_B (a_B + x, b_B - y)$

The payoffs are as then obtained as follows:

A's payoff $= P_A = U_A (a_A - x, b_A + y) - U_A (a_A, b_A)$
B's payoff $= P_B = U_B (a_B + x, b_B - y) - U_B (a_B, b_B)$

The power parameters for A and B are denoted ϕ and $1 - \phi$ respectively. Hence the Nash equilibrium is given by the values of x and y which maximize L, given by:

$$L = P_A^\phi \, P_B^{1-\phi} \qquad\qquad (B1)$$

The first-order conditions are obtained by differentiating L with respect to x and y, and are, after rearranging, given by:

$$\phi\frac{\partial U_A}{\partial x} P_B + (1 - \phi)\frac{\partial U_B}{\partial x} P_A = 0 \tag{B2}$$

$$\phi\frac{\partial U_A}{\partial y} P_B + (1 - \phi)\frac{\partial U_B}{\partial y} P_A = 0 \tag{B3}$$

Equations (B2) and (B3) give two non-linear simultaneous equations in x and y, which may therefore have more than one solution. Some insight into the nature of any solution can be obtained by combining (B2) and (B3) to eliminate P_A and P_B, so that:

$$\frac{\partial U_A/\partial x}{\partial U_A/\partial y} = \frac{\partial U_B/\partial x}{\partial U_B/\partial y} \tag{B4}$$

Hence a Nash equilibrium is a point on the contract curve. This will not in general be equal to the price-taking equilibrium, nor the utilitarian solution which maximizes $U_A + U_B$, although these are also on the contract curve.

Consider the extreme situations where either $\phi = 0$ or $\phi = 1$. When $\phi = 0$, then from (B2) and (B3), since marginal utilities are positive, the solution requires $P_A = 0$. This is in fact the equation of the pre-trade indifference curve of person A, that is the indifference curve going through the endowment point. Hence the solution is the intersection of the contract curve with A's pre-trade indifference curve. When $\phi = 1$, the first-order conditions require $P_B = 0$. This is the equation of the pre-trade indifference curve of person B. Hence the solution is at the other extreme of the contract curve where trader A obtains all the gains from trade.

In comparing alternative solution concepts it should be remembered that the rate of exchange (the implicit price ratio) at which trade takes place is the slope of the line from the endowment point to the point along the contract curve where trade concludes. It is thus the ratio y/x. For the price-taking equilibrium, y/x must be equal to the common ratio in equation (B4). This is of course precisely Jevons's famous 'equation of exchange'. All that can generally be said from (B2) and (B3) about a Nash equilibrium is that for each good the ratio of marginal utilities is equal to the ratio of payoffs. It is therefore instructive to turn to a special case.

Cobb–Douglas utility functions
Consider the special case of Cobb–Douglas utility functions, such that:

$$U_A = (a_A - x)^\alpha (b_A + y)^\beta \tag{B5}$$

$$U_B = (a_B + x)^\gamma (b_B - y)^\delta \tag{B6}$$

For convenience, write the pre-trade utilities of each person as U_A^* and U_B^*. Then after appropriate differentiation and substitution into (B2) and (B3), the first-order conditions for the Nash solution are:

$$\frac{-\phi\alpha}{a_A - x} U_A (U_B - U_B^*) + \frac{(1 - \phi)\gamma}{x + a_B} U_B (U_A - U_A^*) = 0 \tag{B7}$$

$$\frac{\phi\beta}{b_A + y} U_A (U_B - U_B^*) - \frac{(1 - \phi)\delta}{b_B - y} U_B (U_A - U_A^*) = 0 \tag{B8}$$

Even for this special case the first-order conditions are non-linear in x and y, and cannot be solved analytically. However, the equation of the contract curve can be found to be:

$$y = \frac{(b_B a_A - k a_B b_A) + x (k b_A - b_B)}{k(x + a_B) + (a_A + a_B) - x} \tag{B9}$$

where

$$k = \frac{\alpha\delta}{\beta\gamma} \tag{B10}$$

Furthermore, the price-taking equilibrium price ratio, of good X to good Y, $p = y/x$, can be found to be:

$$p = \frac{(b_A + b_B) S}{(a_A + a_B) (1 - R)} \tag{B11}$$

where R is a weighted average of $\alpha/(\alpha + \beta)$ and $\gamma/(\gamma + \delta)$ with weights equal to $a_A(a_A + a_B)$ and $a_B/(a_A + a_B)$ respectively, and S is a weighted average of the same terms with weights $b_A/(b_A + b_B)$ and $b_B/(b_A + b_B)$ respectively.

The utilitarian solution is given by maximizing $U_A + U_B = U$, for which the first-order conditions are:

$$\frac{\alpha U_A}{a_A - x} = \frac{\gamma U_B}{a_B + x} \tag{B12}$$

$$\frac{\beta U_A}{b_A + y} = \frac{\delta U_B}{b_B - y} \tag{B13}$$

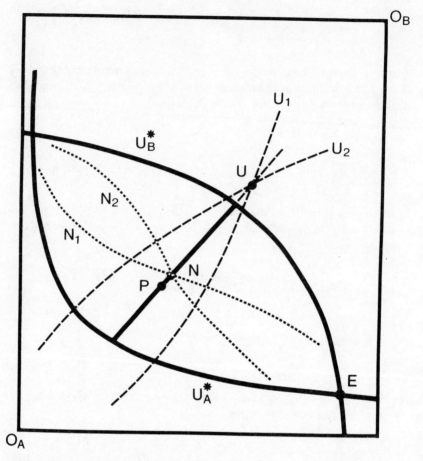

Figure B1   Cobb–Douglas utility functions

The solution, which is also on the contract curve, cannot be obtained explicitly in view of the non-linearity of (B12) and (B13), although if individuals have identical tastes it can be seen that the stocks are shared equally between the two traders.

In view of the non-linearity of the Nash and utilitarian first-order conditions, numerical methods of solution are required. Suppose that $\alpha =$ 0.3, $\beta = 0.5$, $\gamma = 0.2$, $\delta = 0.4$, with initial endowments given by $a_A = b_B$ = 0.9 and $b_A = a_B = 0.1$. The endowment point is shown as point E in Figure B1, where indifference curves U_A^* and U_B^* are the pre-trade indifference curves. Substitution into (B1) gives a price-taking equilibrium rate of exchange of 0.536; the equilibrium position is shown as point P on the contract curve. The associated indifference curves and price line are not shown in order to avoid cluttering the figure. Assuming that $\phi = 0.5$, the loci defined by (B7) and (B8), the first-order conditions for the Nash equilibrium, are shown by the lines marked N_1 and N_2. These intersect at the point on the contract curve where x and y, the amounts exchanged, are equal to 0.473 and 0.283 respectively. A higher value of ϕ would of course move the Nash equilibrium further away from the price-taking equilibrium in a north-easterly direction.

The loci defined by (B12) and (B13), the first-order conditions for the utilitarian maximum, are shown as the lines U_1 and U_2 in Figure B1. These intersect at the point where x and y are 0.256 and 0.501 respectively. This is a clear example of a situation where the utilitarian position makes one individual worse off than before trade. Hence this method of arbitration would not be accepted by both parties. The basic reason for this outcome is that the assumed parameter values imply that both individuals prefer good Y to good X, but the utilitarian arrangement does not allow the person who holds the majority of goods Y to exploit this advantage.

A further simplification

The problem of finding the Nash equilibrium is considerably simplified if it is assumed that trader A initially holds all of good X, while trader B initially holds all the stocks of good Y. The stocks may then be normalized to unity, so that:

$$a_A = 1, b_A = 0, a_B = 0, b_B = 1 \tag{B14}$$

The substitution of (B14) into (B9) gives, after rearranging, the equation of the contract curve as:

$$y = [1 - k\{(1/x) - 1\}^{-1}]^{-1} \tag{B15}$$

These assumptions also imply that $U_A^* = U_B^* = 0$. The limits of the contract curve are the corners O_A and O_B of the Edgeworth box in Figure B1, since, for example, A's indifference curve through the endowment position (now the bottom left-hand corner of the box) effectively coincides with the base of the box. The terms U_A and U_B can in this case be eliminated from the first-order conditions (B7) and (B8), which can then be arranged to give:

$$x = \left\{1 + \frac{\alpha\phi}{\gamma(1 - \phi)}\right\}^{-1} \tag{B16}$$

$$y = \left\{ 1 + \frac{\delta(1 - \phi)}{\beta\phi} \right\}^{-1} \tag{B17}$$

From (B16) it can be seen that if $\alpha \geq \gamma$, then $x \leq 1 - \phi$. Similarly, from (B17), if $\beta \geq \delta$, then $y \geq \phi$. In the situation where trader A has all the bargaining power, that is where $\phi = 1$, equations (B16) and (B17) show that $x = 0$ and $y = 1$. This means that A 'forces' B to give up all the stock of good Y without giving any of good X in return. Where B has all the power, that is where $\phi = 0$, the situation is reversed and A is 'forced' to give the endowment of good X to trader B. This extreme situation arises because each person has zero utility before trade. Positive utility requires individuals to hold at least some of both goods. With extreme asymmetry in the bargaining power, the effective price of the good held by the strong trader can be raised infinitely high.

In the more normal situation where $0 < \phi < 1$, the effective price ratio of good X for Y is the ratio of the amount of Y given up per unit of good X, or the ratio of (B17) to (B16). The price ratio, p_N, is thus given by:

$$\frac{y}{x} = p_N = \frac{1 + \alpha\phi/\{\gamma(1 - \phi)\}}{1 + \delta(1 - \phi)/\beta\phi} \tag{B18}$$

In the special case where tastes are identical, $\alpha = \gamma$ and $\delta = \beta$, then the implicit rate of exchange from the Nash equilibrium is simply equal to $\phi/(1 - \phi)$. Appropriate substitution into (B11) shows that the price-taking equilibrium price would be:

$$p = \frac{\gamma(\beta + \alpha)}{\beta(\delta + \gamma)} \tag{B19}$$

In this case, identical tastes imply that the price-taking equilibrium rate of exchange is α/β. Equation (B18) defines a straight line through the endowment point (the origin in this case) with slope given by the right-hand side. The intersection of this line with the contract curve gives the Nash equilibrium, whereas the intersection of the price line given by (B19) with the contract curve gives the price-taking equilibrium.

Suppose that the parameters of the utility functions are as follows: $\alpha = 0.5$, $\beta = 0.2$, $\gamma = 0.3$, $\delta = 0.5$. Substitution into (B19) shows that the price-taking equilibrium price would be equal to 1.31. But with bargaining power equally divided between the two traders ($\phi = 0.5$), substitution into (B18) gives an effective relative price of 0.76. Trader A would be better off under a price-taking equilibrium. This is because B's preference for good Y relative to good X is less than A's preference for good X relative to Y, combined with the fact that A and B hold all initial stocks of X and Y respectively. With price-taking, the price of good X must be relatively higher than that of Y, in order to induce trader A to supply the needs of B. When ϕ is 0.8, the effective relative price is higher, at 4.72.

References

Amano, A. (1968), 'Stability Conditions in the Pure Theory of International Trade: A Rehabilitation of the Marshallian Approach', *Quarterly Journal of Economics*, **82**, 326-39.

Appleyard, D.R. and Ingram, J.C. (1979), 'A Reconsideration of the Additions to Mill's "Great Chapter"', *History of Political Economy*, **11**, 459-76.

Bailey, M.J. (1954), 'Edgeworth's Taxation Paradox and the Nature of Demand Functions', *Econometrica*, **22**, 72-6.

Barnett, G.E. (ed.) (1936), *Two Tracts by Gregory King*, Baltimore: John Hopkins Press.

Baumol, W.J. and Goldfeld, S.M. (1968), *Precursors in Mathematical Economics: An Anthology*, London: London School of Economics.

Bhagwati, J. and Johnson, H.G. (1960), 'Notes on Some Controversies in the Theory of International Trade', *Economic Journal*, **70**, 74-93.

Black, R.D.C. (ed.) (1977), *Papers and Correspondence of William Stanley Jevons 1873-1878*, London: Macmillan.

Black, R.D.C. (1981), *Papers and Correspondence of W.S. Jevons: Papers on Political Economy*, London: Macmillan.

Black, R.D.C. (1982), 'W.S. Jevons's correspondence with T.E. Jevons', *History of Economic Thought Newsletter*, **29**, 1-11.

Bladen, M.E. (1965), 'John Stuart Mill's demand curves', *History of Political Economy*, **21**, 43-56.

Blaug, M. (1968), *Economic Theory in Retrospect*, 2nd ed., London: Heinemann.

Bostaph, S. and Shieh, Y.-N. (1987), 'Jevons's demand curve', *History of Political Economy*, **19**, 107-26.

Boulding, K.E. and Stigler, G.J. (eds) (1951), *Readings in Price Theory*, London: George Allen and Unwin.

Bouniatian, M. (1927), *La Loi de la Variation de la Valeur et les Mouvements Généraux des Prix*, Paris.

Bowley, A.L. (1924), *The Mathematical Groundwork of Economics*, Oxford: Clarendon Press.

Bowley. A.L. (1926), *Elements of Statistics*, 5th ed., London: P.S. King and Son.

Buchanan, J.M. (1971), 'The Backbending Supply Curve of Labour: an Example of Doctrinal Retrogression?', *History of Political Economy*, **3**, 383-90.

Buchanan, J.M. and Thirlby, G.F. (eds) (1973), *LSE Essays on Cost*, London: Weidenfeld and Nicolson.

Campanelli, G. (1982), 'Whewell's Contribution to Economic Analysis: the First Mathematical Formulation of Fixed Capital in Ricardo's System', *Manchester School*, **50**, 248-65.

Canard, N.F. (1801), *Principles d'Economie Politique*, Paris.

Cantillon, R. (1955), *Essai Sur La Nature du Commerce en Generale*, translated by H. Higgs (1931), London: Macmillan.

Chalmers, G. (1802), *Estimate of the Comparative Strength of Great Britain*, London.

Chipman, J.S. (1965), 'A Survey of the Theory of International Trade; Part 1, the Classical Theory', *Econometrica*, **33**, 477-519.

Clark, G.N. (1938), *Guide to English Commercial Statistics 1696-1782*, London: Royal Historical Society.

Coase, R.H. (1946), 'Monopoly Pricing with Interrelated Costs and Demands', *Economica*, **13**, 278-94.

Cochrane, J.L. (1975), 'William Whewell's Mathematical Statements', *Manchester School*, **43**, 396-400.

Collard, D. (1968), Introduction to *Mathematical Investigation of the Effect of Machinery* by J.E. Tozer, New York: Augustus M. Kelley.

Cournot, A.A. (1927), *Researches into the Mathematical Principles of the Theory of Wealth*, translated by N.T. Bacon and introduced by I. Fisher, London: Stechert-Hafner.

Creedy, J. (1984), 'Public finance', in J. Creedy and D.P. O'Brien (eds), *Economic Analysis in Historical Perspective*, pp. 84-116, London: Butterworth.

Creedy, J. (1985), *Dynamics of Income Distribution*, Oxford: Basil Blackwell.

Creedy, J. (1986), *Edgeworth and the Development of Neoclassical Economics*, Oxford: Basil Blackwell.

Creedy, J. (1990), 'Marshall and Edgeworth', *Scottish Journal of Political Economy* **37**, 18–39.

Creedy. J. and O'Brien, D.P. (1990), 'Marshall, Monopoly and Rectangular Hyperbolas', *Australian Economic Papers*.

Cunynghame H. (1892), 'Some Improvements in Simple Geometrical Methods of Treating Exchange Value, Monopoly and Rent', *Economic Journal*, **2**, 35-52.

Cunynghame, H. (1903), 'The Effect of Export and Input Duties on Price and Production Examined by the Graphic Method', *Economic Journal*, **1**, 313-23.

Cunynghame, H. (1904), *A Geometrical Political Economy*, Oxford: Clarendon Press.

Dalal, A.J. (1979), 'A Note on Mill's Theory of International Values', *Journal of International Economics*, **9**, 583-7.

Davenant, C. (1699), *An Essay upon the Probable Methods of Making a People Gainers in the Balance of Trade*, London.

Davenport, H.J. (1935), *The Economics of Alfred Marshall*, reprinted 1965 by Augustus M. Kelley, New York.

Deane, P. (1974), 'Gregory King', *International Encyclopedia of the Social Sciences*, **8**, 385-6.

Dooley, P.C. (1985), 'Giffen's hint?', *Australian Economic Papers*, **24**, 201-4.

Dunlop, J.T. (1944), *Wage Determination under Trade Unions*, New York: Macmillan.

Dupuit, J. (1844), 'On the Measurement of Utility of Public Works', reprinted in *International Economic Papers*, **2**, 83-110, 1952.

Eatwell, J., Milgate, H., and Newman, P. (eds) (1989), *General Equilibrium*, London: Macmillan.

Edgeworth, F.Y. (1881), *Mathematical Psychics*, London: Kegan Paul.

Edgeworth, F.Y. (1894), 'The Pure Theory of International Values', *Economic Journal*, **4**, 35-50, 424-43, 606-38.

Edgeworth, F.Y. (1904), 'Review of Cunynghame's *Geometrical Political Economy*', *Economic Journal*, **15**, 62-71.

Edgeworth, F.Y. (1925), *Papers Relating to Political Economy*, 3 vols, London: Macmillan for the Royal Economic Society.

Einaudi, L. (1943), 'La Paternita della Legge detta di King', *Revista di Storia Economica*, **8**, 33-8.

Endres, A. (1985), 'The functions of numerical data in the writings of Graunt, Petty and Davenant', *History of Political Economy*, **17**, 245-64.

Endres, A.M. (1987), 'The King-Davenant "Law" in Classical Economics', *History of Political Economy*, **19**, 621-38.

Evans, G.H. (1967), 'The Law of Demand: the Roles of Gregory King and Charles Davenant', *Quarterly Journal of Economics*, **81**, 483-92.

Fellner, W. (1949), *Competition Among the Few*, New York: A.A. Knopf.

Ferguson, C.E. (1958), 'Modified Edgeworth Phenomena and the Nature of Related Commodities, in R.W. Pfouts (ed.), *Essays in Economics and Econometrica*, pp.178-87, Chapel Hill, USA: University of North Carolina Press.

Fisher, I. (1892, 1925) *Mathematical Investigations in the Theory of Value and Prices*, New Haven: Yale University Press.

Fraser, L.M. (1937), *Economic Thought and Language*, Edinburgh: A. and C. Black.

Gärdlund, T. (1958), *The Life of Knut Wicksell*, translated by N. Adler, Stockholm: Almquist and Wicksell.

Garegnani, P. (1983), 'The Classical Theory of Wages and the Role of Demand Schedules in the Determination of Relative Prices', *American Economic Review*, **72**, 309-13.

Garver, R. (1933), 'The Edgeworth taxation phenomenon', *Econometrica*, **1**, 402-7.

Gherity, J.A. (1988), 'Mill's "friendly critic" – Thornton or Whewell?', *Manchester School*, **61**, 282-5.

Gherity, J.A. (1990), 'The International Flow of Mathematical Economics from Lloyd to Thompson', *Manchester School*, **58**, 165-72.

Glass, D.V. and Eversley, D.E.C. (1965), *Population in History: Essays in Historical Demography*, London: Arnold.

Guitton, H. (1938), *Essai sur la loi de King. Etude des relations entre les Mouvement des prix*, Paris: Librairie de Recueil Sirey.

Harsanyi, J.C. (1953), 'Cardinal Utility in Welfare Economics and in the Theory of Risk Taking', *Journal of Political Economy*, **61**, 434-5.

Henderson, J.P. (1973), 'William Whewell's Mathematical Statements of Price Flexibility, Demand and Elasticity and the Giffen Paradox', *Manchester School*, **41**, 329-42.

Henderson, J.P. (1985), 'The Whewell Group of Mathematical Economists', *Manchester School*, **53**, 404-31.

Henderson, J.P. (1989), 'Whewell's Solution to the Reciprocal Demand Riddle in Mill's "Greater Chapter"', *History of Political Economy*, **21**, 661-77.

Hennings, K.H. (1980), 'The Transition from Classical to Neoclassical Economic Theory: Hans Von Mangoldt', *Kyklos*, **33**, 658-81.

Herford, C.H. (1931), *Philip Henry Wicksteed*, London: J.M. Dent and Sons.

Hicks, J.R. (1930), 'Edgeworth, Marshall and the Indeterminateness of Wages', *Economic Journal*, **40**, 215-31.

Hicks, J.R. (1932), *The Theory of Wages*, London: Macmillan.

Hicks, J.R. (1934), 'Leon Walras', *Econometrica*, **2**, 338-48.

Hicks, J.R. (1939), *Value and Capital*, London: Macmillan.

Hobson, J.A. (1900), *The Economics of Distribution*, London: Macmillan.

Hotelling, H. (1932), 'Edgeworth's Taxation Paradox and the Nature of Demand and Supply Functions', *Journal of Political Economy*, **40**, 577-616.

Hotelling, H. (1933), 'Note on Edgeworth's Taxation Phenomenon and Professor Garver's Additional Condition on Demand Functions', *Econometrica*, **1**, 408-9.

Howey, R.S. (1960), *The Rise of the Marginal Utility School 1870-1889*, Kansas: University of Kansas Press.

Hutchison, T.W. (1955), 'Insularity and Cosmopolitanism in Economic

Ideas 1870-1914', *American Economic Association Papers and Proceedings*, **45**, 1-16.

Hutchison, T.W. (1953), *A Review of Economic Doctrines 1870-1929*, Oxford: Clarendon Press.

Jaffé, W. (ed.) (1965), *Correspondence of Leon Walras and Related Papers*, 3 vols, Amsterdam: North Holland.

Jaffé, W. (1983), *Essays on Walras*, ed. by D.A. Walker, Cambridge: Cambridge University Press.

Jenkin, F. (1870), *The Graphic Representation of the Laws of Supply and Demand*, reprinted in 1931 in LSE Reprints of Scarce Tracts, no. 9, London: Longmans, Green.

Jenkin, F. (1871), 'On the Principles which Regulate the Incidence of Taxes', in R.A. Musgrave and C.S. Shoup (eds), *Readings in the Economics of Taxation*, London: Allen and Unwin.

Jevons, T.E. (1889), 'Mr Wicksteed's Notes upon Jevons', *Quarterly Journal of Economics*, **3**, 500-3.

Jevons, W.S. (1957), *The Theory of Political Economy* (with editorial material by H.S. Jevons), 5th ed., Reprinted 1965, New York: Augustus M. Kelley.

Jevons, W.S. (1909), *The Principles of Science*, 2nd ed., London: Macmillan.

Johnson, W.E. (1913), 'The Pure Theory of Utility Curves', *Economic Journal*, **23**, 483-513.

Keynes, J.M. (1972), *Essays in Biography*, Volume X of the *Collected Writings* of Keynes, London: Macmillan.

King, G. (1696), *Natural and Political Observations and Conclusions upon the State and Condition of England*, in G. Chalmers, *An Estimate of the Comparative Strength of Great Britain*, London, 1802.

Knight, F. (1956), *On the History and Method of Economics*, Chicago: University of Chicago Press.

Lardner, D. (1850), *Railway Economy*, London: Taylor, Walton and Maberly.

Laslett, P. (1973), *The Earliest Classics: John Graunt and Gregory King*, Westmead: Gregg International.

Lauderdale, Lord (1804), *An Inquiry into the Nature and Origin of Public Wealth*, London.

Launhardt, W. (1885), *Mathematische Begründung der Volkswirtschftslehre*, Leipzig.

Leontief, W. (1946), 'The Pure Theory of the Guaranteed Annual Wage Contract', *Journal of Political Economy*, **54**, 76-9.

Letwin, W. (1963), *The Origins of Scientific Economics*, London: Methuen.

Loria, A. (1923), 'Review of *Money Credit and Commerce*', *La Riforma Sociale*, **34**, 234.

Lowe, J. (1823), *The Present State of England*, reprinted in 1969 by Gregg International.

McDonald, I.M. and Solow, R. (1981), 'Wage Bargaining and Employment', *American Economic Review*, **71**, 896-908.

MacGregor, D.H. (1942), 'Marshall and his Book', *Economica*, **9**, 313-24.

Mangoldt, H. (1863), *Grundriss der Volkswirtschaftslehre*, Stuttgart: Verlag von J. Engelhorn. Second edition (1871) revised by F. Kleinwächter. First edition reprinted by Gregg International (1968).

Mangoldt, H. (1962), 'The Exchange Ratio of Goods', *International Economic Papers*, **11**, 32-59.

Mangoldt, H. (1975), 'On the Equation of International Demand', *Journal of International Economics*, **5**, 55-97.

Marget, A.W. (1938), *The Theory of Prices*, Reprinted 1966, New York: A.M. Kelley.

Marshall, A. (1876), 'J.S. Mill's theory of value', reprinted in A.C. Pigou, (ed.) *Memorials of Alfred Marshall*, London: Macmillan, 1925.

Marshall, A. (1879), *The Pure Theory of Foreign Trade: The Pure Theory of Domestic Values*, reprinted in J.K. Whitaker (ed.), *The Early Economic Writing of Alfred Marshall 1867-1880*, London: Macmillan.

Marshall, A. (1890) *Principles of Economics*, Variorum edition, ed. by C.W. Guillebaud, London: Macmillan, 1961.

Marshall, A. (1923), *Money, Credit and Commerce*, London: Macmillan.

Marshall, A. (1975), *Early Economic Writings, 1867-1890*, 2 vols, ed. by J.K. Whitaker, London: Macmillan.

Marshall, M.P. (1947), *What I Remember*, Cambridge: Cambridge University Press.

Marshall, A. and Marshall, M.P. (1879), *Economics of Industry*, London: Macmillan.

Meade, J.E. (1952), *A Geometry of International Trade*, London: Allen and Unwin.

Meek, R.L. (1973), *Precursors of Adam Smith 1750-1775*, London: Dent.

Menard, C. (1990), 'The Lausanne Tradition; Walrus and Pareto', in K. Hennings and W.J. Samuels (eds), *Neoclassical Economic Theory*, pp. 95-136, Boston: Kluwer Academic Publishing.

Mill, J.S. (1844), *Essays on Some Unsettled Questions of Political Economy*, reprinted in LSE series of Scarce Works in Political Economy, no. 7, 1948, London: J.W. Parker.

Mill, J.S. (1848, 1920) *Principles of Political Economy*, edited by W.J. Ashley, 1920, London: Longman, Green and Co.

Moore, H.L. (1908), 'The Statistical Complement of Pure Economics', *Quarterly Journal of Economics*, **23**, 1-33.

Moore, H.L. (1914), *Economic Cycles, Their Law and Cause*, London: Macmillan.

Morrell, J. and Thackray, A. (1981), *Gentlemen of Science*, Oxford: Clarendon Press.

Newman, P. (1990), 'The Great Barter Controversy', in J.K. Whitaker (ed.), *Centenary Essays on Alfred Marshall*, pp. 258-77, Cambridge: Cambridge University Press.

O'Brien, D.P. (1975), *The Classical Economists*, Oxford: Oxford University Press.

O'Brien, D.P. (1981), 'A. Marshall 1842-1924', in D.P. O'Brien and J.R. Presley (eds), *Pioneers of Modern Economics in Britain*, pp. 36-71, London: Macmillan.

O'Brien, D.P. (1988a), *Lionel Robbins*, London: Macmillan.

O'Brien, D.P. (1988b), 'Marshall's Work in Relation to Classical Economics', *University of Durham Working Paper in Economics*, **91**.

O'Brien, D.P. (1989), 'Lionel Robbins and the Austrian Connection', *University of Durham*.

Pantaleoni, M. (1889), *Pure Economics*, translated by T. Boston Bruce, London: Macmillan.

Pareto, V. (1895), 'La legge della domanda', *Giornale Degli Economisti*, reprinted in *Oeuvre Compléte de Vilfredo Pareto*, **26**, ed. by G. Busion, 1982, pp. 295-304, Geneva: Librairie Droz.

Pennington, J. (1840), 'Letter to Kirkman Finlay Esq', reprinted in *Economic Writings of James Pennington*, ed. by R.S. Sayers, 1963, London: London School of Economics.

Pigou, A.C. (1905), *Principles and Methods of Industrial Peace*, London: Macmillan.

Pigou, A.C. (ed.) (1925), *Memorials of Alfred Marshall 1842-1924*, London: Macmillan.

Pigou, A.C. and Robertson, D.A. (1931), *Economic Essays and Addresses*, London: King.

Postlewaite, A. (1979), 'Manipulation via Endowments', *Review of Economic Studies*, **47**, 255-61.

Rankin, S.C. (1980), 'Supply and Demand in Ricardian Price Theory, *Oxford Economic Papers*, **32**, 241-61.

Rashid, S. (1977), 'William Whewell and Early Mathematical Economics', *Manchester School*, **45**, 381-91.

Reisman, D.A. (1987), *The Economics of Alfred Marshall*, London: Macmillan.

Robbins, L. (1930), 'On the Elasticity of Demand for Income in Terms of Effort', *Economica*, **10**, 123-9.

Robbins, L.C. (1958), *Robert Torrnes and the Evolution of Classical Economics*, London: Macmillan.

Robertson, R.M. (1949), 'Mathematical Economics before Cournot', *Journal of Political Economy*, **57**, 523-36.

Robinson, J.V. (1933), *The Economics of Imperfect Competition*, London: Macmillan.

Samuelson, P.A. (1942), 'The Constancy of the Marginal Utility of Income', in O. Lange, F. McIntyre and T.O Yntema (eds), *Studies in Mathematical Economics and Econometrics*, Chicago: University of Chicago Press.

Samuelson, P.A. (1947), *Foundations of Economic Analysis*, Cambridge: Harvard University Press.

Samuelson, P.A. (1952), 'Spatial Price Equilibrium and Linear Programming', reprinted in J.E. Stiglitz (ed.), *The Collected Scientific Papers of Paul A. Samuelson, 2*, pp. 925-45, 1966, Cambridge, Mass.: The MIT Press.

Schneider, E. (1960), 'Hans von Mangoldt on Price Theory: a Contribution to the History of Mathematical Economics', *Econometrica*, **28**, 380-92.

Schultz, H. (1938) *The Theory and Measurement of Demand*, Chicago: University of Chicago Press.

Schumpeter, J.A. (1952), *Ten Great Economists*, London: Allen and Unwin.

Schumpeter, J.A. (1954), *History of Economics Analysis*, London: Allen and Unwin.

Seligman, E.R.A. (1921), *Shifting and the Incidence of Taxation*, New York: Macmillan.

Shapley, L.S. and Shubik, M. (1977), 'An Example of a Trading Economy with Three Competitive Equilibria', *Journal of Political Economy*, **85**, 873-5.

Shubik, M. (1959), 'Edgeworth Market Games', in R.D. Luce and A.W. Tucker (eds), *Contributions to the Theory of Games vol 4*, pp. 267-78, Princeton, NJ: Princeton University Press.

Sidgwick, A.S. and Sidgwick, E.M. (1906), *Henry Sidgwick: A Memoir*, London: Macmillan.

Smith, V.E. (1951), 'The Classicists' use of "Demand"', *Journal of Political Economy*, **59**, 242-57.

Smith, V.E. (1956), 'Malthas's Theory of Demand and its Influence on Value Theory', *Scottish Journal of Political Economy*, **3**, 205-20.

Spiegel, H.W. (1971), *The Growth of Economic Thought*, Englewood Cliffs: Prentice Hall.

Stigler, G.J. (1965), *Essays in the History of Economics*, Chicago: University of Chicago Press.

Stigler, S.M. (1982), 'Jevons as a Statistician', *Manchester School*, **50**, 3354-65.

Studenski, P. (1958), *The Nation of Nations*, Washington: New York University Press.

Theocharis, T. (1961), *Early Developments in Mathematical Economics*, London: Macmillan.

Thirlby, G.F. (1948), 'Demand and Supply of Money', *Economic Journal*, **58**, 331-55.

Thorold Rogers, J.E. (1884), *Six Centuries of Work and Wages*, London: Fisher Unwin.

Thorold Rogers, J.E. (1891), *The Economic Interpretations of History*, 2nd ed., London: Fisher Unwin.

Thweatt, W.O. (1983), 'Origins of the Terminology "Supply and Demand"', *Scottish Journal of Political Economy*, **30**, 287-94.

Todhunter, I. (1876), *William Whewell. An Account of his Writing with Selections from his Correspondence*, London: Macmillan.

Tooke, T. (1838), *A History of Prices*, reprinted with introduction by T.E. Gregory, 1938, London: P.S. King and Son.

Turnbull, H.W. (ed.) (1959), *Correspondence of Sir Isaac Newton*, **1**, 1661-75, Cambridge: Cambridge University Press for the Royal Society.

Uhr, C.G. (1960), *Economical Doctrines of Knut Wicksell*, Los Angeles: University of California Press.

Vickrey, W.S. (1958), 'Can Excises Lower Prices?, in R.W. Pfouts (ed.), *Essays in Economics and Econometrics*, pp.165-77, Chapel Hill: University of North Carolina Press.

Vickrey, W.S. (1960), 'Utility, strategy and social decision rules', *Quarterly Journal of Economics*, **74**, 507-35.

Viner, J. (1955), *Studies in the Theory of International Trade*, London: Allen and Unwin.

Viner, J. (1958), *The Long View and the Short*, Gencoe: Free Press.

Walker, D.A. (1967), 'Marshall's Theory of Competitive Exchange', *Canadian Journal of Economics*, **2**, 590-8.

Walras, L. (1874), *Elements of Pure Economics*, translated by W. Jaffé, 1954, London: Allen and Unwin.

Whewell, W. (1829), 'Mathematical Exposition of Some Doctrines of Political Economy', reprinted in *Political Economy* (1968), Gregg International.

Whewell, W. (1831), 'Mathematical Exposition of Some of the Leading

Doctrines in Mr. Ricardo's "Principles of Political Economy"';
reprinted in *Political Economy* (1968), Gregg International.

Whewell, W. (1850), 'Mathematical Exposition of Some Doctrines of Political Economy – Second Memoir', reprinted in *Political Economy* (1968), Gregg International.

Whewell, W. (1862), *Six Lectures on Political Economy*, Cambridge: Cambridge University Press.

Whittaker, E. and Robinson, G. (1924), *The Calculus of Observations: A Treatise on Numerical Mathematics* (4th ed., 1944), Glasgow: Blackie and Son.

Wicksell, K. (1893), *Value, Capital and Rent*, translated by S.H. Frowein (1954), London: Allen and Unwin

Wicksell, K. (1934), *Lectures on Political Economy*, translated by E. Classen and edited by L. Robbins, London: Routledge.

Wicksell, K. (1954), *Value, Capital and Rent*, translated by S.H. Frowein, London: Allen and Unwin.

Wicksell, K. (1958), *Selected Papers on Economic Theory*, ed. by E. Lindahl, London: George Allen and Unwin.

Wicksteed, P.H. (1888), *The Alphabet of Economic Science*, London: Macmillan.

Wicksteed, P.H. (1889), 'On Certain Passages in Jevons's "Theory of Political Economy"', *Quarterly Journal of Economics*, 3, 293–314. Reprinted in 1933 in *The Common Sense of Political Economy and Selected Papers and Reviews on Economic Theory*, ed. by L. Robbins, II, pp. 734–54, London: Routledge and Kegan Paul.

Wicksteed, P.H. (1910, 1933), *The Common Sense of Political Economy and Selected Papers and Reviews on Economic Theory*, 2 vols., ed. by L. Robbins, London: Routledge.

Wold, H. with Jureen, L. (1953), *Demand Analysis: A Study in Econometrics*, New York: John Wiley and Sons.

Young, A (1924a), 'Consumers' Surplus in International Trade: A Supplementary Note', *Quarterly Journal Economics*, 39, 498–9.

Young, A. (1924b), 'Marshall on Consumers' Surplus in International Trade', *Quarterly Journal of Economics*, 39, 144–50.

Young, A.B. (1927), *Economic Problems Old and New*, New York; Houghton Mifflin.

Yule, G.U. (1915a), 'Crop Production and Prices: a Note on Gregory King's Law', *Journal of the Royal Statistical Society*, 78, 296–8.

Yule, G.U. (1915b), 'Review of H.L. Moore's *Economic Cycles*', *Journal of the Royal Statistical Society*, 78, 302–4.

Index